In the Light of Dying

In the Light
of
Dying

The Journals of a Hospice Volunteer

Joan Leslie Taylor

CONTINUUM • NEW YORK

1989

The Continuum Publishing Company
370 Lexington Avenue
New York, NY 10017

Printed in the United States of America

Library of Congress Cataloging-in-Publication Data

Taylor, Joan Leslie.
    In the light of dying : the journals of a hospice
volunteer / Joan Leslie Taylor.
        p.   cm.
    ISBN 0-8264-0425-1
    1. Taylor, Joan Leslie—Diaries. 2. Volunteer workers in
hospitals—United States—Diaries. 3. Hospice care. I. Title.
R726.8.T39 1989
362.1'75—dc19   88-32758
                                                            CIP

In loving memory of my grandmother

Anna Trnka Stehlik

June 27, 1891–October 9, 1981

Disclaimer

Although the experiences recounted in this book are real, the names, descriptions and other identifying characteristics of all persons, places, and institutions have been disguised to protect their privacy. Any resemblance to actual persons, places, or institutions is purely coincidental.

Contents

Contents

Preface

When I first began work as a hospice volunteer several years ago, I was surprised to find that most of my friends and acquaintances were eager to hear about my experiences with dying patients. Many seemed to be searching for a context within which to understand and resolve their own personal losses and fears. Some related stories of the last weeks and months of relatives. One woman haltingly told me of the death of her son many years before, and confided that she had been unable to talk to anyone about her grief until she heard me talk about my experiences with hospice patients. Another voiced her guilty feeling that she had not done enough for her father in his last weeks; she was reassured to hear that this is a common feeling among those who have lost someone they care for deeply.

Later when I shared my hospice journals with a few people, I again found a deep and very personal interest in my experiences. Death was supposed to be an unpopular topic; yet everyone I encountered wanted to know more about my experiences with dying patients. I was encouraged to compile the journals into a book, which is the book you now hold.

In the Light of Dying consists of the journal records of my experiences with ten patients over a period of several years, as well as sections that tell how I came to volunteer with "City Hospice" and how my life was changed by the work. As I worked with dying patients, I found myself reflecting upon my own mortality and ex-

ploring issues of helping and being helped, of what is important in
life and how dying affects living.

You may read *In the Light of Dying* as merely stories of interesting people at a special time in their lives. If you are considering
becoming a hospice volunteer yourself, you may find my experiences helpful preparation for working with dying patients. Or, you
may find yourself dealing with death and dying in your family or
among your friends, and be struggling to comprehend the incom-
prehensible experiences and feelings that arise. Perhaps my experiences will be useful to you whether you are faced with an elderly
relative with a terminal illness, a young friend with AIDS, or are
attempting to help someone else cope with a death, whether sudden or lingering.

What is hospice? Frequently when the word is used we think
of a place where people go to die, which is what the first modern
hospice was. In 1967 Dr. Cicely Saunders (now Dame Saunders)
founded St. Christopher's Hospice in England because she saw the
need for a new kind of care for the terminally ill. She helped to
pioneer a method of pain control that called for regular doses of
painkillers at the level necessary to keep the patient both pain-free
and as alert as possible. She also recognized that terminally ill
patients needed more than physical care and insisted that St.
Christopher's be as homelike as possible and that patients be
helped to live as completely as possible during their final days. Visitors were encouraged and patients brought their own belongings
from home.

Since that first modern hospice was established, the hospice
philosophy has grown and spread throughout many countries. In
the United States most hospice programs are home-care programs.
Most people say they would prefer to die at home, but without the
kind of support that a hospice program provides, too many people
die in institutions. The goal of a hospice home-care program is to
keep the patient comfortable at home, utilizing whatever equipment, medications, and services are necessary.

Although hospice programs in different localities provide services in different ways, all programs (currently over eighteen hundred in this country) subscribe to the basic hospice philosophy of
compassionate care for the dying. Rather than thinking of the final
months of life as an ordeal to be endured, the hospice philosophy

affirms that this should be a time for final pleasures, resolving issues, reflecting upon the satisfactions of a lifetime, and saying goodbye.

The hallmarks of a hospice program, whether home care or inpatient are:

- The goal of treatment is comfort rather than cure.

- Pain control is a priority. Medications are used, but other treatments, such as massage, visualizations, music, heat, activities, and visitors are used as well.

- All symptoms are treated to enhance the patient's comfort. Attention is paid to diet, skin care, bowel and bladder function, nausea, and edema.

- Care encompasses the physical, the emotional, the mental, and the spiritual.

- An interdisciplinary team approach is used. The team is directed by a physician, either the medical director of the hospice program or the patient's own personal physician, and includes, social workers, registered nurses, attendants, clergy and trained volunteers.

- The unit of care is the whole family, which includes friends caring for the patient as well. The hospice team provides emotional and practical support to the family and the patient.

The patients you will read about in *In the Light of Dying* were patients in the home-care program of an inner city hospice program serving a diverse patient population, many with limited finances and without close family ties, which creates a different situation from that found in suburban hospice programs. All of the names and many details have been changed to protect the privacy of patients and their families. The hospice program is identified as "City Hospice," not its real name. The journals are my experiences as a volunteer and should not be considered medical case histories. The focus of the journals is on my interactions with patients and their families, but my participation was only one part, and sometimes a small part, of the total hospice involvement.

Although the journals do not include details about the participation of nurses and social workers, these professionals were in
every case actively involved with the patient's care. The observa-
tions and concerns expressed in the journals are mine as a volunteer and might be quite different from those of the hospice nurse
or social worker. As a volunteer I was considered an integral part of
the interdisciplinary team and encouraged to call either the nurse
or the social worker whenever I had concerns or questions.

In City Hospice each patient's own physician is actively involved in directing the patient's care, with the medical director of
the program serving as a consultant and advisor to the staff. Other
members of the team provide services as follows:

- The nurse makes regular visits to the patient to review the
  patient's condition, monitor pain control and symptom management, and supervise attendant care.

- The social worker visits the patient to assist the patient and
  family in handling practical details such as insurance coverage, finances, funeral plans, and wills as well as psycholog-
  ical issues such as fears about dying, concerns about the
  future, family communications, depression, and loneliness.

- Attendants assist the patient with personal care, such as
  bathing, grooming, and meal preparation.

- The on-call nurse provides emergency nursing services after
  office hours twenty-four hours a day, seven days a week.

Most of the journals end with the patient's death, but Hospice involvement does not end with death; bereavement services, such as
support groups and volunteer counseling, are provided to surviving family members and friends.

Hospice care is paid for by Medicare, private insurance, Med-
icaid and private donations. To the maximum extent possible, a
Hospice program admits patients regardless of their diagnosis or
ability to pay. Because many patients require services beyond what
Medicare or insurance cover and beyond what they can afford to
pay for (most commonly additional attendant care hours), private
donations are used to supplement insurance benefits.

Without the help and encouragement of many people, *In the Light of Dying* would never have come to be written. I am extremely grateful to the staff of the City Hospice program for the excellent training and support I have received in my volunteer work and for the opportunities and experiences I have had. Stephen Levine through his books and retreats provided inspiration and thought-provoking suggestions for me in my examination of the issues of death and dying. I am fortunate to have many wonderful friends who read and commented upon early drafts of the manuscript. Their comments helped me turn a loose collection of journals into a readable book. Thanks to all of you, especially Maryanne Raphael, Dorothy Manning, Nellie Pine, Marjorie Cyrus, Brian Donovan, Barbara Weisser, Christine Vinson, Joel Redon, Jenny Wolf, Susan Potter, and Marcena Brook. A special thank you to Wendy Norins who first encouraged me to create this book. And, my deep appreciation and gratitude to the patients and families who opened their hearts to me and gave me an incredible gift.

1

Sitting Still in the Midst

Today I sat at the bedside of Sylvia in the hospital. She is dying. More quickly now. In the past week her body has melted away, and her sad, gray eyes are large in her hollow face. She hasn't had many friends in recent years, perhaps not in all her seventy-five years, so she has delighted in the attention of my visits, first in her small, bare, senior housing apartment, and then during this past month in the hospital. Here she lives hooked to a tube that empties her stomach of whatever liquids they allow her for pleasure not nourishment, for her intestines are blocked by inoperable cancerous growths. She struggles, hoping for a miracle, not wanting to accept that she is dying, dying no matter what the doctors do, no matter the prayers of her born again Christian sister, no matter the flowers I bring, no matter even miracles.

The pain medications and the illness have taken their toll on Sylvia. Her mind now wanders and she becomes easily confused and incoherent, so the hospital has assigned a nurse's aide to sit beside her bed. The aide gratefully leaves her post when I arrive.

There isn't much to say, so I just sit beside the bed and I look into her eyes. She looks back at me with a smile and shifts her legs restlessly under the blankets. I feel the nearness of death in her restlessness, like waiting in a railroad station on a hard wooden bench for an overdue train. I wait with her for a few minutes, as if we were strangers at a depot with not much to say to one another, but connected in our listening for the roar of an approaching train.

Sitting with Sylvia, I find myself remembering back to before I became a hospice volunteer, before I spent time with dying strangers, all like Sylvia with the prognosis: six months or less to live. It's difficult to remember not being connected, loosely or closely, with one dying person or another. I remember a conversation with a friend whose father had died some months before.

"Sure, I'm glad I was with Dad when he died," my friend told me, "but I cannot imagine wanting to sit at a stranger's deathbed."

"I've learned so much, that I feel lucky to be there. And by the time a patient dies, we're not strangers anymore," I told her. "It feels good to be truly useful to someone just when they need it most."

"And that hardly seems fair, that you should have all these great insights without having to lose your father!" She went on to tell me again about her father's death and about her grief and anger at losing him. I heard in her voice an anxious hope that she would find answers to the urgent questions in her mind, and comfort for the grief and fear in her heart, if only she could understand what I have found at the bedsides of strangers.

"Isn't it awfully sad and depressing to be with someone, knowing that they're just going to die?" she pressed me. "And what exactly do you do for someone who's dying?"

"Every person's different, but the time I've spent with each one feels very precious, and, no, I've never felt depressed. Sad yes, but not depressed. Some people just need someone to talk to. Some need transportation and help getting out of the house. And sometimes, it's the family who needs help coping with the approaching death. I'm sometimes given a specific assignment with a patient, but most of the time, I just show up and do whatever needs to be done."

"But I still don't understand what made you volunteer to begin with."

I don't know exactly why I find working with dying patients more satisfying than anything else I've ever done. And how did I get here?

Keeping a journal was my first spiritual practice, although I wouldn't have called it that when I began. I was only trying to make sense of my busy life as a single parent of two energetic children, my work as an accountant, my various relationships, and my thoughts and feelings about the meaning of life and how I could become a better person and find more satisfaction in my life. The journal kept me in touch with my inner self, and led me to learn to meditate.

At first meditation gave me the strength and motivation to accomplish what I needed to do. I developed my skills as an accountant, gained confidence in the world of business, raised my children, and kept in contact with my inner spiritual self. Eventually, my meditation practice led me to question the very life that initially it had allowed me to pursue so successfully.

There are no simple cause-and-effect explanations for the important decisions in my life. Every choice is inextricably wound into the whole knotty fabric of the rest of my life, so it's impossible to say with any certainty: this is when I first decided thus and such. Or, this experience is what led me to make that decision; yet there are moments that stand out.

The Journal

October 1981
Gramma died today.

All summer I kept meaning to call her. When did I last talk to her? For so many years we spoke at least once a month, but this past year I've been busy, and she stopped calling me. I received her usual birthday card and check in June. Did she call one day while I was out? Weeks came and went, and when I'd think of Gram, it'd be too late at night to call.

Now it's too late for phone calls. I'm not sure what to do. Tears of disbelief churn inside, but I don't cry. Oh, if only I hadn't waited to call. So foolish to put off a phone call to a ninety-year-old grandmother, who loved me deeply and gave me so much. We'd told each other good-bye forever, twice, but did I ever tell her how much I loved her? Really?

I sit on my meditation cushion and I'm filled with a sense of peace, flowing time, and an exchange of responsibilities. I feel responsible to pass on the joy Gramma gave me. I feel in her death a signal for me to begin to do more in the world. Now that she's gone, I'm closer to my own death, only one generation removed from "the top." As long as Gramma lived, I could stay an over-grown child with much potential; now she has sent me out into the world, to do whatever I am going to do.

November 1981
Max is terribly sick. Is eight years very old for a cat? I don't think so and I don't want to even think of him not being here. The vet says I must get fluids into him so the antibiotics will have a chance to work. Max just lies there in the wicker basket, breathing with a great noise of congestion, his beautiful, long orange and white fur now a matted mess. When I pry his mouth open and push in a dropper full of water, he looks at me with trust. He resists swal-lowing the water, but I see in his eyes that he is relying on me to make him well.

My breath comes in short pants matching Max's labored breathing. I feel myself willing him to live, to please get better. Every little while I tiptoe into the room where he is, afraid that he'll be dead, but there he is with that grateful look in his yellow eyes, so I force more water down his throat and scratch the top of his head.

Caring for Max I find myself thinking of Gramma, and as I slowly nurse Max back to health, I feel my regrets for not calling Gramma slowly fade away. Even though I was three thousand miles from Gramma's bedside when she died, and I've felt cut off from her since then, lost in my own regrets and if-onlys, today here with Max, I am enfolded in my grandmother's love and I feel my love for her, too. At last, it's all right that I wasn't there when she died.

Max did recover, and he continued to trust me in a special way. It may seem incredible that caring for a sick cat could substitute for being at the deathbed of a favorite grandmother, but since then I've learned that grief and loss can be ameliorated by direct hands on caring, and on a deep level each loss is connected to every other loss. Gramma's death helped me care for Max and caring for Max helped me say good-bye to Gramma.

June 1982
Melancholy and thoughtful, wondering about my life. It's back to my old question: what's the point? The point of life, my life. And

why do I labor day after day at my job . . . only to . . . perhaps, watch it disappear? What else is there? I cannot bear to think that there's nothing more than this.

I keep hoping my current work as an accountant will somehow lead to a new vocation, but perhaps I must want change more desperately before I can see what there is in me, in my world, without the work I have labored at for now eleven years without ever really choosing. I don't want to do this forever. It's too hard, too exhausting, too pointless, but what else is there? I yearn for work of greater value, more earthshaking importance in the larger scheme of things, and in my frustration I see nothing that's particularly "important."

I am overwhelmed with weariness and loss and sadness, and I feel a plaintive cry rise in me. What is it that I cry for? Some piece of myself? It's the pointlessness of my life that fills me with this feeling of sadness and loss. I long for a Big Reason to do things, a clear measure of a day's work, of a lifetime's tribulation and loss, but I see no such clarity. Accounting feels besides the point, but every other life I can imagine seems equally besides the point. What *is* the point?

My job fills my life, overfills it, leaving no room for anything else. Am I only this: an accountant moving numbers about the page? I never figured out what I wanted to be when I grew up, what kind of work I truly wanted to do. With two children to support and no particular skills, I fell into accounting, as something to do for a little while. But it's been many years and now I feel hopelessly trapped in business. How I long to get out of business! I have no idea what else I could possibly do, but I yearn to be through with the endless pages of numbers and the pressure of arbitrary schedules and deadlines.

I think I want to take care of people, or something. But who would I care for? My children are nearly grown. Who else would need me? And what could I do that would be of some help, to someone?

I don't know what to do. Except to keep trying to sit still in the midst, being willing to see whatever needs to be done and then doing it. I feel so far from that Zen ideal, yet the image of sitting still in the midst is reassuring in this hopelessness.

July 1982

I cannot count the number of leaves that move when the wind moves through the eucalyptus trees, but the resulting song— or is it a dance?—is like the singing of the heavenly multitudes: uncounted, numerous beyond enumerating, beyond imagining, each with the others, all played by the wind. When I watch the tall trees, the branches each filled with leaves all tossing in the wind in unison, I long to know my place in the universe. Where is my branch? And what is it connected to? And where, oh, where are my fellow leaves?

August 1982

I think I may have discovered something.

This morning I read an article about a Stephen Levine who runs something called The Dying Project. He receives phone calls from people who are dying and trying to figure out their lives. I feel a surge of excitement and disparate parts of myself merging.

Meditation has been a powerful force in my life. The focus is life and death, so a natural preparation for dealing with dying.

Before all the accounting I was a psychology major. And now I remember the human potential movement of the late sixties, and the excitement and urgency of that time.

Working years ago at Medicare: I remember how I loved the elderly people I talked to everyday, how easy it was for me to picture being old and frightened.

In seeking new work I've been trying to figure out what would be good for me. Now suddenly, I've turned the mirror away from me and I'm asking a new question: what could I do that would be good for someone else? That is what I've yearned for, and I feel a measure of satisfaction in just the realization. How did I never notice in myself this huge unmet need? To be useful.

I'm not sure what this means or what exactly I will do or become. All the years of sitting on the meditation cushion, breathing in and breathing out. All the years of asking, what's the point? Is there a point? Now I know there is a point.

January 1983

Little pieces of small things, small hopes. I feel like a leaf in a pool of water, feeling lots of little pulls but not yet sensing the direction of the main stream.

I'm parked by the ocean, with gentle, winter raindrops plopping on the windshield, the night air drenched with moisture, not cold, but with the raindrops hinting of winter storms.

Nothing will ever be the same. And nothing will ever change. I feel myself rooted in life—LIFE—with capital letters, with time marching on, impersonally counting off the moments, days, events, years, lifetimes. It feels as if I could hold my breath and never make any choices at all and—poof!—it would all pass. The rhythm is powerful in me now; the heartbeat that transcends day to day, small-minded minutiae and petty concerns is my own.

Everything, my whole rich wonderful life, feels accessible to me here at this moment. The waves charge on into shore—on rushing, on course, certain, undiminished by obstacles. All my worries about what to do . . . and all I really need to do is to listen to this rhythm, and not resist.

April 1983

This morning I reached toward the bathroom shelf and in the next instant there was a tremendous crash and I felt sharp bits of glass bouncing off the tile floor onto my bare legs. It was the little antique glass, cut glass with the ornate design highlighted in gold. Over one hundred years intact, and in a moment it was gone. Picking up the pieces and sweeping up the fine glass dust, I felt the loss of a treasure.

Until the moment of loss I didn't feel attached to the little glass. I've enjoyed its beauty, but have never thought much about "having" it, or not having it, for that matter. Suddenly I'm filled with sorrow and loss and loneliness, as if I'd been deserted by a dear friend. The attachment became painfully apparent in the moment of loss. Perhaps "having" dulls the awareness and it is loss that opens me to see both myself and the object more clearly.

As I sit in the feeling of loss, I really understood that, yes, after a while, all will be lost. At first the realization seemed horrible, but as I sit with it, I notice a kind of freedom in the certainty of loss, and the freedom is here, right now. If I can enjoy each possession for its beauty, and know right in the moment of enjoyment that this too will be lost someday, perhaps I will not be so blinded and dulled by the attachment. Now I understand the Zen story about a teacher who tells the student to see the glass as already broken.

April 1983
I've been reading a Zen book about death. The doctrines are stated with certainty. I resist accepting or rejecting any particular ideas or beliefs about death. I have an inner sense that death is exciting, important, beautiful, just like life is, and there's a mystery about it that compels me to approach and explore. I don't want doctrines; I want to see for myself. In the meantime I read and listen to what everyone says about death, just absorbing all the different beliefs and perspectives. More sitting still in the midst of not knowing.

April 1983
Max is sick again, and this time I don't know whether he'll make it. Same regimen as last time: lots of fluids. I got up several times in the night and gave Max water. Since I had to go to work today, a friend agreed to take care of him.

By midafternoon I was too worried to work, so with everyone at the office thinking I was nuts, I rushed out of the office and ran for the bus. I arrived home to find Max hiding under the couch, barely breathing. I grabbed him and took off for the vet's office. In the car, I looked down at Max. His head was down and his breathing so shallow, I thought he might be dead. I started to sob. Oh, if only I'd stayed home today to take care of Max. If only . . . The alarm, the feeling of inadequacy, of regret: this felt familiar. It was just like when Gramma died and I wished I'd called her. If only . . . Whether Max lives or dies, I thought, I want to have done everything possible.

Several days later
A week of talking to the vet by phone, of going there to sit on the floor by Max's cage, scratching his lowered head. X rays, blood

tests, an IV running into his paw, and they've still no idea what's wrong with him, except that it's not his heart. One day they said he was a little better, but when I saw him, he looked the same. I avoided thinking about the bill that was accumulating. The vet never mentioned the possibility of Max dying, and I didn't really want to see that that was what was happening. I felt helpless, fearful, inadequate.

The vet was talking about doing another X ray in the morning and I wearily wondered how many more days of not knowing, of waiting to hear who knows what were ahead. I saw the pained look in Max's yellow eyes, and I cringed to see the painful way he breathed. He moved toward my hand when I moved away for a moment, so I knew he was comforted by my petting. Then suddenly, he sat up and raised his paw at me. My heart froze at the look in his eyes. No more the look of grateful trust; now his look said, "Leave me alone." I came away in tears. I knew in my heart that he was dying.

I sobbed and sobbed. Not only was my dear, sweet cat dying, I wasn't even taking care of him. Helpless, lonely, exhausted, eventually I fell asleep.

At 1:00 a.m. the phone rang. Bleary-eyed and dull-witted, I listened to the vet. Max was having more difficulty breathing and was in a lot of pain. Choices: cut him open to see what was going on, wait until morning to see if he survived, or put him to sleep. I knew there was no point in surgery and I couldn't bear to think of him struggling through the night in pain. I never dreamed I would say, "Okay, please kill my cat." I remembered the look in his eyes when he raised his paw at me, and I told her not to let him suffer any more.

It was nearly 2:00 a.m. and quite wet, on the verge of either raining or clearing when I left the house. After I'd walked a long time through the deserted streets in the damp darkness, I looked up and saw the moon, brightly shining through the dissipating clouds. All at once the knot of fear and anxiety in my stomach eased, and I took my first full breath since I'd hung up the phone. I said to myself, "I did the right thing." No conflict, just the way it was.

It's raining harder now. I'm alone listening to the rain pounding on the window, and I think how Max can't hear it anymore. I remember how he would meow and complain if he were stuck outside in the rain. Oh, Max, you can rest now! The eternal sunshine is perfect for catnaps. Run free now and be happy.

Although I didn't know it until much later, the difficulty I had in accepting Max's approaching death and the anguish and pain and loneliness I experienced were very much the same as what many families of dying patients experience. The medical establishment, for people as well as for cats, keeps family members at a distance, and there's little opportunity for actual physical caring such as I'd experienced the first time Max was sick. I've often wondered if I'd been caring for Max at home under the guidance of a sympathetic veterinarian, whether I might have been able to ease Max's pain, and my own, enough to allow him to die naturally.

May 1983
My first workshop in, as a friend calls it, "the death biz." The Stephen Levine workshop. The room is filled with perhaps two hundred people: many nurses, social workers, therapists; quite a few people with illnesses. Everyone is "ahead" of me: they have lost a friend or relative, do work with dying people, or have cancer themselves. I feel a little shut out because I'm not dying right now. Then there are a lot of people all very excited about "conscious dying," and talking importantly about their "awareness." These last embarrass me; I fear I am like them.

Stephen asks how many have or have had cancer; many hands go up and I find myself staring at the back of the young, very healthy looking woman in front of me who raises her hand. I'm startled to see that cancer does not necessarily show; how ordinary all these cancer "victims" look. How easily it could be me, raising my hand. Would I understand any more if I had cancer? Listening to people tell of their experiences, and ask questions of Stephen, I begin to realize how little anyone understands about death, and how much fear there is in everyone.

As Stephen talks, answering questions, leading the group through exercises, telling stories, I come back to how I felt when I first read the article about him. I know I can work with dying people, knowing only what I know right now. I'm still intimidated by all these "conscious diers" and professionals, and I still have no idea exactly what I might do for anyone dying, or how, but I'm certain I can do it.

Two days of listening, questioning, wondering. Everything Stephen says about dying is what I do just living. Investigate; use your experience to learn. Resistance causes pain; watch where you're holding; pain can be a great teacher. This is the "Braille method"; we don't know. This sounds like my own muddling through, looking at everything, examining, hoping to see truth in everyday experiences, yearning to grow in spirit. But I don't talk as beautifully as he does.

Exercises: looking into the eyes of a stranger, sending and then receiving love; this reminds me of encounter groups. Feeding and being fed, a very powerful exercise for many people, but it only reminds me of how much I enjoyed my children as infants. A meditation: breathing in and out of the heart center, the warmth and patience breath; how wonderful to feel that even I have patience in my heart.

A young man speaks of how he had volunteered to work with AIDS patients, but then had backed away in fear, and how ever since, he has been filled with guilt and remorse, but still wishes he could do this work. Stephen says we must recognize that feelings of unworthiness will always be there. The ability to serve and work with the dying grows slowly, and, he cautioned the young man, it cannot be rushed by charging in with bravado.

Later in the park after the workshop
How beautiful it is with the late day sun making all the flowers and trees glow with inner radiance. I ask myself, have I ever seen an inadequate plant? Even the simplest blade of grass seems lovely and perfectly complete. Even bruised or sickly plants, even dead plants are lovely; at least I don't blame them. Why then do I feel inadequate?

I absorbed all the stories and ideas of everyone at the workshop and I watched my feelings ebb and flow. I listened to everything with an uncommitted waiting to see for myself. But how will I do that? I'm doing the best I can, all I can, spiritually, but I don't know how to show anyone that inner core of knowing I'm on the right path. I have no experiences with death, no training, no skills to offer.

Enough thinking about working with the dying, enough books, enough workshops: it's time to *do*, though I'm not sure exactly where or how or what to do.

December 1983
This morning was my interview at City Hospice with the volunteer coordinator. I'm going to be a bereavement volunteer! After the training sessions, where I'll learn about grief and how to help bereaved people through the difficult first year after death, I'll be assigned to a bereaved person. I'm still very, very nervous, but at least I've taken the first step.

January 1984
Ever since last evening's Hospice meeting, when I was assigned two clients, I've been rehearsing scenes in my mind. Nervous, very nervous, yet excited, too. And anxious to get on with it.

Most volunteers have either had a relative die in the hospice program, or are in professional training to be therapists. I've had no personal experience with hospice and I'm not on the way to becoming a professional anything. I'm just trying to figure out something about life and death, and I want to do something useful.

later
I telephoned Margaret, my first bereaved client. My hands are shaking. My voice sounded relaxed, gracious, experienced, understanding. I managed to survive the call and I have an appointment to see her on Monday.

For the next nine months I was a bereavement volunteer, working with those who'd lost a loved one, attending the monthly volunteer support meetings and the monthly bereavement social, where those who'd had a family member die in the City Hospice program get together for a pot luck dinner and new volunteer assignments are frequently made.

Once I got into the work I began to lose my nervousness and found that I really could do something more important than accounting: I could be a real help to people going through difficult times. I loved the quality of transition and change that I found bereaved clients struggling through, but after awhile, I began to feel I was coming into people's lives after the main event, in time only for the rehashing and if-onlys.

That October I attended a six session training program and applied to be a volunteer with dying patients. The training sessions dealt with pain control, symptom management, and other background information. Once again I was interviewed and once again I was surprised that I was accepted.

In November I was assigned my first dying patient, Edith.

2

Edith

Edith was a typical hospice patient: an elderly woman with cancer of the colon, alone in the world without much in the way of
financial resources, friends or family, living a very narrow life, just
the sort of bleak existence I imagine in nightmares of my own old
age. Edith was also an exceptional person, who in retrospect
stands out from all the elderly, dying women I have known since
then. I don't know how much of Edith's uniqueness lay in the fer-
vor with which I approached my first patient, and how much she
really was unique.

The relationship that unfolded between Edith and me was
probably partly due to that peculiar juxtaposition of my predilec-
tion to love my first patient and her relief and wonderment at having a stranger come into her lonely life. Throughout the months I
spent with Edith, over and over again, I was struck with how little
I actually did, and yet how deeply she responded. My not having
enough experience with death and dying to have any set ideas
about dying made me perhaps the most useful friend she could
have.

I felt somewhat uncomfortable about popping into the life of a
stranger at such an intimate time in her life, and I admitted that
had I met Edith earlier in her life, I would never have become close
to her. After a time of knowing Edith, when her tedious and boring qualities became unimportant and I felt myself connected to
her, heart-to-heart, I came to realize that though we may be at-
tracted to friends and lovers for their personalities and interesting

lives, and what they have done or become, it's this bare heart-to-heart connection that we really want.

Dying offers many incredible opportunities, but the first is what Edith shared with me: the most exciting moment of a life, when all the pretenses and distractions have fallen away. How lucky I was to be there just as that moment approached for Edith.

The Journal

November 21
The volunteer coordinator called to tell me about my first patient. "Although Edith is still ambulatory, she's been very depressed since September when she was told she had an inoperable cancer of the colon, so it would be good for you to take Edith out in your car. It might improve her spirits. Her personal physician has prescribed antidepressants, but the City Hospice nurse has let him know that Edith is not taking them on a regular basis."

"Edith is seventy-one and has lived all her life right here," she continued, reading from the chart. "She never married and has no family and few friends. She's quite isolated and lives in a very rigid and limited way. The nurse says that she's obsessed with her bowel functions and she talks incessantly about what she has eaten or not eaten and the digestive results."

A City Hospice attendant comes for four hours a day, Monday through Friday. The attendant gives her a bath, changes the bed, and goes to the store to buy TV dinners and other simple foods for Edith.

Nervously, I agreed to call Edith.

November 25
I called Edith to set up a time for a visit. She sounded depressed and low and seemed unenthusiastic about a visit. "I'm nothing great, you know. Have you been told the situation?" I assured her I was fully aware of her situation and I hoped I would be able to help her in some way.

She sounded very sick. "Would you mind calling another time because I'm getting ready to get out my dinner so I can eat it in an hour?"

But she then proceeded to come alive and tell me about her Thanksgiving and to ask me about mine. She even asked me exactly what I had served for Thanksgiving. This lady does have an inordinate interest in food! We agreed on Friday at 1:00.

November 30
The first day I climbed the stairs to Edith's small apartment, clutching flowers that I hoped would cheer Edith and diminish my nervousness, I was breathlessly prepared, determined, to love any dying person. I had spent several years leading up to this moment and I was so anxious to get on with it, that I could probably have loved Attila the Hun if he lay dying in a small downtown apartment.

Actually meeting Edith was something of a shock. I don't know what I expected, but Edith was so ordinary, her life so bland, and her dying was right in the context of her bland, ordinary life.

She greeted me enthusiastically at the door in a bathrobe, and led me into the small studio apartment, and settled herself back in the narrow bed. Edith is a thin, drawn woman with soft, wispy hair framing her hollow face; she looks very ill. She was touched by the flowers, but she wearily sat down on the bed and gestured toward the kitchenette. "There's a vase in there. Would you mind?"

The room was perhaps twelve or fifteen feet square, with the small kitchenette, a bathroom, and a large walk-in closet. The room was austere, with little furniture or decoration: a cheap dinette set covered with a plastic tablecloth, a hard wooden rocker, a tall old-fashioned dresser, a television on a metal stand with casters, and a single bed. The old, yellowed shades were drawn, giving a further air of gloom to the room, but propped up on the high dresser, on every dinette chair, and elsewhere about the room were rag dolls, large and small, smiling their eternal embroidered smiles.

While I was still in the kitchenette, putting the flowers in water, Edith began a litany of all her sufferings, past and present. "My main problem has always been bowels not moving. You may not believe it, but I was born constipated." I thought she meant for a long time, but before I could respond, she continued, "Oh, yes,

Mother said even the doctor found it hard to believe, but I truly was constipated right from the moment of birth. The doctor prescribed senna tea and I've been drinking it all my life."

"Did the senna tea work?" I asked, returning to the main room with the flowers, now crammed into the one small, dime-store vase Edith owned.

"Well, a little, but I have never in my life had a normal bowel movement, not like other people. Oh, what beautiful flowers! Yes, set them on the table over there so they won't get knocked over."

As I listened to Edith tell me about her constipation, I flashed on all the moving, ethereal conversations with dying people that I had read of or heard about at workshops. Edith had not read books or attended workshops, so she knew nothing about how she should be, what she should say, or how she should die. After the initial shock of hearing the intimate reports of a stranger's bowel problems, I just sat back and absorbed everything about her. Everything I had learned in all the workshops seemed rather irrelevant, and all I could do was be there with Edith and let her take of me what she needed.

By the time I met Edith, she was already opening up to the attention that City Hospice brought her, and one might even say, enjoying the excitement of being ill. Yes, in a bleak, lonely life, serious illness brings excitement and attention, the two qualities every life needs in some minimal quantity. And she was ready to talk.

For the first hour, I barely spoke. She seemed intent on bringing me up-to-date with a complete account of her life and her physical condition. She lay propped up in bed, often closing her eyes while she spoke.

"When I was ten I was knocked down by a dog and lost my two front teeth. I was coming home from school and this large dog jumped out at me, terrified me, and knocked me right to the ground. There was blood everywhere, and my permanent front teeth were gone. We were poor, but a dentist took pity on me and made me false teeth. For weeks I had to go to that office after school and sit in the waiting room with all the rich children having their teeth straightened."

I barely had a moment to utter a murmur of sympathy before Edith launched into the next chapter of her tale of woe. "And then my father died when I was twelve." She and her mother were

cheated by her father's partners and discriminated against by his
relatives, because her mother was Jewish. They were poor and
alone in the world. They kept to themselves and lived a quiet life.

When Edith finished high school, she worked as a clerk in an
office downtown. I heard how lonely she'd been after her mother
died, sometime during the fifties, and I heard the full details of
the past two years since her cancer was diagnosed. She included
details of meals eaten through all the years and all the sufferings;
her memory for food is incredible. "I was having a hamburger at a
place I went once in a while, and that time I had the mashed potatoes, but my bowels objected." The colostomy was difficult for
her; two accidents, one in a department store while buying a bathrobe, were humiliating. Eventually, she had surgery to close the
colostomy that made things less messy, but caused the bowels not
moving problem to return.

She pointed to a large portrait of herself holding a rag doll,
which was prominently displayed on the bureau. "That's when I
looked like a human being," she said forlornly.

"Why, Edith, you're still a human being," I reminded her. I
didn't tell her, but I thought she was more attractive now, despite
the ravages of her illness; the tightly smiling face of the younger
Edith, with the angular features and the hairdo that looked like
plaster of paris, lacked the softness of the hollow face before me as
she lay back wearily on the pillows. There was something very sad
about that lonely lady with the rag doll who looked down from the
dresser. I could easily envision all of the long lonely hours Edith
had spent in this drab, Spartan room with only the vacantly staring, button-eyed rag dolls for company.

She went on to tell me about her dolls. "They just seem so
lovable, and they've been good company for me. On their birthdays
I used to buy them new hair ribbons. See, this one is my favorite,
so I wanted her in the picture with me. The coupon was for a
picture of your family and since Mother was gone, I told them,
'She's my family.' " As she talked, I watched love sparkle in her
eyes and bring a soft smile to her lips. I felt tears playing at the
corners of my eyes as I realized that loving a rag doll was better
than not loving at all.

Her friend Frances, who had invited her to Thanksgiving dinner, has been a friend since childhood. "I like Frances, but she's

very busy and awfully difficult to get a hold of. And she yells at
me. She thinks being sick is all in the mind. You know, I don't
even know you, but because you don't yell at me, it's easier to talk
to you about feelings."

"Sometimes it's easier to talk to a stranger than a long time
friend," I told her. "It's probably upsetting to Frances to see how
ill you are, which makes it hard for both of you to be open with
your feelings." She mentioned a younger friend who had moved to
Chicago three years ago when she lost her job. They've corre-
sponded a few times. "I really miss Linda now that I'm sick. Oh,
she'd be running over here all the time, if she were still living
here."

She told me about going to a spiritualist church after her
mother died. I asked her if she had ever been able to communicate
with her mother. "Twice, but in a dreamlike state." I told her I
thought we were more open to that kind of communication in a
dream state than in the ordinary waking state. Encouraged by my
understanding of her belief in the spiritual realm, she continued,
"Spiritualism also deals with healing. I went to a medium when I
first felt sick and the medium described my illness very precisely
and advised me to seek medical help. Now it's too late for healing.
I'm going to die."

"Even when it's too late to heal the body, the heart can always
be healed," I reminded her gently. She nodded and sighed.

Off and on during the conversation she talked of her impending death. "I'm not afraid to die, but I can't bear the thought of
suffering for as long as a year. I have suffered enough! Every night
I pray the Lord will take me soon." I reminded her that the Lord
would take her in His own time, that it must not be time yet, that
perhaps there was more for her to do. She couldn't imagine what
that might be, but she seemed reassured by my words. I marveled
to hear how easily Edith's words for the spiritual realm rolled from
my lips.

She was worried about having to go to a nursing home. "Try
to take this experience one day at a time," I suggested and assured
her Hospice would help her stay at home as long as possible and
that not all nursing homes were terrible.

We discussed her need to deposit her checks next week. I told
her I could either make the deposit for her, or take her to the

bank. "I want to go myself if I'm at all able." I suggested that she consider direct deposit, but she resisted the idea.

Near the end of our visit she told me about a man she had gone out with for several months sometime in her fifties. "He was a janitor in the building where I was living." Her stories of their evenings together and a trip they took to see a waterfall, not to return until 3:00 in the morning, made me think this brief fling had provided Edith with the closest thing to adventure in her whole life. "I had to break off the relationship because he was only interested in my body," she confided. "I'm glad I never married. There's one part of marriage I just know I wouldn't have liked. Even though I never did it. I can be frank with you, Joan," she said, glancing pointedly at me. "I mean the sex part. Sometimes when you read things you feel certain things in your body, but that's all; I never wanted to marry. Never."

I had no idea how to respond to this confession of a true maiden lady, but Edith seemed to need no response. Having revealed this essential piece of her inner life, she asked me to go downstairs and get her mail out of the box. When I returned with her social security check, I lowered the blinds and she asked for a glass of water. "The nurse told me I needed more liquid to make the bowels move." I reminded her that since she was less active now, she might not move her bowels as frequently. She is also bothered by nausea and has been using suppositories to control it. Almost everything has stayed down over the last few days, yet the feeling of nausea, or the fear of it, remains.

When I said good-bye to her, I leaned over and gently kissed her cheek. How soft and warm her skin was. I promised to call her Monday about going to the bank and left her my telephone number in case she felt lonely over the weekend. She continued to talk even after I had my coat on and was standing ready to depart. Now that I had my coat on, I found the small room oppressively hot, but it was difficult to slip away while Edith talked on.

It was 5:00 and the streets were full of hurrying commuters. I walked through what had probably been familiar territory to Edith. I stepped onto a crowded bus and became aware of the vibrant, robust quality of everyone on the bus. As I looked into the full, rosy faces of the commuters, I thought of Edith, both the younger

Edith in the portrait with the rag doll, and the dying Edith I had just left. The robust bodies around me, even the muscular, young male body that I was pushed up against as more people crowded onto the bus, every single body seemed as fragile and temporary as Edith's dying body. I remembered the barely-there quality I saw in Edith and was surprised to see that same quality in the faces around me. I thought of how often Edith must have ridden the buses and sat tightly staring ahead just like these people. It seemed only a moment in time before everyone on the bus, myself included, would wither and die, like Edith was doing. I saw a tightness in one woman's face that reminded me of the look in the young Edith's face in the portrait.

Having sat close to a dying woman, having heard the confessions and sufferings of a true maiden lady, I felt a welling of compassion for every human being on the bus and throughout the world. I saw each person as unique and as just another human being; I saw foibles and virtues; I saw how each person lived; and I saw how each would die.

There was not a lot about Edith that was fascinating, in the usual sense of getting to know a new person. She had done little, had little, wanted little, so what was there? Edith was so stripped of all the accoutrements of a social being that she had only herself, a generic human being, to offer. What does it mean to be human? I had always confused accomplishments, intelligent conversation, creative works, jobs, responsibilities, and relationships with being human. With Edith, I had felt at moments as if I were suffocating in her depression, her narrowness, her boring blandness, but bumping along in the bus, when I heard these judgments in my mind, I remembered the look of love in Edith's eyes when she talked of her dolls, and I knew Edith was no different from me, or from anyone else.

At a deep level any human being can be a mirror for another, but most of our lives we stay in our separate unique lives. It was Edith in her bareness, who would teach me this, who would show me that my judgments of her were only unflattering reflections of my own shortcomings. That first day, I was only beginning to recognize that to know Edith was to see all my own fears: dying of cancer, alone in a bare room, in poverty, after a sad and lonely life that never really gave much of anything.

December 4

Edith was dressed in a sweater and skirt and ready to go when I arrived. "I want to get to the bank so bad!" she anxiously cried. "I just hope I can make it! I feel kind of dizzy." I assured her she would make it and helped her into her coat; she added a scarf and a beret pulled down over her ears. With her checks and bankbook in my purse, I suggested she didn't need to take her own. She seemed to consider leaving it, but ended by taking it. "I always take my purse."

Very slowly, we made it down to the lobby, out the front door, and down several steps to the street. I'm not sure who was more nervous, Edith with her sturdy cane or me, praying I wouldn't let her fall. The building manager passed us as we left the building. She had apparently not recognized Edith, but Edith called to her and she came over. "Here I am, just barely crawling. My friend is helping me get to the bank. I've been very ill and am under the doctor's care," she added. The manager seemed quite shocked to see how sick Edith looked and I thought that Edith somehow enjoyed shocking her with her illness.

Once in the car, Edith relaxed a little and said it felt good to be outside. She oohed and aahed over the large Christmas tree in the park and pointed out various neighborhood restaurants that were good, or used to be good, or were too expensive. "On Wednesdays that place has a special: soup, salad, and the whole dinner, even coffee." Despite much traffic, luck was with us and there was a free parking space on the corner next to the bank. We entered the bank and crossed the lobby slowly; she carefully endorsed each check at the counter. Standing in line I realized that I was carrying the cane!

A very friendly teller waited on Edith. Edith told her, "I don't have much mind anymore," and the teller smiled and said that of course Edith had a mind. Sure enough, when the teller counted out the bills and change, she made a nickel error and Edith caught it.

On the way out of the bank Edith heaved a sigh, "Well, I made it! I wanted to do it myself, at least one more time." I told her she would probably do it again and in the meantime, we might think about going someplace more interesting than the bank. "Well, I might like to go to the supermarket someday so I can see the TV dinners myself," she replied. Not exactly what I had in mind as an outing.

Back at her apartment even before removing her coat, she washed her hands. When I reached for a hanger to hang up her coat, she followed behind to make sure I had gotten the right hanger; she replaced the one I had removed and reached for an identical one, two hangers down the rack. She seemed glad to take off the support hose, garter belt and heavy shoes, and to put on her pajamas.

She told me over and over again how much she appreciated me taking her to the bank. I was overwhelmed with how deeply grateful she was, for what seemed to me only a small favor.

Many of Edith's stories revolve around food. After her father died, she remembers looking out her window into another family's window and watching them eat mush three times a day. She marveled that they could survive on just mush but they did, "And I guess their bowels moved all right."

As her mother's money came close to running out, her mother told her they would soon have to kill themselves. "Mother would allow no charity, but fortunately, there was one more insurance policy. We got a few more checks, so we didn't have to kill ourselves." All this was delivered in the monotone of a curious but uninvolved observer of her own life.

After she retired, she spent her days at the court house, attending criminal trials, mostly lurid rape trials, I gathered. "Oh, yes, I was a regular. All the clerks and bailiffs knew me. Even some of the judges."

As I rose to leave she told me, "I wish the doctor hadn't told me I was dying! I've been depressed ever since. Maybe it'd be easier if I didn't know."

"I think the depression will lift little by little," I told her.

"I feel so good while you are here with me, but it's harder when I'm alone. It's funny. We've known each other only a short time, but I consider you a very, very good friend, and I pray for you every night."

Her birthday is Friday. Already she has several cards. She told me she hopes Hospice won't bring her a cake, but she made a point of telling me mocha is her favorite kind.

December 6

Edith's birthday was today and there was a little party for her. I arrived past the appointed time, all sweaty and out of breath, but Edith barely said hello. She was eating her lunch, a chicken TV dinner on its foil tray, and I gathered that she doesn't like to be interrupted or distracted while she eats. I conversed with her Hospice attendant and the home health aide, who had come for the party. When Edith finished eating, the attendant brought her a cup of hot water, into which she placed a rather shriveled and ancient looking tea bag. After a while Barbara, the social worker, arrived with the cake.

Edith enjoyed the party in a low key sort of way and talked of how she always used to eat out on her birthday, even when she had to do it all alone. Barbara asked her questions to draw her out and Edith told of her early memories of the city and how when she first went to work and ate in a Woolworth's, she was terrified if a man sat next to her and only the thought that she had paid for her lunch kept her in her seat. She said she got used to being around men in public, but never felt comfortable with them beyond that, probably because there had been no man in her home after her father died.

After everyone else left, I stayed on at her request. She thanked me for the *Reader's Digests* which I'd brought earlier in the week. She said she'd been thinking about "that woman in New York" (my mother-in-law) and how my daughter didn't want to hurt her feelings and so let her grandmother renew it even though she never reads it. She said, "That woman did good even though the granddaughter didn't like the magazine and the granddaughter did good, too, not to hurt her grandmother's feelings. And now I am reading it, so it's okay."

The little nurse doll I brought was a perfect present for Edith. She was as pleased as a little girl. I told her the nurse doll was to remind her that I am thinking of her even when I am not with her. This seemed a poor consolation to offer Edith here alone in this small, dim room, hour after hour, with only her dollies, but it seemed to please her very much.

December 9

Edith called me to ask if I would pick up her prescription at the pharmacy. When I delivered the prescription to Edith, she meticulously paid me for it. "Money no longer matters," she said, "and now that I don't spend much on food, I have plenty." Interesting that on such a small income she feels she has plenty. I guess she has plenty for what is within her control: mainly TV dinners and canned fruit. And what is outside of her control, like full-time nursing care, should she need it, is so far outside her control and beyond her means that she doesn't even think of it.

In the weeks following her birthday, Edith seemed to slip more rapidly and to sink deeper into depression. I visited frequently and called her in between visits. She called me occasionally. "I can't get out of the tub myself anymore, so I have to let Ellen (the hospice attendant) help me," she told me one day with a note of resignation in her voice. She always answered the telephone sounding as if she might expire at any moment, but once she had a chance to talk a little, her voice would grow stronger.

Edith continued to be depressed and to feel badly about being depressed despite all the antidepressants. I told her not to worry about it, that depression can be a healing of the heart and is very common among people in her situation. Hospice concentrates on treating symptoms: pain and depression among them. I wondered if it wouldn't be better for Hospice to help the patient deal with the symptoms and attendant feelings of helplessness as a part of the dying process, but I didn't voice my concern.* Depression is difficult enough without feeling bad about it, as Edith does. She's alone all weekend so she's glad when the attendant comes on Monday and she can have a bath. I continued to remind her to take the experience a day at a time, even an hour or a moment at a time, but I heard a growing panic about the future in her voice.

I tried to sit and listen to Edith as much as possible without judgment and without preconceived notions of how she should deal with her illness and impending death. I really didn't know what she should be doing, which seemed to be a helpful attitude to maintain.

---

*As I became more experienced as a volunteer, I learned to call the social worker or nurse whenever I felt such concerns. Had I called the social worker in this case, I would have been reassured to hear of the deep concern of the Hospice team for Edith's emotional state and of the many hours of counseling she had received from the social workers.

December 14
Edith seemed less "boring" to me today. She is opening up more all the time. She said she had no interest in Christmas, but she was pleased that I'd brought a few Christmas cards for her to send her friends.

She dictated a note to her friend in Chicago: "I am not at all well. I don't know how long I'm going to be around. My health problems have come back. Hospice is taking care of me. I wish you a happy holiday season. Keep well. God bless you always." She signed her name to the card and supervised how I sealed and addressed it.

Ellen had a family emergency so a new attendant has been assigned to Edith. She admired the new attendant's industrious cleaning, but she missed Ellen. And Ellen made better poached eggs.

December 23
I visited Edith on my way to a holiday party. She looked thinner and weaker, and sadder, too. Depression saps her energy and her interest. She was in bed and I encouraged her to sit in the rocking chair while I was there. She moved slowly but managed by herself. She put her feet up on the edge of the bed and agreed that it felt good to be out of bed.

I realized that she had been alone all weekend and made a mental note to schedule my visits on weekends as much as possible. How lonely these four walls must become.

She asked me to open two cans for her, apricots and asparagus. She directed me where to find the can opener and containers. Opening the cans was a long process because Edith has a very old and inadequate can opener. I commented on this and she replied with a stubborn pride in her voice, "Well, I've used it for a long time." How disruptive illness has been to this narrow and completely planned life.

She felt anxious about whether she would make it to Frances's for Christmas dinner. I told her that I thought she would make it and that the trip to Frances's would do her good.

As I helped her back into bed, she said impulsively, "I wish we were sisters!"

I kissed her soft, warm cheek. "In God's family surely we are sisters, Edith."

December 24, Christmas Eve

The Hospice nurse called to tell me Edith had fallen during the night and had not been able to get up. The attendant had found her when she arrived in the morning, and Edith was now in the hospital. Her blood pressure was very low, and she wasn't doing well.

I arrived expecting to find Edith full of complaints, but she barely stirred the whole time I was there. I spoke to her and after many repetitions of her name and telling her who I was, her eyelids flickered, and a lone tear of recognition rolled down the side of her face. I had no idea what to do. I stroked her limp hand and watched her breathe. She lay there with her mouth open and I thought how embarrassed she would be to see herself like this.

Using the number obtained from the nurse, I called Edith's friend Frances who was expecting Edith for Christmas dinner. Frances seemed to appreciate my call in a distant way.

December 25, Christmas morning

I awoke wondering whether Edith had survived the night. At the hospital I found her awake and smiling, but still unable to say more than a word or two. I asked her if she remembered my visit the evening before and she nodded, yes. The nurse said she had eaten breakfast. Country-and-western-style Christmas carols were piped into the room, which I found annoying, but Edith smiled when I mentioned the music, so I guess she liked it. A plant with a small teddy bear implanted on a plastic stake amidst the leaves sat on the windowsill. "Who sent you this, Edith?" I asked.

She replied with difficulty, "A lady."

A small, cheery woman dressed in a Santa-like coat and cap came in with a cart of newspapers. She asked if Edith would like to hear a song and proceeded to sing "O Holy Night." I joined in as best I could.

Edith drifted off to sleep and I told her I would return later in the day.

December 25, Christmas evening

The nurse was just preparing to move her when I arrived. I saw pain on Edith's face while the nurse shifted her. I wondered how much was physical and how much the humiliation of being exposed with a catheter protruding between her dead-white, swollen legs. After the nurse left, she closed her eyes and seemed to be asleep. I spoke to her and at several points she made a small sound of recognition. When I left she struggled to say "good night."

December 26
I spoke with the Hospice nurse, who had visited Edith this morning. "She was mostly unconscious. She has an infection in her blood, possibly caused by perforation of her bowel. Antibiotics can control the infection, but she's very weak and low," the nurse told me. "This kind of infection can come on quickly and may have been what caused her to fall."

I arrived at the hospital at 1:00 to find a small, stout woman feeding Edith. I introduced myself, but in reply she only nodded, so I had to assume the woman was Frances. Edith was sitting up and smiling brightly. I didn't know whether to stay since Frances was already there, but Edith seemed so glad to see me that I stood awkwardly at the end of the bed for a minute. As soon as we had completed greetings, Edith asked me, "Did my mother have anything to say to you?"

I was a little taken aback, but I saw the earnest look of entreaty on her face so I said, "No, did she have anything to say to you?" Sadly and with disappointment, she said no and stretched her hand toward me. There were tears in her eyes as I took her hand in mine.

I continued to hold her hand while Frances fed her. "Don't worry, Edith," I told her. "Just enjoy your lunch and rest."

Frances seconded that and added firmly, "And get well!"

Edith talked of her mother, how much she missed her, and how lonely she was. From time to time she asked me again if her mother had called. "Does my mother know?" she inquired in an anxious voice.

"Yes," I assured her, "your mother knows and she's with you always in spirit. You aren't alone." After the days of silence, she talked on and on with urgency, and she cried tears of grief for her mother. Some of her words were garbled and at times she repeated what was said to her.

When Frances had to leave I walked out into the hall with her to let her know that she should call City Hospice if she needed anything. She told me nervously that she was going out of town for a few days. "Life has to go on," I assured her, and she seemed relieved that I didn't criticize her. As we were talking a tiny, old woman lugging a cane in one hand and a shopping bag in the other approached. It was Edith's neighbor Ruth, who had brought Edith food and visited her at home. She stayed only a moment, making more of a pro forma appearance than a real visit. Perhaps at that age there is fear that dying is catching.

After everyone else left, Edith reached for my hand and settled down for a real visit with me. It felt very peaceful and intimate to sit there with Edith, holding her hand, which felt as if it were on fire. She continued to talk about her grief and loneliness for her mother, going over and over her mother's death. "She was getting sicker, so I called the doctor. He took so long to come and then he barely looked at Mother. When he told me there was nothing he could do for her, I cried and cried. I was so frightened. I could not bear the thought of Mother dying! I sat by her bedside for days and days watching her get worse and worse. I prayed harder than I had ever prayed. I just didn't know what to do!"

"Were you with her when she died?" I asked.

"No," she replied with deep sadness in her voice. "I had to go out to the store. I was only gone half an hour, maybe less, but when I walked in the house, I knew. I knew she was gone." Edith sunk into the memory of the profound grief that she had suffered thirty years ago, but the look in her eyes told me she was experiencing it again right now.

Suddenly the sadness turned to anxiety and she turned to me and demanded, "Did you come to the funeral?"

I reminded her that I had not been with her then, and that her mother had died a long time ago. She began to cry softly and continued, "Do you think the funeral was all right? I was in shock, I didn't know what to do. Mother had always been the strong one. Do you know who came to the funeral?"

"No, who came?" I asked more softly than ever.

"Oh, I can't remember! There weren't very many. We never had a lot of friends. Were you there?"

"No, but I'm here with you now."

"Oh, thank God for that! They told me I would get over Mother's death, but, you know, I never did. I was so lonely, I could hardly keep on. There wasn't anything I wanted to do, and there wasn't anyone I could talk to. I wanted to die. Even after I went back to work, I just didn't care anymore."

"Oh, Edith, how terrible that must have been," I replied. "I wish I could have been with you then."

"Please stay with me!" she implored reaching for my hand again. "I'm so afraid. I don't want to be alone."

I assured her, "I will visit as often as I can and even when I'm not here, I will be with you in spirit. And, Edith, your mother is with you, too."

She drifted in and out of a light sleep, waking every few minutes to ask me about the funeral, or to tell me something about her mother. When I started to tiptoe out around 3:30, in came a latter day Lady Bountiful, bearing a bow-bedecked plant in one hand and a shopping bag in the other. Her black, fur trimmed coat was obviously expensive, and her stylish hairdo seemed out of place in that room. "Is this the room of Edith Moore?"

I gestured toward Edith and said, "This is Edith." I tried to think of something to say to send the woman away, but she brushed past me and glided toward the bedside with the plant, chirping in an artificially cheery voice, "Hello, Edith, I've brought you a Christmas present." She turned to me and informed me, "I'm a volunteer." She made the word sound as if a "volunteer" were a very superior creature. I wondered what agency had sent this woman.

Lady Bountiful startled me out of the peace and intimacy of the past few hours with Edith. A volunteer, she said. Why that's all I am, I thought with a sinking heart. A volunteer. I could see by the look on Edith's face that she looked on the new visitor as only another person to be with, who might offer her news of her mother. As I fled the room I told myself that surely I was a better volunteer, but for the moment at least, I was disabused of any notions I might have about my unique contribution to Edith.

December 27
Edith was dozing over a liquid lunch when I arrived. I spoon fed her the remaining sherbet and helped her drink grape juice with a straw. She continued to talk about her mother today and she

seemed tormented about her mother's death so I asked her what she was worried about. She said, "What about me? What will become of me?"

"Don't worry, you will be taken care of. The nurses will be here whenever you need them, and I will come as often as I can. Hospice will see that you are cared for." I gave her what reassurance I could, but my words sounded thin and ineffectual even to me.

"I'm afraid! Please stay with me. You're the only one who stays with me." I reminded her of all the visitors yesterday, but she could not remember any of them. The urgency in her voice and the frightened look on her face made me wish I could sit here and hold her hand all day and all night until she dies. I am saddened by the realization that this woman who has lived so much of her life alone and lonely will probably die that way, too.

Yesterday her hand burned with fever; today it was cool. The nurse said her temperature was only 97.2 . As she lay dozing and talking of her mother, she burped and up came the grape juice. I wiped up as best I could and called for the nurse. While we waited for the nurse, Edith lay there quietly, without much concern for the vomit that remains on her chest. She looked at me and asked, "Is this hard for you?" I assured her that it wasn't, that I was glad I had been here when this happened. I could feel her appreciation for my inept but eager care.

After what seemed a very long time, the nurse arrived and proceeded to change Edith's gown and all of the bed linens. I was pained to see Edith's bruised and withered body exposed on the bed. The nurse cleaned bowel movement off her, too, and I thought of how such a short time ago, bowel movements had been Edith's major concern; now she was totally unaware of the workings of her body. She has not once mentioned bowel functioning since she's been in the hospital although she does still weakly attempt to resume her food litany from time to time.

After the nurse left, she said, "I think I will go to sleep tonight and die." She does not like to be alone, especially in the morning. She said she thought about calling me this morning.

When I asked her something, she struggled with words for a moment, then said, "I don't know. My mind. . ." I assured her it was perfectly natural for her mind to wander and to just rest and let the thoughts pass in and out. Not to worry.

At 3:30 she was dozing so I moved to go. Her face registered pain at the thought of my leaving. I assured her I would be back later. My car was in a tow-away zone and I needed to be apart from Edith for a short time. Being so much with Edith who feels totally alone, I felt pulled into that lonely space. Her loneliness was so intense that I wondered if perhaps someone else should visit her in addition to me. I wondered if I were doing the right things or whether I should be helping her in different ways. I thought about calling City Hospice.

Why did they give Edith a CAT scan this morning? Surely the diagnosis was clear at this point and I cringed to think of her discomfort and trauma at being carted down to X ray. Why do they do these things to a dying person? I thought comfort was supposed to be the goal now.

December 27, early evening
Edith was asleep and the room was dark; dinner sat untouched on the tray. I turned on a small light and spoke her name; she roused but seemed disoriented. I asked her if she wanted dinner. She said yes, so I carefully removed the pillow holding her on her side and slid the pillow out from between her knees and straightened her legs. Very slowly I raised the head of the bed a little and stopped. I was nervous about moving her without asking the nurse. Slowly I raised her a bit more and she began to vomit. I caught as much as possible in a towel and pressed the call button as I grabbed another towel from the bathroom. As I cleaned her up, she smiled gratefully, though she continued to burp and vomit.

The nurse, a young, pregnant woman came in and apologized for not having come to feed Edith earlier. I explained what had happened and she said the special fluids Edith had had to drink for the X ray combined with other fluids had been too much for her. I helped her change the bed and Edith's gown. Actually assisting in the changing was less painful for me than watching. As we were finishing, Edith's doctor came in, glanced at Edith in bed, mumbled something about having been out of town for a few days and asked the nurse if Edith had been sitting up in a chair. How remote that idea sounded. The nurse said no and told him about the vomiting. He turned to Edith and said, "We'll get you something to help you feel more comfortable tonight," and walked out. For a while I kept thinking he would be back to examine Edith, but then I realized that those few mumbled words, spoken on the run, were the whole visit.

Once tucked under the clean sheets, Edith fell off to sleep. I sat in the chair and watched her face. How much more peaceful she looked than even this afternoon.

The longer I've been with Edith the more I see that it doesn't matter who Edith is, and now I see that it doesn't matter who I am. I asked Edith this afternoon if she remembered my name. She thought a moment and said, "Mimi." I told her, "Joan," and she seemed to remember for a moment. All the particulars of our individual lives and personalities have fallen away in the hours we've been together.

When I left this afternoon I felt alone and overwhelmed with the need for someone to be with Edith, to comfort her in her loneliness, so I called Hospice to see what practical arrangements were being made. The person I spoke with was very matter-of-fact and said she had spoken to the funeral director. It startled me, but gave me perspective on all the dying people City Hospice assists. I was amazed no one had encouraged Edith to make arrangements for power of attorney. (I later found out that the hospice social worker had tried to get Edith to make a will and sign a power of attorney, but Edith had resisted giving up this kind of control, even though she knew she was dying.)

December 28

Just as I arrived, the nurse was getting ready to feed Edith, so I offered to feed her. The nurse said to go easy because they had added pureed food to her diet to see how she would do. She hadn't vomited anymore today.

The nurse said Edith had been asking for me today, but I think she may have misinterpreted some of the dialogue of Edith's remembrances of her mother's death. Almost at once she told me, "One of the ladies is gone now." When I asked her who, she replied, "Hellissima," and when I asked her what my name was, it was also, "Hellissima." She was somewhat dismayed that she did not know my name, but then went on to tell me about Hellissima, who I think was a nurse for her mother. She talked more today about her mother's funeral. "Do you think it was nice?"

With some anxiety, she told me, "My mother is lost!" I reminded her that her mother had died and been buried after the beautiful funeral and that her spirit was in heaven. With a sigh of relief, she said something about "the heaven books," as if she had just figured something out.

She ate a little of everything but not much in total. When I asked her if she wanted some meat, she said, "I should because they want it in my diet." She has been such a "good girl" all her life that she cannot stop now. A lot of gas during and after eating.

She told me, "We had so much to say, but I didn't say anything at all!" I didn't know whom she was talking about, but when I asked her if she wished she had said something, she replied wistfully, "Oh, yes."

Almost immediately after eating, she dozed off into a light but peaceful sleep. She stirred when the nurse returned; she mumbled a few words and smiled at me. I lowered the head of the bed. She looked peaceful, but there were still unresolved issues about her mother's death, or was it about her own death? Was her mother's death a metaphor for her own?

December 29
I arrived just before 5:00 to find her sleeping, but she roused easily and talked of dreaming some happy dreams, and some sad ones. She dreamed of being alone in an apartment. I mentioned what a nice apartment she had and she replied, "Did I?" She seemed to have no memory of it. "So many dreams. . ." She sounded weary of dreaming.

Dinner arrived, all liquids tonight, and I sat her up to feed her. What a lovely, intimate thing it is to feed someone! I had given her only a few spoonfuls when a dour-faced nurse came in and told me not to feed Edith, that she would feed her herself later. Something about choking and not wanting to force her. Despite my assurances that I had fed Edith before and would not force her, she persisted. Edith listened without concern. I left the tray and sat down beside Edith. We talked for a while and soon another nurse came in and wondered why Edith was not eating. She was surprised to hear of the other nurse's admonitions. The "choking" was actually the vomiting of two days ago! Edith remarked with humor, "Too many nurses on the floor." Although Edith's care at this hospital had been very good, the incident reminded me how difficult it is for a large, inner-city hospital to provide the personalized kind of care Hospice would like to see for all patients.

After I fed her very little, she'd had enough and lay back resting and burping. Very soon she fell asleep, and I sat for awhile watching her sleeping face. When I rose to leave, she awoke with a start and began talking anxiously and incoherently of her dreams.

"What are you worrying about, Edith?" I asked her, adjusting the blanket.

"What is going to happen to me?"

"We will all continue to take care of you and you will heal your heart. Try not to worry."

"But I'm afraid of the other land!"

"Trust in God, Edith. He will take care of you. No one knows what death is really like, but I think it will be just fine for you." I reminded her of when she went to the spiritualist church and she brightened. I promised to return the next day and she smiled with a peaceful sigh.

December 30

Edith was quiet and peaceful today. No mention of her mother in two days now. Perhaps she has resolved her feelings about her mother's death. "It's light and dark now," she reported.

"Let the light into your heart," I told her. "The light is love. Feel your breath flowing in and out, all by itself. Just rest and let your heart be open." She put her fingers on her chest and had a look on her face like she now understood something very important.

Many fewer words today. She still smiles broadly and tends to agree with whatever is asked. Like a small child, choices confuse her. It is better to ask, "Do you want some soup?" rather than "Do you want soup or Jello?"

A little later she told me, "Don't close my eyes."

December 31

Calls from City Hospice. I talked to a nurse and the volunteer coordinator. It felt good to share a little of my experience. I feel more like a member of the team now.

Edith was sleeping when I arrived at 5:00 and when I roused her, she indicated that she didn't want to eat, or even to sit up. Soon the nurse came in and told Edith that it was time to eat. I fed Edith soup and ice cream. She seemed very distant and sad tonight. She said very little and kept her eyes closed most of the time, even while eating.

Being with Edith is harder now than when she talked a lot. I realize that the discomfort I feel with her silence is my resistance to her dying, really dying. I sat there in the silence, watching Edith sleep, and I felt separate from her and at the same time connected to her every breath.

January 1

I arrived shortly after lunch to find Edith dozing but somewhat wakeful. Today one eye was closed while the other was half open. Does the one not close properly or does the other fall shut?

She didn't talk much today. She responded yes or no, but nothing more. For a long time, I sat just watching her, not knowing what to do or say. My heart was so full of feeling for Edith, that I began talking to her from my heart, without thinking too much about what I was saying.

"There's not much need to talk anymore, is there?" She opened her eyes and looked very directly at me as if she were surprised that I knew what she was thinking. "You seem to be moving much closer to God now," I continued. "Prayers need no words and God can hear prayers directly from your heart. My heart can hear your heart, too." And for those few minutes, I do believe it was true.

What an amazing experience to abandon ordinary thought and rely totally on words from the heart. Even more amazing to see how easily Edith heard my words.

January 2

Edith will be transferred tomorrow to the hospice inpatient unit at another hospital. The nurse said she has been sleepier, but has been eating well.

She was sound asleep, snoring with her mouth open. She awoke and seemed glad to see me. She struggled to say something. I asked her what she was trying to say and she said the first sentence I have heard in several days, "I am trying to tell you, it is going pretty good." She gave a couple odd short yawns and shuddered as if something hurt her. I asked her if she could tell me what was hurting and she said, "No," in a small sad voice.

I asked her if anyone had come to visit today and she replied, "Frances." So she was less sleepy and out of it than the nurses assumed.

While I was feeding her, the social worker came in to confirm the ambulance to the Hospice inpatient unit tomorrow morning. Edith looked a little frightened. I reassured her and promised to visit her tomorrow after she was transferred. She ate quite a bit and remained alert throughout dinner and for a short time afterwards. A young doctor came in to say good-bye. It was obvious that Edith liked him very much for she just beamed. Although he seemed uncomfortable and awkward in his good-bye to her, I sensed how much he cared for Edith. I felt him struggling to find appropriate words, but there were none.

January 3

Edith was transferred this morning. The volunteer on duty gave me a tour of the hospice inpatient unit.* Everything seemed shabby and cramped, but everyone was very friendly. Pat, Edith's City Hospice nurse, was there and we discussed her progress. I felt very happy to be part of Edith's Hospice team. They asked *me* what she had been eating!

Edith looked a little dazed, but she looked comfortable in her new room. A man retched in the next room and she looked at me. Other than that she gave no sign of noticing the sounds in the hallway. From her bed, she can see into the hall, but she made no effort to see the steady stream of people passing. I remembered how she was concerned that no man move onto the same floor of her apartment building and wondered whether the male nurse

*This hospice unit was a contracted care facility at a local hospital. City Hospice provided training to staff on the unit, but the hospital supervised staff and controlled all other aspects of care. Although the care was generally better than in most nursing homes and hospitals, hospice staff often wished for an inpatient facility more in tune with the hospice philosophy of care. Hospice nurses and social workers visited patients regularly and monitored their care.

made her uncomfortable. Those concerns may all be in the past now.

I fed her her lunch and spent a few more minutes with her. She ate only a little and then rested with her eyes closed. One eye still stays halfway open. I told her that I wouldn't be able to come tomorrow, and she seemed concerned, but only slightly.

January 5

Edith was sleeping when I arrived and I had to call her name twice before she stirred. It had been two days since I had seen her, and she looked more gaunt than ever.

The whole time I was with her, she barely opened her eyes, even when I fed her. Every television on the floor, except Edith's, was tuned loudly to a football game. I asked her if the noise bothered her, but she made no answer. Edith was distant and separate from everyone, even me. The television cheers were depressing to me. I felt an enormous loneliness well up in me, and I missed the closeness of the days in the hospital.

She ate very little and her stomach rumbled and gurgled. Occasionally a look of pain crossed her face. I spoke softly to her, "Soften around the discomfort. Create a space around the edges of where it feels bad and breathe into the space." She stirred in recognition and, I think, relief at my words.

January 6

Edith did not rouse despite my repeated efforts. A nurse helped me turn her and she stirred with pain. I asked her if she wanted some soup. She seemed to say yes, but by the time the spoon reached her lips, she was too deeply asleep to notice. After calling her name over and over again without any response, I set down the spoon and sat down beside the bed.

In a little while an energetic nurse came in. I told her that Edith was too deeply asleep to eat. She proceeded to call loudly to Edith and to shake her leg: "Honey! You must eat now! Wake up, Honey!" Then she opened the milk shake and began to feed Edith though Edith was obviously in pain and resisting. The nurse noticed the pained expression and promised to bring a pain suppository. She left me with the milk shake and went to attend to other patients.

I encouraged Edith to take a few spoonfuls of the milk shake, but I gave up quickly because I saw how hard it was for Edith to swallow, and she kept drifting off. I couldn't bring myself to force her to eat. What an intrusion! I was beginning to understand that death creates a curriculum for the dying, and for Edith, withdrawing from food, which had been the focus of her pleasure, was the current task in her curriculum.

Soon I set the spoon down and again sat beside Edith. Pain flickered across her face repeatedly. Where was the promised pain medication? I talked to her softly, soothing and reminding her to soften around the pain. She had a lot of phlegm in her throat and upper chest, and I wondered about all the dairy products on her dinner tray. Not much attention seems to be paid to diet in hospitals. Diet is either liquid, pureed or regular, without any further sensitivity to the patient's specific condition. I thought that removing dairy might reduce the mucus in Edith's chest and let her breathe more comfortably.

After about forty-five minutes the nurse returned with the pain suppository, and I helped her turn Edith. Poor Edith cried in pain while I held her bony frame. She had lost more weight and her skin hung in folds on her bony frame. The skin on her buttocks was extremely red. The nurse applied a lubricant and inserted the suppository.

"Why isn't she on an egg-crate mattress?" I asked the nurse. Hospice always used the rumply, blue foam mattresses to prevent bed sores.

"Oh, I don't know, but she's turned every two hours, so it's not necessary," she assured me.

After Edith was at length settled, the nurse was determined to feed Edith some more. With a coaxing, but firm manner, she managed to get Edith to finish the milk shake, a glass of juice and some milk. It was more a matter of the nurse pouring liquids into Edith's mouth than feeding her. Was this good for Edith? Surely Edith was past the need for a healthy diet with lots of protein and plenty of vitamins.

After the nurse left, Edith settled into a deep sleep. Her stomach grumbled and gurgled, but the pain suppository must have gone to work because Edith slept peacefully. As usual television sounds came from every direction and various buzzers, bells, and loudspeakers intruded. At the hospital there seemed to be a little more protection from sounds, but here the rooms were so small, it was like being in the hall. Edith's bed faced the hall, and fortunately, the room opposite was vacant or another patient would be directly facing Edith.

I kissed Edith on the forehead and said good night; I don't think she was aware of my departure. I left feeling disturbed, with many questions about her care. I had hoped that the special Hospice unit would provide especially good and sensitive care, but I see it is pretty much like any hospital with too many overworked nurses, working from charts rather than from current patient needs, more geared toward improvement, cure, and discharge than supportive care of the dying. And here, everything is old and cramped which makes everything harder, and more depressing.

January 7
I called Pat this morning about my concerns with the care Edith is receiving. She wasn't surprised to hear of these problems; apparently the quality of care at this facility has been disappointing to everyone at City Hospice. She planned to visit Edith today and said she would get her an egg crate mattress and make sure she wasn't force fed anymore. Forcing Edith to eat seemed wrong to me, but I was easily intimidated by the nurse into thinking that perhaps there was something I didn't understand about patient care. I was relieved to find that an experienced nurse like Pat agreed with me. I guess my instincts aren't so bad. (I later found out that the nurse who had fed Edith was new and had not yet undergone the Hospice training.)

Edith was resting, but she roused easily when I arrived mid-afternoon. The egg crate mattress was in place, and she looked much more comfortable today. Pat's visit had obviously had an effect.

Speech was difficult, but Edith mouthed "good to see you." Her stomach gurgled loudly and the phlegm in her chest made her cough, which seemed to aggravate the discomfort in her stomach. She seemed to be in less obvious pain today, but every now and then, she would grimace. There was now a bald spot on one side of her head from constant contact with the pillow. She dozed off occasionally, but remained alert throughout most of my visit.

A gray-haired man in a clerical collar carrying a Bible prominently like a talisman came in. Fingering his collar, he introduced
himself, "Hello, there, I'm Roger Jones. I'm a retired navy chaplain, and I come here once a week as a volunteer."* Once again, as
with the lady at the hospital, I heard an implication in his voice
when he said the word "volunteer," that he was doing something
extraordinary and that I should be impressed. He seemed more
inclined to talk to me than Edith. When I told him she could hear
and understand him perfectly, he spoke to her loudly as if she were
hard of hearing. " Well, how are you today?" I could hear discomfort in his voice. Edith obviously understood that this was a min-
ister and listened attentively although she couldn't respond.

"God bless you," the chaplain intoned as he fled out the door.

January 8
Only a brief time to visit today; a friend waits for me downstairs
in the lobby. As soon as I walked into Edith's room, I felt a calm,
settled feeling, not unlike the feeling of walking into a room full of
people meditating. It was the same feeling of being absorbed into
a deep and powerful silence that felt right on the edge of eternity.

Edith was sleeping, but opened her eyes briefly when I called
her name. I sat beside her, watching her breathe; there was a slight
catch in her breath now. This being with a dying person is a terribly intimate experience that transcends the ordinary criteria for
relationships. I scarcely know Edith and we have nothing in common. If sitting beside a virtual stranger like Edith feels this intimate, what would it be like to be with a friend?

January 9
It was late by the time I arrived and I wondered whether it was
worthwhile to visit Edith this late. The hall was quiet and Edith
was asleep. "Hello, Edith," I greeted her, and she opened her eyes
briefly and acknowledged my presence. Her breathing became
faster and I think more frightened. I smoothed her hair and whispered soothing words, the same ones I found myself intoning day
after day. "Nothing to do, nothing to worry . . . just breathe.
Even though breathing feels a little harder now, it still happens all

---

*The chaplain was a hospital volunteer, not a Hospice volunteer.

by itself. . . Just watch the breath . . . breathing in . . . breathing
out, just rest and watch . . . be very soft . . . and keep your heart
open."

I sat beside her and watched her as she slept. Her breathing
seemed more difficult tonight; the catch I'd noticed last night was
more pronounced, and she seemed to be breathing quite rapidly,
though she was relaxed and asleep. I synchronized my breathing
with hers: it was too fast so I began to breathe one breath to every
two of her breaths. Breathing with her, I was intensely aware of
how alive she was. It seemed incredible, for the moment, that she
would ever stop breathing. I reached out and placed my fingers
lightly on her forearm; I was overcome with the strength of the life
force coursing through this wasted and sick body. I sat for a long
time with my fingers on her arm, feeling the rhythms of her pulse,
her breathing, her just being alive, being Edith. I watched her
breath and my own breath. I thought about how she really was
going to die, how all the rhythms would cease and her spirit would
slip out of the body.

After a little while I got up to leave, not sure I'd done much
for Edith. This visit was more for me. I silently promised to visit
earlier tomorrow. Always before, I had told Edith I would be back
tomorrow, but a friend pointed out that a day would come when
she would die before I could return and I would be left alone with
my promise. "Good night, Edith," I whispered, with tears rising
in my throat. She barely stirred.

January 10
Once again it was late afternoon by the time I arrived. As I
reached the nurses' station, the young nurse at the desk greeted me
with enthusiasm: "Oh! You are the Hospice volunteer! I am just
now calling City Hospice. She died today at 4:30." It took me a
few minutes to realize that it had been only forty-five minutes
since Edith had died.

I had never seen a dead person, and as I walked down the
familiar hall to Edith's room, I wondered what to expect. What
would she look like? Would I get upset? The moment I entered the
room I was touched by the presence of death. Although Edith was
exactly as she always was, lying to one side with her mouth open,
irrevocable change was blatantly obvious. The fact of death rushed

up to greet me in that small room. There was a gray stillness about her face, perhaps a certain emptiness about her features. Her eyes were slightly open.

There was no look of pain on her face; I hoped that meant she had died without pain or struggle or fear. I stood beside the bed, looking down at her body. For a moment, I thought I could see the sheet rising and falling as if she were still breathing, but then I realized that the sheet was totally still. Everything was still except for my pounding heart and shallow breathing, which seemed conspicuously loud. I tried to remember what I had read about the time soon after death. Was her spirit still lingering near her body? I couldn't tell. Silently I urged her to leave now, if she were still here.

After only a few minutes, the nurse came in carrying large plastic bags. She proceeded to clean out the drawers and closets, gathering Edith's few personal belongings, chattering away to me all the while. She seemed glad to have me there to tell about all that they must now do and what a nice lady Edith was. It seemed odd to be having this conversation with Edith lying right there in the bed.

I returned to the desk to talk to the hospice nurse who had called. Hospice would contact the coroner, Edith's personal physician, and Frances, who must come and sign before the body could be taken to the mortuary. After talking to the nurse, I wandered back down toward Edith's room. I would have liked to sit beside her for a few minutes, but the nurse was still bustling about the room and I felt hesitant to say that I wanted to sit with a dead woman. I stood in the doorway listening to the nurse and looking at Edith's gray and silent face. Again I wordlessly implored her to leave now, and hoped that she couldn't hear or see all this chattering and stowing of things in plastic bags.

The nurse came out with all the bags and closed the door behind her. It seemed odd after all these days of visiting Edith that there would be no more visits to make, that I wouldn't be coming back here tomorrow. I was filled with the image of her gray and silent face, but I didn't feel anxious or sad or even surprised. I didn't feel either incomplete or complete. The nurse said something about too bad I hadn't come earlier today, but I didn't feel any particular regret about that, or about anything. I was still living the experience one day at a time. Sitting day by day with Edith, my heart had been opened in a new and deeper way. I trusted my heart more, too, and felt somehow a little bit clearer about everything.

Good-bye, Edith, my friend. And my sister.

Epilogue

The journal ends on the day Edith died, but the story continued a little longer, and my learning even longer.

Sitting as close to Edith as I did in those final weeks, I had little sense of the context of her life. She became for me a human being without context. She just was. It was several weeks after she died that I found myself once again walking up the dark stairs to her apartment and back into her life.

Edith's friend Frances had gratefully accepted my offer to help close up the apartment. As we opened the door, the musty, stale odor of the room, closed up all these weeks and weeks while Edith lay dying in the hospital, assaulted us. I felt as if we were walking on a grave site and I could hear the rustling of ghosts and spirits in the still air.

Frances's first concern was finding Edith's will. Although she was the only person to take care of winding up Edith's affairs, and there was no "estate" to divvy up, without a will in hand, dealing with the bureaucracy was full of frustrations and delays. While I was still standing in the middle of the room trying to regain my equilibrium amidst the whirling of memories and the whisperings of ghosts, Frances anxiously pulled a battered suitcase from the back of the closet. Inside was a small, gray metal box that opened with the key she found in Edith's purse. Nervously, she sorted through the contents of the box, discarding numerous bulky envelopes on the table in her search for the will.

"Oh, thank God!" she cried with a sigh of relief. "Here it is! She did write a will after all." As she read through the single handwritten sheet of lined paper, I looked at the envelopes on the table and realized they were full of twenty-dollar bills! Frances was so relieved to find the will, she showed little interest in the envelopes full of money, but agreed I should count it.

The envelopes were the window kind that must have contained her social security checks and each one was labeled with the name of the month and inside were cryptic notes in Edith's handwriting on scraps of paper. She had obviously squeezed all this money out of her meager allotments, but why? One envelope had a note about her funeral costs, but the other notes mentioned "food money" and "extra." Altogether there was nearly nineteen hundred dollars. I would never know why Edith had accumulated this secret hoard of cash, that could have paid for additional attendant care, but like all recipients of SSI and Medi-Cal, she lived in fear of losing her benefits, so even had she stayed at home longer, she might never have mentioned the money. She was used to doing without.

I returned the money to the envelopes and turned to help Frances with the packing and sorting. Edith had so few belongings that it took only a few hours to empty the dresser, the kitchen cupboards, the closet. The shelves and drawers were filled with rolls and rolls of toilet paper, aluminum foil, and waxed paper, clothes she had never worn and rows and rows of sturdy shoes, and stacks of envelopes, the kind the phone bill comes in. All of her belongings were old and cheap, and there was an impersonal quality to everything. Her kitchen with dime-store, plastic dishes and cheap aluminum pans reminded me of the furnished kitchens in rented summer cottages. I thought of my own apartment full of books and photographs, old letters and journals, sea shells and plants, souvenirs and treasures of my life, not much longer than half of Edith's, and I was chilled by the contrast. There is part of me that would like to live in a little room with only the bare essentials: ah, the simple life. But then I start accumulating the sea shells, rooting new plants, and writing it all down. There goes the simplicity.

"Oh, here's the photo of her mother, she always kept by her bed." Frances held out an old fashioned, sepia-toned photo in a small oval frame of a stout woman in a heavy coat. I strained to see the woman Edith had loved, but the photo was small and unclear.

After we had sorted everything into piles, Frances gave me a ride home and thanked me for helping her. On the way home, she talked about her lifelong friendship with Edith. Despite all the years and all the shared holidays, Frances said Edith would some-times retreat into her own private life and resist her overtures. She told of one time several years ago when Edith went for weeks re-fusing to answer her phone, and then without explanation called her again. "I would always know it was her because the phone would ring once and then stop. She was on limited phone service, so that was the signal for me to call her. Now that she's gone, I still find myself listening when the phone rings, wondering whether there will be just one ring, whether it's Edith. But then the second ring comes, and I remember."

I never expected to see Frances again, but a few months later she telephoned me to tell me she had wound up Edith's affairs and wanted to make a donation to City Hospice of the money we had found in Edith's closet. "I know the money is mine, but I really don't need it. Hospice was so wonderful to her, that I know she would be happy to see me give it to Hospice."

She came up my steps bearing a huge flowering plant for me and an envelope with the check for Hospice. We drank tea together and talked of our dear friend Edith. While Edith was alive, I never knew how Frances felt about me, whether I might be intruding on their friendship. She told me she had tried to be a good friend to Edith, but sometimes Edith had made it difficult for anyone to be close to her. Somehow my being with Edith at the end made it easier for Frances to be close to her, too.

Just before she left, she reached into her purse and pulled out a small plastic bag, "I thought you might like this back, perhaps to give to another patient." It was the little nurse doll I had given Edith for her birthday!

3

Jeanne

I met Jeanne less than a week before she died, and saw her only twice; yet the grief I felt when she died, and the sense of sadness that has stayed with me ever since, has been profound, and out of proportion to my involvement.

Why did I mourn so deeply the loss of a woman I had only met? Perhaps it was because Jeanne was a startling reminder that death was not an event reserved for old women. She was only a few years older than I and one of her children was the same age as my daughter. Unlike Edith, she had a family, friends, and a full life.

The Journal

May 1, a new patient
Jeanne is a forty-eight year old mother of two teenagers. She was until recently a teacher at a local school. She has liver cancer with metastasis to the bone, and she is receiving chemotherapy, but is also trying alternative therapies. She had a double mastectomy some years ago, so this illness is not entirely a new thing. Jeanne and her family have fought her illness very aggressively, and her doctor, who is one known for prescribing full treatment until the very end, has now given her six months or less to live. After visiting her, the Hospice nurse thought her spirits were good, and said Jeanne was not in much pain, but her energy was low. The nurse

47

discovered that Jeanne was quite actively dying and seemed very confused about what to do. She hasn't thought much about the possibility of dying and hasn't dealt with the fact that the effects of chemotherapy on her body prevent her from having the energy to perhaps put her life in order. Her husband Greg is the strong silent type who probably hasn't dealt with Jeanne's impending death either.

At her physician's suggestion, Jeanne sees Julia at the Women's Health Center, a nonprofit organization, where she receives massage, counseling, and other therapies. I'm to call her to offer a ride to her appointment on Tuesday, which is all she has requested for now. It's hard for her to ask for help.

Call to Jeanne

She was pleased to hear from me and accepted my offer of a ride on Tuesday. She said, "I've only had this 'bugaboo' three weeks and I'm hoping to get better and be able to drive and share rides again." I told her I was glad to give her a ride, and I left her my telephone number so that she could call if anything came up over the weekend.

I feel an urgency to establish a rapport with Jeanne so that, hopefully, I can be supportive to her in whatever time she has left. She has so much to do: accept that she is dying, put her life in order, and say good-bye to her family and friends. I wonder how much time she has.

May 5

Jeanne lives in an attractive home on a quiet, tree lined street with a sweeping view of the city below. As I walked up the front steps and rang the door bell, it was difficult to imagine anyone dying in this lovely home, with the welcoming front entry. I could picture guests arriving for a dinner party, and I could imagine children racing up the steps and swinging open the teal blue, carved door, crying out, "Mom, I'm home!" but it was hard to imagine the mother of the family dying, here in what was easily the American dream of a safe solid home, a good place to raise a family and live the good life.

The deep notes of the door chimes sounded within, and in a minute Jeanne opened the door and greeted me with a tired smile.

She looks older than I expected. She is tall with prominent, warm dark eyes that are quite yellow from jaundice. "Please come in. I'm so grateful you could come. I'm all ready; just let me get my purse." She walked with difficulty but managed without any help from me.

I felt rather nervous on the drive to the Women's Health Center. The conversation seemed too trivial, too light, but I didn't know what to say to Jeanne, Jeanne with her dark, sad eyes looking wearily out upon the busy street we sped down. We could have been any two women thrown together by chance, getting acquainted. "Do you have children, Joan?"

"Yes, two: a daughter who is nineteen and a son, fifteen," I replied.

"Why, Tommy, our oldest is nineteen, too! Where is your daughter going to school?"

"She's a freshman at Cal Berkeley."

"Oh, how lucky she was able to get into Cal. She must be a smart girl. Tommy just never applied himself in high school. He's bright enough, but he paid no attention to his grades, so he's going to city college this year, and hoping to get into a university in the fall. He seems to be working harder at school now, but he still doesn't have much discipline. His younger sister has always been a better student, and she plays sports, too. They're both good kids though. I worry too much, I guess."

"I worry, too," I admitted. "My daughter's a good student and has nice friends; she has common sense and has always shown good judgment. Yet, the world is full of so many dangers and pitfalls. It's not easy, even for a smart kid, so I worry about her."

The Women's Health Center was in an unfamiliar part of town, so our conversation was interrupted by having to look for the street to turn on, and then finding the address. The center is housed in a large corner house in a working class neighborhood, not a likely locale for a center dealing in massage, meditation, and alternative healing practices. Jeanne ascended the few steps, leaning heavily on the porch railing, and we entered a dimly lit hallway with notices of meditation class schedules and posters in muted colors on the walls. The scent of incense hung in the air. Julia, Jeanne's therapist, greeted us before Jeanne had a chance to sit down in the waiting room, and led her to another room. I spent the hour reading the Women's Health Center literature in the cozy, book lined waiting room. I found myself thinking of Edith, and wondering whether she would have liked to come to a place like this.

After the appointment Julia came into the waiting room with Jeanne. Jeanne with difficulty lowered herself into a rocking chair, and smiled at me. When I returned her smile, our eyes held for a moment and I had the feeling we were close friends, rather than strangers who had only just met.

Julia had a list in her hand. "Can you please tell Hospice that Jeanne needs a home health aide? She's too weak to be alone so much."

Jeanne looked dismayed at Julia's pronouncement, and protested, "I'd rather to be alone. So many people calling—it tires me out. And whenever someone comes, I must get up and answer the door. It's easier to be alone." She looked at me again, hoping I would understand.

"A key for Hospice people needs to be arranged, so Jeanne won't have to answer the door," Julia continued. "What else can Hospice do? Perhaps a massage by a Hospice volunteer would relieve the pressure in her abdomen."

"They are after me to have a family meeting," reported Jeanne wearily. "It's too much. I can't do it this week. The kids are too busy and I'm too exhausted. Can you tell Hospice I need to put the meeting off until next week?" she implored me. "I'm too tired to even call. Maybe next week I'll feel better."

I suspected that Hospice wanted to hold the family meeting soon because Jeanne might not have much time, and if she had not acknowledged her impending death, chances are the family had not either, but I agreed to talk to Karen, the hospice social worker.

Julia set Jeanne's next appointment for next Tuesday and gave her a book to read, but Jeanne seemed uninterested.

In the car on the way home, Jeanne and I talked again, but now that we'd been together at the Women's Health Center, and it had been acknowledged between us that Jeanne was very sick, we both relaxed into the easy intimacy between friends. With Edith, I had always known that I would never have known her or been close to her were she not dying, but with Jeanne, I knew we would have been friends under any circumstance, and the fact that we were only meeting now that she was so ill added a note of urgency to our conversation.

"You know I've had to tell my whole story to so many people these past few weeks, that I just can't do it again right now," Jeanne told me apologetically. "I hope you understand. I wish I weren't so tired."

"Oh, Jeanne, please don't feel you have to tell me anything. I do understand, and I don't need to hear your whole story to know you. We can just proceed without stories and get to know each other along the way."

"I'm so glad you understand," Jeanne responded with obvious relief in her voice. "I'm just so tired . . . and there's so much happening. Tommy and Jill have had the flu, and now all this Hospice business. I just don't know."

"This is a really hard time for you," I suggested. "Of course, you're tired. It's hard enough to be sick yourself, but to be dealing with sick children on top of your own illness. . ."

"Yes," she continued, grateful for my understanding of what she had to cope with, "for weeks everyone has been coughing and feverish. Even Greg, my husband, was home a day or two, and Tommy and Jill were really sick. And Jill—she's fifteen—seems to refuse to fully recover. She stayed home from school long after she was over the flu, and she seemed to be calling for me day and night. The other night I insisted she come down to dinner, and she refused." Jeanne paused and then continued with a catch in her voice, "I didn't mean to yell at her, but I worry about her. She's more dependent on me than Tommy ever was. I wanted to comfort her, but I ended up yelling at her, and she cried and stayed in her room."

How well I knew that shock of hearing my voice raised in anger at just the moment I meant to express love to my child. The tears in Jeanne's voice, brought a lump to my throat. "Jill is probably frightened to see how sick you are, which makes her want to retreat to a time when she was small and you took care of her."

When we walked in the door, the sound of teenage music greeted us. The stereo in the living room was tuned to a pop station and Tommy was in the kitchen on the phone with the hospice social worker, Karen. He paced the kitchen floor as far as the telephone cord would allow, and gestured with his free hand. "No, I don't think tonight will work . . . . sure I know it's important, but my sister has a game tonight, and I'm not sure what time my dad will be home either. Oh, here's my mom! You can talk to her about it," and with that he offered the receiver to Jeanne, and explained, "It's the social worker from Hospice. She still wants to have the meeting tonight. Maybe you can explain to her. . ."

Jeanne sunk wearily into a chair at the dining room table, and shook her head, "I'm too tired, Tommy. Joan, can you talk to her? Tell her next week would be fine, but not this week."

I took the phone to relay the messages from Julia and to talk to Karen about the family meeting. She was dismayed, "I don't think the family realizes how sick Jeanne is, how little time there may be! I'm afraid to wait until next week. See if you can convince Jeanne to have the meeting tonight. The daughter can be a little late to the basketball game."

So I spoke with Jeanne and Tommy, and they reluctantly agreed to have the meeting tonight. "Tell her it will have to be short, because Jill can't be late for the game," Tommy instructed me.

After I hung up the phone, Tommy introduced himself to me. "Hi, I'm Tom. Thanks for taking my mother to the doctor." He was articulate and concerned about his mother. "Do you want some more of that juice, Mom?" Jeanne told him my daughter was at UC Berkeley.

"Great, hey she must be my age! Does she like it? Boy, she must have applied herself better than I did in high school. I never really thought about college . . . and stuff like that, until it was too late. But I'm getting it together now. I've applied to several schools for the fall, but this . . . this illness is making me really think seriously about a lot of things."

"It's natural," I told him, "for you to be doing this kind of thinking and you can call upon Hospice for help in thinking these things through. I'm going to leave my telephone number, so you can call me, too, if anything comes up that I might be able to help with."

"I'm tired," Jeanne interjected, "and ready for a nap. I'm sorry, Joan. Maybe we can talk another day."

"That's fine, Jeanne. I'll call in a day or two and you can count on me to take you to the Women's Health Center again next week."

Tom helped Jeanne stand up and she turned to me with outstretched arms and a tired smile. We embraced and she told me with feeling, "Thanks so much . . . for everything. Tommy, can you help me upstairs?"

"Just a minute, Mom," and he followed me to the door. He seemed reluctant to let me go. "I hope I'll see you again," he said with a sudden lost and lonely undercurrent to his voice.

"I'll be back," I assured him, and then as Tom opened the door for me I waved to Jeanne waiting at the foot of the stairs.

"Thanks for coming," he said, suddenly sounding more grown-up again.

May 6 and May 7
Calls to Hospice. The family meeting was delayed one more day. Meanwhile, Jeanne realized that she was dying very quickly, and at the meeting she spoke very plainly. The whole family now understood. All the confusion of busy lives fell away and they dropped everything else to care for Jeanne. Nothing concrete for me to do. Jeanne will never leave home for visits to the Women's Health Center so I cannot even do that. Karen said to just keep calling or to drop by, perhaps with a casserole or some flowers.

I called Jeanne's house. Tom answered. "Oh, yes, I remember you. Lots of hospice people are coming now. No, there's nothing we need. Our aunt is here to help, and the hospice people are great. Yes, I've got your number. Thanks for calling." The family was mobilized to care for Jeanne, and I felt useless.

May 9
I dropped by with flowers. Jeanne's sister Cara answered the door and welcomed me in. She led me upstairs to Jeanne's bedroom where Jill was sitting with her mother. Jeanne had aged forty years in the four days since I had seen her, and she had withered to a small gaunt, balding figure lying on her side in the middle of a king-size bed. Her face was gray and yellow all at once.

Jill sat cross-legged next to her, stroking her face and hands while a black-and-white cat cavorted about the bed. A vase of red roses stood on the bureau. I didn't know quite what to say to Jill. She seemed older, more mature, than fifteen, but I could see the soft, vulnerable child in her, the child Jeanne had told me she worried about. She seemed calm and quietly happy to be with Jeanne.

I scratched the cat's head, and told her to call me if there were anything I could do, but I knew that I was a stranger here and had no role in Jeanne's death.

When I moved to leave, Jill rose with the same gracious quality that Tom had exhibited when he showed me to the door, and again when I called. I was getting a deeper feeling of Jeanne by meeting her family.

I left feeling sad that there really wasn't anything for me to do, with Cara cooking dinner in the kitchen, Jill attending to Jeanne, and Greg and Tommy no doubt out shopping or running errands. They are a close, loving family who will care for Jeanne by themselves and provide support to each other, too. Once they understood what was happening, there wasn't a moment's hesitation. The whole house was infused with the warm, gracious spirit of this family.

May 11

Jeanne died yesterday. The news didn't surprise me. Glad I stopped by the day before on Saturday.

May 12

I was getting ready to go to the dentist when it hit me: a week ago today, I had not yet met Jeanne and now already, she was gone! Waves of grief swelled in me for a woman I scarcely knew. It was on my calendar for today to take Jeanne to the Women's Health Center.

Oh, may you be healed, Jeanne! And may your children be healed and loved, as they have loved you. I grieve for the loss of your life, for the loss of the opportunity to know you and to be with you as you died. I'm flooded with tears, remembering how our eyes met in a smile at the Women's Health Center just last week, and of how you hugged me when we parted. I just know we would have been friends, if there had been just a little more time. I mourn the loss of the friendship I saw in your eyes, the friendship that never had a chance to develop. I'd have been a good friend to you as you died, if only there had been a little more time, for you and I to create a form for our friendship, and for your family to get to know me.

So much of the grief I felt for Jeanne was for the loss of everything that had never been: the loss of unrealized potential. Losing what is held dear is painful and sad, but for me losing what had only been hoped for, what had never been at all, was the loss that hurt.

As I cried for Jeanne I realized that I hadn't cried such painful, copious tears when Edith died. I was so much a part of Edith's dying and the intimacy was so complete that it seemed that nothing was lost or missed. But when Jeanne died, I felt even the chance to know her was ripped from me, that anything I might have been able to do for her was lost, anything we might have shared was lost, and I was lost, too.

Oh, Jeanne, I came to see you the day before you died, but it was too late. You were just a small figure on a large bed, receding into death while your daughter sat beside you and stroked your face with loving young fingertips. I wish I could have sat there on the bed with you, too, but I was just a stranger bringing flowers. And you were a woman dying too quickly.

4

Four Children Remembered

Although my experiences with Edith make a better story, it was my brief time with Jeanne that loosened the hold of my mind on the old grief in my heart for my four unborn children, lost in miscarriages years and years before. When I found myself several months later at a retreat with Stephen Levine, that grief was finally accessible. Knowing Jeanne and losing her gave me a second chance to deal with my own losses that I had not been able to deal with when they occurred.

The retreat with Stephen Levine (a separate event, unassociated with City Hospice): Dying into Life, I think was what it was called. Ten days of being with several hundred people, everyone working on issues of grief, loss, childhood abuse, rape, unhappy relationships, sexuality, cancer and illness, pain and dying. Going through the exercises, listening to the stories of people dying and people working with the dying, I had begun to see my small child self, that I carry in my heart, as worth loving. I never realized how much of my life I'd devoted to hiding this ugly child self from others. After all, if I had to be sent to my room as a child, then I had better keep that ugly, inadequate child well hidden. I went about my adult life, and even my work with dying patients, hoping to grow beyond that child who'd been dismissed as unacceptable and who cried alone in her room. The retreat had allowed me to love myself and to begin dealing with many of the fears and pains of my life.

On one of the last days of the retreat, someone announced that there had been a miscarriage that morning. A woman who lived there where the retreat was being held had lost her baby. Her family and her close friends had loved her and grieved with her, and she had showed them the perfect little being in a sac. Hearing this story, I was filled with grief for my four lost babies. And in hearing how another woman had been loved and cared for in her loss, I noticed in myself the deep sense of failure that I had carried in my heart all these years. No one had thought my miscarriages were worth the sorrow that I felt, so I assumed I was not only incapable of bearing babies, but too immature and selfish to face the miscarriages bravely. Everyone said I should try again, but that only sounded like I hadn't tried hard enough, and that this tragedy was my fault.

I remembered my mother-in-law flushing the first one down the toilet, telling me it was too soon for me to have another baby, anyway. Maybe it wasn't so smart to get pregnant again so soon, but yes, I did want that baby. I was dazed, shocked, and grief-stricken: wasn't miscarriage something that happened to other people? And I remembered the hoping, the praying each time that it wouldn't happen again, and then how each time I tried harder, and each time the new loss became all the accumulated losses along the way. I remembered the hospitals, the pain, the guilt, the loneliness, and the unspeakable grief. In those days, miscarriage was treated more like a malfunction of the mother than a death, so they ran tests on me, and sliced open my abdomen to ferret out the trouble in my innards. Nothing was discovered. I was stitched up and told to try again. My husband tried to cheer me on, but I felt his unspoken criticism and he refused to consider that he could possibly have any role in the cause of the miscarriages.

The year of the last miscarriage I wrote a poem.

There are four dead children
    there—
    wherever it is
    dead children go.

I hear them
    laughing
    crying
    calling to me.

I see them
    growing tall.
    One would be
    nearly three.

I cannot reach them
But I love them
Oh! What a fate
    to die unborn
    without a taste
    of life.

And so I wait
    for a living child
    hearing the cries
    of my dead children.

Not very good poetry, but it was an expression of the grief I didn't know how to ease. I remember how everyone cringed and shrank from me when I tried to share the poem with my husband and a few close friends. They said I should be grateful for the daughter I already had and to stop being so morbid.

After the fourth miscarriage, the doctors said I could try again, but I said I couldn't. I couldn't bear to go through the possibility of another miscarriage. I refused to become pregnant again and in a matter of months, we were rushed through the adoption process, and we adopted the son that I had been incapable of bearing.

The years passed and I buried the grief deep in my heart, deep under my anger at the insensitivities of those around me, under my envy of women who popped out babies year after year, under my guilt and disappointment, and under all the intervening losses and disappointments, dashed hopes and sorrows. I did not think about those four lost children very often and when I did, it was in an abstract, distant way. There was an unresolved grief in my heart, a grief that I couldn't get at, but that cast its long shadow across everything I did.

That morning at the retreat, for the first time in years, I felt the fullness of the loss of my babies who were never born. Tears rose to my eyes as I told a small group what I was feeling. A man who had himself recently lost an unborn child held my hand. The grief felt as fresh as when I lost the babies, but this time someone heard my sorrow and I was comforted. And this time it was not my fault; without the guilt, and the sense of failure and inadequacy, I looked directly at the loss and felt all the grief that had been stuffed away for fifteen years or so. I cried, and I felt grief stream from every pore in my body. So much grief, so many tears. It was frightening to live in the outpouring, but even as I cried, there was a feeling of relief that, at last, the grief was released from my heart.

A little while later, I was surprised to find myself walking around bursting with love for all my children: my daughter, my adopted son, and the four little ones who were lost. I'd always wanted six children and had felt deprived because I hadn't had the big family I wanted; for the first time ever, I lived in the fullness of being the mother of six children. Love, truly greater and more spacious than my tears and my pain, filled my heart and I wrote this letter.

To my four children who died so long ago, before you were born, but not before I loved you: thank you. Thank you for coming into my heart, into my life, and teaching me so much. Thank you for inhabiting my body, ever so briefly. Though our parting was not of my choosing, wherever you are now, I send you my love, which grows and blooms in my heart more profusely than the tears and the grief of losing you.

Though I never held you in my arms, nor suckled you at my breast, I have loved you. I have loved you, as I have loved your sister Marcelle and your brother Jordan. You'd be teenagers now, had you been born. We'd have been laughing and crying through your adolescence now: school work, new clothes, rebellions, and hormones bursting out all over. Instead, I'm here in this world loving you, and you four are. . .

I don't know . . . perhaps reincarnated on this plane, knowing the joys and sorrows of the earth, or perhaps you're someplace else, in another realm, beyond my conscious knowing. I don't know how all this works. But wherever you are, please, please know that I love you.

I ask your forgiveness for keeping my heart closed to you all these years. I have missed you so.

May your hearts be open and loving. May you be happy, my dear children. May you be free of pain. May you seek the truth and may you know God. I love you.

For the rest of that day, I felt the presence of my four little children and I loved them. I heard their voices, I felt them walking beside me, and for that one afternoon they practically lived in the flesh. I felt the essence of childhood, the wonder, the excitement, the innocent sense of adventure, and I knew that these four would always be children. They wouldn't grow up and become insurance brokers and accountants. They'd never endure pain and they'd never acquire the scars of surviving in a harsh world; instead, they'd always be the children in my heart.

I came home from the retreat knowing how very precious a life is, whether it is a lifetime as a human being, or just three months as a fetus. And I knew that I could love deeply even in the brevity of an interrupted pregnancy, or in meeting Jeanne in her very last week on earth.

5

The Little Old Ladies

The little old ladies are like pigeons, so common, so much a part of the landscape in any major city, that they're taken for granted. Individuals don't stand out, and if they do, they are the crazy ones, the ones that embarrass us and make us look into their faces. The pigeons flutter about the statues, scavenge for crumbs in the parks, cooing and pecking, waddling with their distinctive walk, and we are aware of their presence, but we place no value on pigeons, and may even complain that "someone ought to do something" about the dreadful mess the pigeons make. We see the little old ladies: small hunched figures, wearing unseasonably heavy, faded coats, and sturdy shoes on their shuffling, plodding feet. They carry shopping bags left from another era, and deep inside their pocketbooks, they sequester small coin purses from which they extract coins to pay for single bananas, small containers of plain yogurt, cheap tea bags, and day old bread.

I've stridden quickly past these solitary, slow-moving figures, my long healthy legs propelling me through my busy life, and right past them. Would I ever be this old, this slow, this sad? I certainly hoped not. I've reassured myself that I live an interesting life. I have many friends, I take reasonable care of my health, and I feel quite capable of coping with whatever challenges life sends my way. Surely, I won't find myself in a faded, ill-fitting coat, creeping along a city street while healthy young women stride by without seeing me.

Women now in their seventies and eighties were raised with one basic purpose in life: to raise families and to care for others. With the advances of medical science they have outlived that one function by many, many years, and find themselves with idle, lonely years on their hands. (Men, too, but these I rarely met; men tend to die before their wives, of heart attacks that provide no opportunity for a hospice death.)

When I became a hospice volunteer, I knew that most of the patients would be old; this was as it should be. But I wasn't quite prepared for the fact that the patients I was assigned would be overwhelmingly female. Certainly, there were men in the Hospice program, but the patients I saw were mostly female. Many of the women I met lived alone with only peripheral connections to relatives and friends, and had what appeared to be empty lives with little purpose and less satisfaction. Edith was an old woman, but it was only later that I saw she was quite different from most of the women I came to know in Hospice. Edith had lived most of her life alone; she'd never had a busy, exciting, productive life. She'd carved out her own unique niche in the world, where she'd lived and grown old with her rag dolls. Edith didn't lose much in her final years, for she'd never had very much.

Later I met women who had once been wives and mothers, who'd had friends and children and grandchildren, who'd cared for others and been important to them. And yet, just like Edith, they lived the last ten or twenty years of their lives, alone, without anything important to do, without anyone to depend upon them, but unlike Edith they were unprepared for this kind of life. Some reacted with anger, others with fear, and many with depression.

What are old women supposed to do with themselves? After they've raised the children, adored the grandchildren, then buried and mourned their husbands, and grieved for all the departed friends and relations? After there's no one left to cook for and tend to, after everyone has died or moved away and the house stays clean? Is cancer a result of all these wasted years at the end, or a solution? What do we, the young and the busy of this society, have in mind for the little old ladies, as we call them? We've tried to make them invisible, and they have cooperated by withdrawing from an active life and blending anonymously and blandly into the background, like so many gray pigeons huddled under the eaves.

The appellation serves to diminish them further: little old ladies. This is the name we use as an insult: "What an old lady's dress she was wearing!" "He sure carried on like a little old lady!" The "little old lady" has found a place in jokes and stories, and she certainly isn't a heroine. She reminds us of a large fear we cannot face, so we call her "little," and make a joke to cover up our discomfort.

My generation is the generation of women's lib. We were raised to be wives and mothers, but we've turned our backs on the passivity of these roles, and we've become assertive in "doing our own thing." We've stopped being victims of other people's needs and desires, and we've discovered our own needs and desires. So why do we cringe when we hear older women moan about what sacrifices they've made, and how inattentive their children are? Do they make us modern, liberated women uncomfortable because they remind us of how we were before we became liberated, and who knows, might become again, if ever we were to slacken our assertive pace?

I met these women whom we call little old ladies. I went into their homes and into their lives. I heard their stories and I knew them as unique individuals. Instead of being fully myself looking in on the life of an anonymous stranger, I would become mesmerized until I was no one in particular, just any human being struggling to fathom the mystery of old age, disease, and death, entering deeply into the life of a very particular human being. I sat with them and was absorbed into their lives. Sometimes I would depart choking from the weight of their grief and depression. At times I was filled with fear and loathing for the future I saw all too clearly for myself. And I saw underneath the superficial sameness of their lives to the true human sameness that I share with them. The more I saw of the endless varieties of human experience, the more I saw that in the end it doesn't matter so very much. What does matter, and matters very much, is how it's been done, and how it has felt.

Perhaps I paint too one-sided a picture of my time with the elderly women. I was that anonymous searching person, but at the same time I was a particular middle-aged woman filled with the compulsion to make my life meaningful and to be of use. It was the intensity of my spiritual search and the determination to be of service that gave me the itch to get in deeper, to do more, to learn more of what death was all about, and what the living could do about it.

When I returned from the retreat with Stephen Levine I wanted to do something more than regular volunteer work, and City Hospice was having to reduce staff to meet a fiscal crisis. I volunteered to work one day a week with Barbara, who was to be the only social worker to contend with twenty-five hospice patients.

Barbara accepted my offer enthusiastically and set out to teach me everything about social work that I could possibly learn in one day a week. She combined a wealth of experience with her ever fresh enthusiasm for each new patient. Working with Barbara was an incredible education. Every Thursday morning she would telephone to give me an update on the patients I was seeing and make suggestions for issues to raise in my visits that day. I would write her notes and sometimes call her afterwards, especially when I was overwhelmed with frustration or feeling discouraged. Despite her heavy caseload, she always made time to talk with me and gave me the encouragement I needed. With Barbara's guidance and support, I was elated to discover that I really could be of service, and that I had something of value to offer.

Because of the fiscal crisis, City Hospice not only had to reduce staff, but also had to temporarily restrict services to Medicare patients. Because private insurance and Medi-Cal don't come close to covering the true cost of Hospice services, these people could no longer be accepted in the program. Under normal conditions, City Hospice uses private donations to ensure that all patients, regardless of financial situation or type of coverage, are able to receive Hospice services. The effect of this change was to create a homogeneous patient census: all over sixty-five and mostly women. All were hungry for contact with people and needing the attentions of Hospice staff and volunteers. At first I was afraid that an unending round of sad old people, all dying alone, would be depressing, but as soon as I left the abstractions of statistics and generalities, and opened myself to the individual people, my fear passed. For instance, the idea of incontinence was horrifying to me, but handling the actuality of incontinence in someone I knew and cared for was only something else I could do to help.

Since Barbara couldn't visit patients as often as was necessary, my role became broader than the traditional volunteer role, and she involved me actively in the ongoing issues of patients, such as final financial arrangements, feelings about attendant care, saying good-bye to friends, and letting go of the concerns of life in order to face dying.

I had mixed feelings about my new role. I loved being more intimately involved with the patients and their families, and I loved learning about social work from a gifted pro like Barbara. But I wasn't always comfortable with the more active, initiating posture. Everything I'd learned so far had taught me to set aside my own ideas and opinions and to be open to the patient's process.

Most patients, Barbara felt, didn't know what issues to tackle until Hospice came into their lives, so she encouraged me to take an active role in helping people identify and deal with issues before it was too late. Barbara was always respectful of patients, and I was never uncomfortable with any approach she took with any patient in all the time I spent with her; however, it was uncomfortable for me to do the same things.

Throughout the summer and fall, I worked with patients and continued to reflect upon my role. Gradually, my confidence in my skills and my trust in my own intuitive feelings grew. I began to develop my own unique way of working with patients, that was perhaps more initiating than before, but still in keeping with my desire to respect the lives and deaths of the patients and not cloud anyone's final moments with my ideas and beliefs about how she should die.

At the time, the patients were each unique to me, and it was only later that I noticed similarities. I dove into their lives and was fascinated with whatever was going on for them. I observed the minutiae and the consequential, the details of daily life and the general sentiment and flavor of their final weeks and days. The journals for this period are a jumble of patients, just like my Thursdays: first one patient, then another, then another, then reflections on what on earth I was doing and could I ever learn social work. To preserve the individual lives of the patients and to spare the reader a nightmare of trying to keep track of who's who, I have extricated and condensed the individual stories, and offer them now, one at a time.

These women each deserve their own stories; yet the stories together tell a larger story that reaches beyond their individual lives and right into my life, your life, and every woman's life. It's not a romantic story. It's one of depression, chronic illness and disability, poverty, fear, loneliness, boredom, and grief. But it's not unmitigated sorrow either. Dying, it turns out, is like any other time in life, and it's full of laughing and fun, as well as the sadness we expect. I listened, and these women stepped out of the impersonal gray landscape that they shared and that defined their lives; they became individual human beings, they grew, and they approached death bravely and openly. As I sat listening to Anna and Rosa, Lucille and Elizabeth, Mary and Soo Ying, I was hearing their own very personal stories, but these are also the stories of my own grandmothers, and my mother, my friends, and myself.

The temptation is to say my life will never be this narrow, this sad, this lonely, but I know that no one ever intended to end up like this. Perhaps when my generation becomes old we'll have a greater repertoire to call upon, but I'm not sure whether all of the education and opportunities I have had, all of the interests and activities I have cultivated and the friends I have made will make any difference. When I am old and it's painful to walk across the room, will I have any more interest in getting out into the world than the women I've met in Hospice? When all of my friends have died or become infirm, will I be any less lonely? When my eyesight fails and my hearing goes, will I have any more enthusiasm for new books and the latest films? After a long life of watching the new become the old, and last year's promise turn into this year's disappointment, will I be any more open to the new ideas of those a half or a third my age who think they know about life?

Or will I, too, like Anna, fear everyone and everything and die fighting off those who might help? Or, will I, like Lucille, spend my last weeks allocating and reallocating my few hoarded dollars? Will I drift into charming senility like Elizabeth, or will I whine and complain like Mary?

I don't know. I've seen little pieces of these lives. I've heard stories. I have helped sometimes, just a little. I have been drained and I have been enriched. I have learned and grown, but I don't know how I will be, when I am an old woman dying alone.

6

Anna

Anna was the angriest patient I ever had, and possibly one of the angriest people I've ever known. Life had not gone well for Anna. There had been many losses, and many disappointments, beginning in her youth in Russia, and continuing throughout her long life in exile. With the tremendous tumult and losses of such a life, it's not surprising that Anna was angry and untrusting.

I always had the feeling that, despite the losses and changes, Anna had coped with life rather well until she began to grow old. She had a sharp wit and although her humor had grown quite black as her illness progressed, she appreciated those who could laugh at her jokes.

Pain is an important issue for many patients, but for Anna it was THE issue, and she couldn't deal with it. She suffered excruciating pain, but refused to take sufficient pain-control medication. Time after time, the hospice nurses talked to Anna about the importance of taking her pain medications. Anna's physician was called, the medical director was consulted, but no one could convince Anna to take pain medication regularly. Some days she would take the medication and some days she wouldn't. Despite the continuous efforts of the whole hospice team, Anna never achieved good pain control. Instead the pain ran rampant and she raged against anyone who tried to help her.

I do not ordinarily tolerate being yelled at very well, but somehow my determination to be of help overrode my aversion to being yelled at. The attendants and nurses grew wary of her rages and either approached her timidly or treated her coolly, all of which only increased her sense of being abandoned, and her rage. Had I been one of the attendants assigned to spend eight hours a day with Anna, I would have done no better than they had. I know this. It was the unique position I was in, coming on a regular schedule, but for short times without difficult tasks to accomplish, that left me free to be whatever she needed. Barbara's direction to me was to confront Anna with how she treated attendants and to work with her on the need to take pain medication. No one expected Anna to be radically changed by my intervention, or anyone else's, but it was necessary to find ways of dealing with some of Anna's anger, just to keep attendants in place.

Why did I want to help Anna, who treated me so badly and fought all my efforts? Her rage was transparent to me: when Anna yelled and screamed, all I saw was a very frightened and lonely lady, and I knew she needed to be loved. But wouldn't it have been easier to help someone who welcomed me more wholeheartedly? In my heart I knew that those who welcome help, do receive it, and that those like Anna who cannot reach out are those that need the most. And when the tiniest measure of caring gets through to someone like Anna, it's a miracle.

It is my need to be needed, my hunger to do something worthwhile, that brought me to this work, but with many patients I am uncertain whether I have helped or not. With Anna, I am absolutely certain that I helped, and that certainty was Anna's gift to me.

The Journal

June 27

"Anna is an eighty-eight-year-old Russian lady, with lung cancer, who lives alone, completely homebound with no family," Barbara told me in the car on the way to Anna's. "She has a great deal of pain, but no one can convince her to take enough pain medication, or to stick to a medication schedule. She complains continually about her pain, her situation, her attendants, and her fears of poverty. She needs more attention than I can give her, so I'm hoping you can spend some time with her and help her work through some of these issues."

"Has she no friends or relatives at all?" I asked.

"Well, she has one friend, Nadia, who barely speaks English. She pays the bills, and visits Anna pretty regularly. When Anna was on the verge of death, Nadia was right there; but after everyone gathered at bedside to say good-bye, Anna rallied. One of her greatest fears is running out of money, so she's talking about selling some of her antiques. She has beautiful things, all brought from China, where she lived most of her life. Maybe that's something you can help her with. She has quite a bit of money in savings, but she has spent most of her life worrying about money, so she is not likely to change now, no matter what we do to reassure her."

We parked on a busy neighborhood street, and rang the bell to Anna's apartment. A buzzer sounded and we passed through a gate and up the stairs, where the attendant met us at the door. The apartment was full of antique carved furniture, mirrors, and screens, and there were numerous pictures of Anna as a fashionable young woman.

Anna is a very frail lady in a pink nightie, perched like a bird on a huge couch. She talked very softly to Barbara about the new nurse who visited her this morning and cut dead skin off her foot. She was very impressed: "This is real nursing!"

Much talk of finances. A nursing home would cost $2,200 per month; twenty-four hour care at home would cost closer to $3,000. She was worried about running out of money, and wanted to sell some furniture and jewelry. "What will happen to me when I run out of money? Will they throw me in the garbage can?" Barbara explained that Hospice would continue to provide twenty hours a week of attendant care, plus regular nursing and social work visits. Although she would need to pay for the additional attendant hours she needed, when her savings got down to $5,000, the Cancer Society would help and when she was down to $1,500, Medi-Cal would help, too. Despite Barbara's reassurances, Anna continued to worry about finances, as she no doubt had done all of her life.

Barbara told Anna that I would visit her next Thursday and that I also would begin investigating places to sell her antiques. I wondered how she would feel if her beautiful things were all sold.

She obviously liked and trusted Barbara but she had not much interest in me, yet another new person, at a time of many changes and new faces. "It's wonderful when you are here," she told Barbara sadly, "but then you go, and I am all alone."

July 4

In pain, "I don't want to talk about medicine! I don't want to talk about pain! Four years I've been sick and no help." I felt helpless to deal with her pain, since she did not want to talk about it or hear any suggestions.

"One time, I took the medicine in the morning and I slept all day long! I'm too skinny to miss lunch like that. And my mind crazy! No more pain pills. I suffer anyway. No relief."

"Anna," I told her, "You should talk about this with the Hospice nurse. She will be able to help you to find a way to take the medications without such unpleasant reactions." Many people have these problems when they first begin taking pain medication, but it's usually for only a little while and then the body adjusts. Anna's physician and the Hospice nurse had already discussed this with Anna, but she didn't believe anyone.

"Someone took my pills, my nervous pills, stole them!" The attendant was summoned from the kitchen to fetch the shoe box of pills prescribed by Anna's physician. There they were: the nervous pills. She took one, and then apologized, "Oh, everyone will think I'm crazy! Accusing someone of taking the pills." I assured her it was natural to feel confused with so many pills and bottles. Her command of English is quite good, but sometimes her Russian accent obscures the meaning when she speaks softly.

Pointing to a small tapestry of Venice, she said, "I wish I were there." A little lighter talk ensued and I had a glimpse of a woman who had traveled and who loved art. But then she spoke of the Russian home that Barbara was investigating as a place for her to go. "When you have money, people take good care of you; but without money, just the welfare, they don't care at all."

"That's not necessarily true," I protested. "Besides, you aren't out of money yet, so try not to worry."

"Everyone says don't worry, but what about when my money is gone? It will be gone before I am. Will they put me on the street?"

"Never, never, never," I told her firmly. "I understand how it is to worry about money; I do it myself, but please try not to worry now. Medicare covers most of your costs. Use the money you have to pay for the extra attendant hours. Hospice will make sure you are well taken care of, no matter where you are, even if you have no money," I told her.

"You can not visit me everyday. It is far, that place." She used the same phrase when I asked her about Nadia: "She can't come everyday; people have their lives." And someone brought soup: "Not every time, but sometimes." A feeling of never getting enough comes through.

Suddenly she said, "There's a lot of fog out there today." Anna was through discussing her fears.

Pain in her hand was making her irritable. "Burning." She apologized for crying and for jumping at me.

No mention of selling furniture so I didn't bring it up.

She went out yesterday with a neighbor. She was glad to get out, but it was "too much" and she came home exhausted. I said she must have been happy to get back to her own couch. She said, "There is no pleasure in being here. It's like a cage."

I left exhausted after about an hour. Being with Anna is frustrating and hard! I came away feeling as if I'd spent an hour trying to hug an angry porcupine!

Throughout the summer I visited Anna nearly every Thursday. Gradually she opened up to me, and gradually I came to know her. Frequently, she would be in pain when I arrived; but a combination of pain medication and tea and conversation would ease the pain, so that by the time I left she would be in gentle spirits. The hours I spent with Anna were exhausting and often frustrating, but I became very fond of her despite her rages and despite her stubborn refusal to let anyone help her. Attendants came and went. She gave them all a hard time and reduced most to tears. The hospice nurses continued to work with Anna's physician in an effort to get Anna's pain under control, but Anna continued to refuse regular medication.

One day, I arrived while the attendant was out shopping, and Anna, with her thin hair in curlers, met me at the door. Seeing the bouquet of pink roses in my hand, she greeted me, "Should not spend money. Too expensive." Although she couldn't say so, she was obviously pleased that I had brought her flowers, and she glowed with pleasure in the attention.

August 1
Anna was napping when I arrived but sat right up, glad to see me. It was too soon to know how Liza, the new attendant, would work out. Each seemed to be feeling the other out. Anna was defensive about how she had treated prior attendants. I suggested that when she was not in a lot of pain, she should take the time to get to know Liza, to explain how she liked things, and not to wait until she was in pain. More discussion about pain medication that went no place. She was afraid of being buried alive, afraid of hallucinations, afraid she would wander outside in the night, etc., but she was still talking about it and said she was tired of the pain. Maybe if she could trust an attendant, she would take the medication.

We talked again of "pleasure." She kept saying she had no pleasure; I pointed out the small pleasures she had like her lunch today with Nadia. Pain and relief from pain were part of this "no pleasure, no relief" judgment. "Well, yes, the medication helps a little bit, but it doesn't last. Always the pain comes back!"

"Maybe you should think of it like housework, something to be appreciated when done, but always needing to be done again. The medication does give some relief, but you must take it regularly," I pointed out. Does her stubborn attachment to "no pleasure, no relief," make it hard for her to take medication that is not a cure, but only some relief?

August 7
Over the weekend Anna called the on-call nurse at 2:00 a.m. to say that there was a note on her door saying she was dying. She also called the police. She now has a night attendant. Liza, the day attendant, is working out well, but she returns to school in a few weeks.

She was feeling very badly when I arrived. She had just awakened in pain and coughing. First she was freezing and then she was too hot. Liza was matter-of-fact and cheerfully efficient; she made us tea. "I want toast!" Anna demanded. Anna's rudimentary command of English syntax made everything she said sound like an order.

Anna was obviously miserable throughout the tea and toast, so I let the conversation lag while she ate. She smoked a cigarette; "My only pleasure," she muttered, coughing all the while.

I asked her how the night attendant was working out, hoping she would share some of the fears and imaginings that had led to requesting a night attendant, but all she would say was that it was costing too much, and she would have to cancel it in a day or two.

First fearful talk of money in a long time. "What happens when my money is gone?" I reiterated that other help would be available when she had spent some of her savings. "But what then? Will they let me stay here?" I assured her Hospice would do everything to help her stay at home as long as possible, that it might be for the whole time. I suggested keeping the night attendant for a while, now while she needs it. "But what if it is worse later on?"

"Try to let the future be. Just do your best right now," I told her. "Your basic hospice services are assured, and additional help will be available to you later on."

"You know, I've helped plenty of people, even given money. I had friends, many friends, and when they were sick, I helped. One friend wanted to leave me her house, but I said, what do I need with a house? I was foolish. And now they are all dead and there's no one to help me." She paused. ". . . except one friend . . . and you . . . and the other lady, I forget her name . . . Barbara."

She rubbed ointment on her hand. "But it's no help, only help to those who sell it." She saw that I didn't understand her and she said it again.

"Oh, yes, their wallets are fattened by sales of the ointment. But I hope it will help you, too, at least a little." She smiled, satisfied that I had gotten her joke.

After a little while with a softer look on her face, she said, "I'm feeling a little bit better now." This was not the first time she has acknowledged when she felt better. She usually feels terrible when I first arrive and as the visit progresses, she feels better. Tea and conversation may be healing for her. She misses Barbara, who has been out of town, and seemed disbelieving of my assurances that Barbara would return next week. Anna needs people contact desperately, especially continuing contact. She easily feels abandoned and has been easy to abandon for her attendants when she has treated them so terribly. How dreadful to have to endure a succession of strangers when she's ill and to have to suffer "abandonment" over and over again. Maybe having all her friends and husbands die felt like abandonment, too. The enormity of Anna's sadness overwhelmed me.

August 15
As I came into the living room, Anna was slowly and painfully making her way across the room with her walker. The phone, under the coffee table, rang so I reached for it, nearly upending the walker. At that point I didn't have high hopes for the visit. It was the attendant coordinator calling to say Liza's replacement beginning Monday would be Mary, Anna muttered something about being "dead by Monday" and collapsed moaning onto the couch. She was coughing, short of breath, and in obvious pain. "Give me a pain pill!" she demanded of Liza.

"I am starving!" Anna insisted, but Liza protested that she could find nothing that Anna could or would eat.

Liza disappeared and I waited with Anna for whatever. To talk to her while she was in such pain seemed silly. She lay back on the couch and put her feet up, and began interrogating me about, "food from a hospital." I had no idea what she was talking about and I cringed to watch her frustration in communicating while she was in pain.

"They can't cook, none of them. I can't eat. I'm starving. You should see what they give me. Waste of food."

"Yes, that's very hard, not to be able to cook for yourself anymore, but Liza is doing her best to make whatever you want. Is there something in particular you want?"

"It's no use. I'm starving!"

"Anna," I began tentatively, "Your taste may be changing because you are sick."

"No!" she insisted angrily. "Such bad food they give me." Her voice trailed off into something about food from a hospital.

"Oh, was there something you had in the hospital that tasted good?" I inquired hopefully.

"No, no, no! Can you get me food from a hospital?"

After a while, I figured out that she wanted food from a hospital because she thought they knew how to cook for patients. I tried asking her what food she wanted, what she thought a hospital would have that would be better and she became enraged with me. "I don't know what they cook! I only want to try! I am desperate!"

"I'll ask Barbara," I assured her. She would not rest and insisted I call Barbara at once. I called, so she could see that I was trying and I fervently hoped Barbara would have suggestions for calming Anna. Barbara wasn't in the office, but by the time I returned to the living room, Anna had decided she wanted Liza to go buy the Russian dumplings called *plemany* and asked if I would drive Liza to the supermarket.

Liza and I went to the market in search of *plemany*, knowing that *plemany* would also not please her, but hoping the effort would help her in some way. Liza understood that food was not really the issue, that though Anna said she wanted to die, she fought it and food was just another way of fighting.

By the time we returned, the pain medication had taken effect and Anna was feeling better and was quite contrite. She kept marveling at how well the pill worked. "I am so glad you stayed! When you first came, I felt so terrible, so much pain. I was sorry you were here. I dreaded having to talk to you." I assured her that she never had to talk to me, that I could be with her without talking.

Without the pain, she had lots to talk about: selling two vases this morning, friends who had died, a postcard from her last attendant, etc., etc. She felt abandoned by attendants who returned to school, and by Barbara going on vacation. "And you, are you going any place?" She likes her night attendant, how vigilant she is, but she has a difficult time understanding her black dialect. The thought of Anna with her Russian accent and the night attendant trying to communicate made me smile mentally.

Usually I leave when it's time for her dressing change, but today she insisted I stay. "You should see how it's done. Just in case," she told me. Quite an experience: I'd never seen a bedsore, at least not like that. The "sore" is not a skin abrasion, but rather a huge, gaping red hole. In Anna's case, the bed sore was on her buttock, which was practically the only flesh left on her thin body. Bedsores are normally preventable with good skin care: use of an egg crate mattress, keeping the skin dry and clean, and encouraging the patient to change positions. When Anna was admitted to Hospice she already had this bedsore, but with the careful attentions of the Hospice nurse and attendants, the skin deterioration had been arrested, though not cured.

Liza was efficient and gentle; Anna lay on her side and never flinched. Liza described what she was doing: irrigation with hydrogen peroxide, then a rinse with saline, then packing the hole with gauze strips soaked in a medicated solution, then covering it over with a thick gauze bandage.

I helped Anna back to the couch. She held my hand firmly with her good hand. Her skin felt soft and warm and the firmness of her grasp left me in awe of the strength of this little woman with the huge hole in her buttock, pain in her body, and agony in her soul. She walked more slowly and with more difficulty this week.

She puts up such a fight and drags everyone into the fray, but somehow ends up endearing herself to the few who survive her tantrums. My sense was that fighting and resisting were so much her style that she would continue in this way right up until the last. Despite that, I saw her a little more open to the idea of pain medication and to being cared for. Next week with a new attendant would bring new challenges, but for the moment I felt encouraged. I made a note to call the nurse so that she could talk to Anna about pain control, now while she might be willing to listen.

Seeing the dramatic change in Anna's whole being after she took the pain medication, I understood now why hospice places so much emphasis on pain-control medication. When I'd first become a hospice volunteer, I had not completely understood the hospice emphasis on pain control in the larger context of emotional and spiritual issues. Now I really understood that when a patient is in excruciating pain, everything feels hopeless; there are no other issues as long as pain is dominant. The medication creates an environment, or at least the possibility of one, where other issues can be dealt with. I was able to talk to Anna today only after she was feeling some relief from pain, so that she could listen and think, at least a little. When she was in pain, she only yelled.

August 22
I arrived at 4:00 just as Mary, the new attendant left. She's not timid so she may endure Anna's Russian wrath. Anna seemed relieved when Mary left. "Oh, dahling, so good to see you! Sit down, sit down."

"So, Anna, how is it going with your new attendant? She seems very nice."

"Oh, she smiles and speaks sweetly when you are here, but I heard her tell the nurse how terrible I am. I'm not such a terrible person, and I try not to complain, but these girls they send me. . . They are so lazy! They don't care about me. I call: Help! I have pain! And she does not come for a long time. So slow and lazy. And I cannot trust any of them. Always, they are eating my food, even taking things! Look, see how I must keep the tea bags where I can see them, but they wait until I'm asleep. You, dahling, do you want tea? Help yourself, if this new girl has not stolen all the tea already."

"Anna, the attendants do their best, but sometimes when you are in pain, you frighten them when you yell at them, and it's impossible for them to please you." I knew better than to take at face value Anna's complaints about attendants. Anna was an exceedingly difficult patient, trying the patience of even the most experienced hospice attendants. Even as I sympathized with her, I knew that no one was stealing her tea bags, or ignoring her cries for help.

"Yell? Everyone says I yell, but I don't yell. Just so nice I call, 'Please help me, dear,' but then when no one comes, I must call a little louder." Anna's voice was filled with righteousness, but there was an undercurrent of defensiveness. "It's not easy. I try, I do, but these girls, they are so stupid. No one believes me, but they believe all the lies these girls tell about me."

"Being sick is hard, I know, and you do try. I believe you, Anna. When you are in pain, it's not easy to be nice to people, and how frightening that must be to call for someone who does not hear you." Barbara had told me she suspected that Anna may have been hospitalized and given shock treatments at some time, perhaps when she first emigrated to this country. Barbara had used the phrase, "full-blown paranoia." Listening to Anna, I wondered whether she was being paranoid. Some of her fears and complaints were certainly irrational, but as I listened to her, whether she was being irrational or not became unimportant. Her fear was real, whether the cause was real or not.

"Anna, perhaps you would feel safer and better cared for in the hospice inpatient unit. It's. . ."

"They want to lock me up!" she interrupted before I could tell her anymore. "Put me in a small room. Handcuffs. Oh, I would surely go mental! I would. . ."

"Oh, Anna, this place is not like that. There are no handcuffs, and no one is locked up. The nurses are very gentle and caring, and they are always there. You just ring the bell and someone comes right away. You would never have to be alone anymore."

"No, I won't go! They do experiments on people in these places. No experiments on me." Terror, sheer terror propelled her. She was afraid of being called crazy, of being crazy. She was afraid of dying, and afraid of staying alive. She was caught in a whirlwind of terror, and the more she talked, the less her particular fears and circumstances mattered.

"There aren't any experiments at the hospice inpatient unit; it's for people who are sick."

This was not one woman being afraid; this was the essential, final human terror, that terror we spend our lives avoiding and pretending we can prevent. To be born is to know on some level the fragility of human life, and how little control we have over what happens to us. Yet we live acting as if we were powerful enough to stop the hand of death; we take our vitamins and stay out of the rain, we put locks on our doors and money in the bank. Then one day, like Anna, we see that our own personal efforts are useless, and that in the end we must turn to forces beyond our rational control, and whether that be the compassion and love of others, or inner spiritual strength, or what some call God, it is terrifying. Trusting in God may be okay as long as we think we are in control anyway and won't need extra help, but to trust in God, knowing that is all there is, is frightening beyond all imagining. Anna in her fear was so exposed to me and so vulnerable that though every nerve in my body, mind, and soul yearned to comfort her, I knew that anything I said might only add to her fear.

"No, I won't go to that place!" She was shaking and her eyes darted about the room, as if "they" might be concealed behind the curtains, ready to jump out and carry her off.

"Anna, no one can make you go. The choice is entirely yours. It was just an idea. You can stay right here as long as you want." I didn't know what to say. Whatever I said sounded like false reassurance, so I stopped talking and sat in silence hoping that Anna would somehow feel the enormous desire in my heart to comfort her.

"Dahling, hand me cigarettes, please." She took a cigarette from the crumpled pack and let me light it for her. "Oh, thank you, dahling. My only pleasure."

After only a few puffs on the cigarette, she began to cough and put it out. "I'm so tired. I will lie down for a while. Help me, dahling." She reached for my hand and I helped her walk from the couch to the bed.

She lay down with a sigh and I covered her with a blanket. "No, not like that!" Her voice was suddenly sharp. She pulled at the blanket and struggled to sit up. "You have spoiled it! No, don't touch it." She struggled to fix the blanket, not looking at me.

"Anna, just tell me how you want the blanket."

"Here, hold this end." At length it was fixed, but then shortly, she was too hot and wanted it off.

"Oh, dahling, stay with me a little while!" she implored, reaching for my hand, but almost at once, discarded it exclaiming, "Oh, your hand is too hot!"

She began to worry about how the night attendant would get in. "Does she have a key? I can't remember! What if she rings the bell and I can't walk to open the door! What if I fall!" She insisted I call Hospice. By then it was after five, so my call was put through to the on-call nurse who assured me that the night attendant had a key.

Anna continued frightened and worried, and would not be reassured. Cigarette after cigarette. Finally, I told her, "I will stay with you until the night attendant gets here at 8:00."

She was obviously relieved by my offer, but she struggled, "Oh, I cannot ask that!" Such conflict: she wanted me to stay, even needed me to stay, but allowing me to stay was hard for her.

"You didn't ask. I offered to stay," I told her. Her need not to be alone won out, but then she needed a way to thank me.

"The green vase! I want to give it to you!" she informed me.

"Oh, Anna, I cannot accept such a gift." I declined and declined until she seemed about to throw the vase at me.

"After I die, someone will take all these things, so it does not matter. I *want* to give it to you. If you don't want it, give it to your daughter." After I reluctantly agreed to accept the vase, she rested more easily. She supervised my wrapping of the vase in a disposable bed pad. Off and on during the rest of the evening she assured me that she would not tell Barbara about the vase and told me not to tell anyone either. Her paranoia now enveloped me since I had come close enough to her to rescue her from the specter of her fear swallowing her.

Even with the issue of my staying and the vase settled, she was a nervous wreck with worry, so she took a "nervous pill." After it had a chance to work, she felt calmer and remarked at how much better she felt. We spoke of the difficulty with the blanket, and I used that as an example of what happened with the attendants. She believed me that I wanted to do it right, but couldn't do what she wanted unless she could tell me clearly, and with her nerves on edge, she could not tell me. I emphasized that it was a painful experience for both of us and that I was sure the attendants felt the same way. She was less willing to believe that the attendants meant well. She admitted that it was the pain and nervousness that made her yell at me and that she felt badly about that.

She talked for a long time; my role was just to be there and to listen. She talked of her fear, not of dying, but of being alone. "What if my mouth be so dry and there's no one to give me drops of water?" And, "What if I fall? And cannot get up." She talked of "thinking" about having an attendant from 4:00 to 8:00, "so expensive."

She told me with bitterness and contempt of her three husbands. Her story was set against the drama and upheaval of the Russian Revolution. Listening to her talk, I felt as if I had entered a time warp: I had read about the revolution, but I never expected to hear a firsthand report of the era, especially from a White Russian, one who had lost her homeland and a whole way of life.

"I didn't want to get married. He was in his fifties and I was such a young girl, just out of school, but my mother had chosen him, so I had no choice. He was an officer in the Russian Army and very soon he was killed. The revolution . . . it was terrible. We had to run away to Siberia."

She spoke matter-of-factly but the image of fleeing to Siberia explained a lot of Anna's paranoia. Sometime later she married another man, also an officer. "He drank a lot, this one," she explained with disgust and bitterness, "and pretty soon he died, too."

"When did you leave Russia?" I asked.

"1919. We had to. The revolution." She and her third husband fled Russia to live in China until 1949 when the Chinese Revolution sent them fleeing again, and they came to the United States. She did not speak much of the years in China, but I have the feeling they were good years and that she was happy there, at least as happy as one can be living in exile.

She talked of how she took care of sick people and showed me several letters expressing appreciation. "See, I'm not such a bad person."

"You don't need letters to prove that. I know you're a good person," I assured her. The letters were from 1970 and both from the same woman, but she said she had many more "of the same character."

Fear of convalescent homes. Fear of being alone. So much fear. Fear of keeping me too late. Afraid she could not wait until next week to see the doctor. And afraid of the doctor. Talk of cancer. "They say I have a cancer, but I don't know." She remembers that she fell in the park and has never recovered. She dozed briefly.

As it got closer to 8:00 she became more agitated. "The night duty is sometimes late. Maybe she won't come." She kept trying to send me home, yet I knew she didn't really want me to go.

Once the attendant was there, she could not bear my presence another moment. "Go now! It's very late. Hurry! No, don't waste time kissing me." Disregarding this instruction, I kissed her good night and watched the look of pleasure on her face. "Drive carefully, dahling."

I wondered how much longer she had. Listening to her rattling breath and watching her frail body, I half expected her to die tonight, but her will was still terribly strong. She insisted upon doing everything she could herself, yet she kept me, or anyone handy, busy fetching, handing, reaching, checking.

I left, wishing that I could have stayed with her forever, until she died, so that she would never have to be alone, but how tiring those four hours I spent with her were. I came home with a headache, and felt drained of everything I had, yet I was very glad I had stayed with her just when she really needed someone to be with her.

Not being able to remember things caused at least some of her anxiety. Her memory failed selectively. She clung to her little pieces of paper with telephone numbers, and the letters from 1970 that tell her who she is. The loneliness of not remembering who you are. I sensed Anna may have had a very small sense of self-worth all along, and the illness, not being able to do things, and not being able to remember, had swept away her already-fragile sense of self-worth.

The green vase sits on my coffee table. She wanted me to remember her after she died. I told her I would remember her without any gift at all, but I think that by accepting the vase I made it possible for her to let me stay with her when she really needed someone.

August 24 call to Anna

Anna's attendant had not shown up this morning. Anna was worried, but not hysterical. The on-call nurse was finding a replacement. I assured Anna that they would find someone.

"I'm afraid I will fall. I can hardly walk."

"Stay put, Anna. Only walk when you have to, and then go very slowly and carefully." I told her.

"Okay, dahling."

August 25 call from hospice

Anna died sometime early this morning. I had been just about to call to see how she was doing today. I was a bit surprised because although she had felt miserable, she looked to me as if she would fight on and on. I felt myself wishing I had gone over yesterday. Along with the regret was the joy of having spent those four hours with her on Thursday, and of having kissed her good-bye. And I was glad I had allowed her to give me the green vase. She really had so much to give, but she did not know how.

And I was glad she had died at home.

September 1 Anna's funeral

Entering the Russian Orthodox convent was like stepping back in time. A small woman in a babushka stood outside the door, and as soon as I opened the heavy door and stepped inside, she drew a massive chain across the doorway. An ancient nun in the foyer handed me a white candle and directed me upstairs, where I found Barbara standing somewhat awkwardly with a candle, and the service about to begin. Barbara and I stood out like aliens. Barbara whispered that the chains were on when she arrived and she had worried that I would not be able to get in.

Anna's Russian friend Nadia gave her a lavish, funeral: a metallic, pewterlike casket, a pale blue, lace-trimmed gown, and masses of pink and white roses mixed with carnations. Only a handful of mourners attended, and most of them looked old and tired. There aren't many left in the Russian community to bury the dead. Candles flickered and the smell of incense was overpowering. The room had no seating and apparently the custom was for everyone to stand throughout the rather long service.

A bearded, young priest, looking as if he had just stepped off the set of "Fiddler on the Roof," with a long, silver-gray cape and a swinging incense burner, chanted in Russian in front of the casket, while elderly nuns chanted in thin voices from behind an ornately carved screen, like unseen angels. Occasionally, one would emerge from behind the screen and snuff out one or two of the innumerable candles burning throughout the room. Beautiful pictures and icons, all terribly Russian and very old, covered every square inch of wall space and various surfaces as well. The diminutive nuns, like dwarfs living in this dark otherworldly place, wore full black robes with high headpieces weighing down their small hunched figures. One crossed the floor using miniature crutches, her sheepskin bedroom slippers visible beneath her habit. Another carried a heavy wooden cross that I feared would topple her.

All during the chanting and incense burning, I noticed what looked like a bowl of rice pudding on a stand by the coffin. Later in the service, the nuns officiated and small portions were placed in paper cups. Nadia passed out cups of the pudding to some of the mourners. Walking as if her feet were too weary to carry her, she came over to explain something to Barbara and me, but she was so distraught that she spoke in Russian to us. All I caught were the Russian words for "I don't know." I think she meant that she did not know whether we should participate in this part of the service.

Several nuns and a few mourners approached the casket and even picked up the cross in Anna's hands and kissed it and then knelt before the casket. The priest continued swinging the incense burner and chanting in Russian.

Finally, the casket was closed with a resounding clank and was carried out by the pallbearers; everyone else followed with the chanting continuing. Rose petals fell from the casket and littered the stairs. Barbara and I followed and for a moment, I was certain we would step out on a Russian street, but outside I was jolted back to the present time and place, and everyone dispersed for the ride to the cemetery. With his cape and cassock removed, the young priest left the church quickly, carrying a large brief case. Barbara and I said good-bye to Nadia who hugged us and thanked us profusely for coming, with tears making her already scant English even scantier. I was surprised she even remembered me, but she hugged me as warmly as she did Barbara.

Barbara and I went for coffee and took a few minutes to share our feelings about Anna and the funeral. We were both amazed at the lavish funeral. I was certain I could hear Anna protesting "too expensive," but Barbara pointed out that in the Russian community, a good funeral is important. She related that earlier when it had appeared that Anna would die quickly, she had been concerned about a dress to be buried in and Barbara had told Anna and Nadia not to worry, that there were plenty of dresses in Anna's closet. They had tried to explain to her, but until she saw the beautiful blue satin gown, she did not realize how inappropriate a dress from the closet probably sounded to the two Russian ladies.

We talked of the difficulty in establishing a relationship with patients like Anna and then how quickly it is all over, and there is nothing to do but to go on to the next patient. Would I always feel so ready to leave the casket of one patient to meet the next patient? This work is a bit like making sand castles at the tide line: the satisfaction must be found in the doing, for nothing lasting can be expected, and the same work must be done over and over again.

7

Lucille

Lucille was eccentric. Also fascinating, intriguing, and appreciative of the attention of hospice and family visitors. After a lifetime of independence, she reveled in the attention she commanded as an invalid holding court. Lucille married at age forty-eight and her husband died very soon thereafter, so she lived most of her life alone.

Not all visits with Lucille were delightful; her moods were mercurial and she could become demanding and frustrate anyone who tried to please her. As I tried to ameliorate her bad humor one day, I realized that being a difficult patient was part of her eccentricity and she had no interest in improving her personality.

Cancer had reduced Lucille to a wraithlike skeleton, and she kept her sister and everyone else running at the sound of the antique bell she kept beside her in bed. Lucille, like most dying patients, had a desire to maintain control over her life, and as her illness progressed, this desire surfaced in various ways. She had just written a new will when I first met her; yet she spent the remaining weeks of her life, revising her will and reallocating her estate. Being able to make and revoke bequests gave her a feeling of importance within her family, but I suspect that she would have preferred to take her savings with her.

My assignment was to help Lucille let go and say good-bye to her family. She needed to resolve conflicts with her relatives, and Barbara hoped that by talking with me, she would be able to let go of old resentments and disappointments, and die at peace. Everyone at Hospice sympathized with Lucille's sister Eleanor, and I hoped that I would be able to help Lucille see the wisdom of treating Eleanor with more respect and appreciation. This was my agenda. It was not Lucille's, so I found myself alternating between the social worker role of encouraging her to do what experienced professionals felt she should do to have a satisfying death, and watching Lucille do exactly what she intended to do. If she let go, I never saw it.

The Journal

June 18
When I arrived, the hospice nurse was examining Lucille in the small bedroom, so I waited in the living room. The apartment was spacious but bland and austere. There were a few nice pieces of furniture, but most of the furnishings were more functional than tasteful. The few pictures on the wall were all too-small, inexpensive prints that added nothing to the room.

She greeted me like one more in a long stream of bothersome strangers. "Now, what are *you* here for?" Lucille is a woman of presence, despite her physical frailty. She knows she's nearly blind, but she doesn't admit how hard of hearing she is. Despite her initial resistance, she soon relaxed and talked openly.

"I think my lawyer is a shyster," Lucille announced. "I wanted to give $1,400 to each of my grand nieces, but then I changed my mind and told him to change it to $1,200, but I don't think he changed it."

"Your will should be exactly as you want it," I told her. She said that her niece, who's an attorney, will be coming this weekend. "Maybe you should go over the will with your niece to make sure that it's what you want."

"My niece Ann and I are very different and we're both stubborn, so we tend to get into screaming at each other." She doesn't trust her niece to handle her will.

She told me grandly, "I'm going to buy some things for myself: a nightgown, a bathrobe, a Sony Walkman, and whatever else I need. I wonder if anyone can find a robe to fit me, only eighty-four pounds now." A neighbor is helping her send things to the Salvation Army, but Lucille thought perhaps she was throwing too much out, and thought that maybe her wedding dress had disappeared.

I asked her whether she needed more than four hours of attendant help. She said she was fine, and that she really liked Wanda a lot, but if Hospice wanted her to have more care, she would accept it. It sounded to me as if she were waiting for someone else to decide she needed more care. "Do you get lonely?" I asked.

"Oh, no, I'm used to being alone. I've always been a loner."

She told me about her nephew Carter, who is obviously a favorite of hers, and who comes to see her several times a year. "There's no need for him to come again. I said good-bye to him the last time he visited." I heard in her voice that she'd like to see him again.

When her brother (Carter's father) died ten years ago of cancer, he left her three hundred dollars a month. "So I've been pretty well off. Everyone says how lucky to have a legacy, but to have a legacy, you have to have a loss." The monthly checks remind her of the loss.

"I asked Wanda to read some poetry to me, but she thought it was too worldly. You know she's very religious."

"Would you like me to read to you?" I asked.

"Oh, would you? The book's right on the bureau." She loved hearing me read her favorite poems and was asking about another poem before I could finish the first one. Some poems she knew almost entirely from memory. I read her Edna St. Vincent Millay and Matthew Arnold, Emily Dickinson, Chaucer, and a few of Shakespeare's sonnets. I said when she got her Sony Walkman, she could listen to tapes of poetry. She also mentioned something she'd heard by Chopin, so tapes could expand her world quite a bit.

I told Lucille I would come another day. Not really believing me, she said, "Oh, please come again! I *really* hope you will. I loved the poetry." I told her I definitely would come again, that it was a promise, and she smiled like a child promised ice cream.

When I became a Hospice volunteer, I imagined myself reading to patients, but until Lucille, I never met a patient who had any interest in being read to. Watching her facial expressions change as I read made me realize what it must be like to go blind.

June 25

I called to set the time and her sister Eleanor confirmed with Lucille: I was to come at 11:00, but when I arrived I found Lucille in bed, proclaiming, "I'm very busy!" Brusquely, she told me, "My bookkeeper is on her way over, so I've no time for idle visiting or poetry." I suggested we visit while she was waiting for the bookkeeper. Sounding like a busy executive she indicated I should sit down. Eleanor retreated to the living room.

"Well, are you going to read to me?"

As I was reaching for the book, Eleanor silently reappeared in the doorway. She said she wanted to speak with me after I was through with Lucille. Lucille interjected sharply, "You don't need to talk to anyone in private about me, Eleanor." Eleanor retired meekly to the living room. I read a poem or two and then the doorbell sounded.

"Oh, please come another day when I have lots of time."

The bookkeeper was ushered in to Lucille's bedside, and I could hear Lucille demonstrating the features of the electric bed for her. I had been there less than ten minutes.

I asked Eleanor if I could come back this afternoon. Eleanor said Lucille might be napping then, but she wanted to speak with me. Eleanor was a sweet-tempered, warm person, in contrast to Lucille's demanding, brusque nature.

Eleanor admitted that Lucille can be demanding, which is easy to believe. Even though the night attendant is there, Lucille wakes Eleanor. She said she intends to return home after this weekend and just spend weekends with Lucille from now on, but this was not clear.

When I returned that afternoon Lucille, Eleanor, and Wanda were having tea and cake in the living room. All Eleanor wanted to know was whether attendant help could be found for the weekend. When someone says, "I want to talk to you," I always imagine I'm about to hear deep inner feelings or to be asked to help solve life and death problems, but the concerns are usually quite mundane. I called the attendant coordinator, who said he will do what he can to arrange someone for the weekend.

Lucille wanted me to read poetry again, so I read for a while, with Lucille attentive in a straight-back chair, Wanda knitting, and Eleanor looking weary. "Visiting is too tiring; poetry is better," Lucille pronounced. I think after a lifetime of being self-sufficient and independent, she likes being the demanding patient, the center of attention, who can even command a private poetry reading at her whim. After I had read a few short poems, she announced that she was tired and rose resolutely from her chair. Her faded nightgown hung straight from her proud shoulders to the floor, without revealing any hint of flesh on her rail-thin body. Like an apparition she moved slowly and wordlessly, back into the bedroom. Her departure signaled the end of the visit.

July 1 phone call to Barbara
Lucille still wants to make a new will. Since there's very little money to be disposed of and no one to contest anything, Barbara suggested I encourage her to just let Eleanor know what she wants done with her things. Everyone is becoming concerned about Eleanor's health. She still hasn't gone home because Lucille keeps asking her to stay on.

July 1
Good visit! First with Eleanor and then with Lucille.

Lucille was having a bath, but Eleanor seemed glad to talk with me.

"Lucille slept all night long," Eleanor told me. "The Hospice night attendant is very attentive and kept coming in to check on Lucille, but I'm used to waking up, so I still didn't sleep well."

"You would probably sleep better at home in your own bed," I suggested. "I thought you were going to go home."

"Well, Lucille didn't want me to go, so . . . I stayed."

I reminded her that she must take care of herself, not do more than she can manage. She agreed and seemed glad to talk about how difficult Lucille can be.

"Has Lucille resolved her problems about her will?" I asked.

"She hasn't mentioned it for several days, so I think the issue must be settled."

Then with tears welling in the corners of her eyes, she told me, "You know, my daughter died just last year. She was only forty-nine years old . . . cancer. It was awful . . . to watch her suffer like that. . . . I took care of her myself for three months at home." Obvious grief just below the surface threatened to overwhelm Eleanor.

"How painful that must have been for you," I replied, stumbling over the words, feeling a sudden congestion in my throat as Eleanor's grief, still raw and painful, spilled over and enveloped me, too. I had the feeling that Eleanor hadn't talked about her daughter's death very much. I touched her arm, knowing that with Lucille dying in the next room, there really wasn't anything I could say to ease Eleanor's grief.

Just then the hospice attendant came out of the bedroom with towels and sheets in her arms and announced that Lucille was ready to see me. I went into the bedroom to find Lucille in a fresh nightgown, sitting up in the freshly made bed with the antique bell near her scrawny hand. I talked with Lucille and told her, "You're wearing out your sister. I think you should encourage Eleanor to go home for a few days."

At first she pursed her thin lips and stubbornly maintained that she "needed" Eleanor, but after we talked for a while she ended up expressing her concern for Eleanor, and as if it were her own idea, she volunteered that Eleanor should go home.

"I need a new will," she informed me. So the issue was not settled at all.

"You can probably skip a whole new will and just let Eleanor and Ann know what you want done," I suggested, but Lucille was unconvinced.

"My niece Ann gave me a beautiful nightgown, but I'm going to tell her to take it back." After asking for a new nightgown, now she just wants to wear her old ones! I commented that she wasn't the easiest person to please. She agreed with pride, and said, "I always like to have my own way."

She talked of her temper tantrums and I suggested that she express her feelings before she became upset so there'd be no need for tantrums, but she insisted, "I feel better after a tantrum." Another note of pride.

A chance remark that I made about enjoying people's attention, and that she "deserved" it, elicited a comment from Lucille that, "You get what you deserve, and if you deserve cancer, you get it sooner or later."

"Many wonderful people get cancer. No one deserves cancer," I insisted.

July 8

Lucille complained that she has a hard time hearing her temporary Hospice attendant, who speaks somewhat softly. "She mumbles." Wanda is due back Monday, and Lucille misses her. Eleanor has gone home for a few days: thank goodness, before she ended up ill.

Lucille was calm, loving and peaceful today. She talked a lot, rambling on about many subjects. She was uncomfortable with the night nurse kissing her, but when she was "especially nice" yesterday, Lucille kissed her!

She was happy to live until her birthday and she wanted to see her nephew, who is coming to visit this week. Those two things she wanted to live for. "I spend most of my time now contemplating God."

We talked of families. She told me about the lovely old photo on her wall, which was of her family around 1904. Even as a little girl in a white dress and high-laced boots, she carried herself with a regal pride. The smaller child beside her in the photo, like a shadow, was Eleanor.

She asked me to hand her a razor, and when I hesitated, she assured me, "Come on, hand it to me. I'm not intending to slit my throat!" She shaved her chin and cheeks, then asked me for lotion and rubbed lotion on her face and hands: busy, busy, busy.

She spoke of a vision she had had: "I was in a pink room with a pink drawer full of jewels. It was beautiful, and it made me think of how I could have had pretty things, but I never did." She spoke again of the nightgown Ann had bought her: "I don't want any pretty things now. Too late to change. Dress should suit the circumstance," she proclaimed adamantly. I told her dress might alter the circumstance.

July 15

She was in irritable spirits today, in contrast to the peace and benevolence of last week. I think two things were probably at the root of her mood: first, some kind of disappointment in the eagerly awaited visit from her nephew. She wouldn't say what that was: "Yes, it was somewhat disappointing, but don't bother about that; it's none of your business." The last was said with a smile, but despite my encouragement to express her disappointment, she would not budge. The second cause of her bad humor may have been pain. "I want my mind perfectly clear for the meeting with my lawyer this afternoon and I'd rather be a little uncomfortable." I suspected she had skipped or reduced her pain medication this morning.

At least twice, our conversation got momentarily caught on a barb of her general irritability. Even poetry did not suit her today, and she stopped me after just one short poem. She was lonely and restless, and sought an unobtainable comfort.

As she talked about her will and of a picture she wanted a friend to have, I realized that disposition of her possessions was her occupation, and should it actually get accomplished, she would have nothing to do, and she would die. She can busy herself making wills indefinitely, I suppose. It seemed tiresome to me and a bit silly for her to keep reallocating her few small possessions, but I began to understand that control of day-to-day activity and giving it meaning and importance may be the force of life fighting off death.

She was quite resentful of my "assumptions" today. I said something about her being a careful person and she retorted, "You know nothing about it! I'm a careless, hasty, destroyer of things!" I had the impression that if I knew too much of her essence, she thought she would lose control, so she clung to her disappointment with her nephew and would not let me say a single, nice thing to her.

I left her listening to Chopin on the tape recorder. Once I had adjusted the volume to suit her, music was more pleasing to her than conversation. Wanda was in the kitchen, perhaps keeping her distance from the bristly Lucille, at least until she was summoned by Lucille's bell.

July 22
Lucille didn't want any visitors today, but I had to stop by with some paperwork from Hospice. Eleanor said that would only disturb her . . . but that was okay (I heard the undercurrent that it really was not okay, but Eleanor was accustomed to passively enduring whatever others requested of her). Given the chilly response

to my call, I decided that it was a good day to bring flowers. Remembering how she liked pink, I wanted pink roses, but the best I could find was white with pink edges. I arrived with the papers and the bouquet of roses, and was invited in, more or less cordially, by Eleanor. Wanda took the flowers and I sat down on the couch with Eleanor, who was in a house coat. We had just begun to talk when Lucille's bell sounded and Eleanor, with obvious weariness, shuffled in. In a moment she returned to report that Lucille had decided she wanted to see me after all.

She may have thought I was the nurse for she began with complaints of a sore throat and wanted to know what to do for it. I suggested something cold to drink. She thought maybe hot would be better. I doubt if a nurse could have pleased her either. Wanda brought the flowers in to show her. Lucille was quietly pleased. We had conversed only a few minutes when she decided she wanted me to make a phone call for her. I ended up in the middle of Lucille insisting on calling a Midwestern relative, and Eleanor telling Lucille, "You can't call Louise now. You know she's a working person," and both acting annoyed with me.

"Well, I can try!" insisted Lucille stubbornly.

Eleanor pulled out Lucille's folder of phone numbers, written in the two-inch-high shaky print of the near-blind Lucille. I commented to Eleanor that Lucille had had me look through these lists last week. She seemed to misunderstand and said, with great annoyance, "Well, here, if you think you can find it, go ahead."

Eleanor found the number; I dialed the telephone and then handed the receiver to Lucille. When there was no answer, Lucille handed me the receiver and announced, "So there! There's not a thing you can do for me, and I'm far too busy to listen to idle chatter today!"

I was at a loss for words. How I wished I had something great to say at that moment, but I was filled with the enormity of truth in what she said: there was not one thing I could do for her, partly because she was dying, despite what anyone did, partly because she was stubborn and wouldn't allow anyone to do much, and partly because I was uncertain what was best. Awkwardly, I told her I would visit another day.

Eleanor nearly pushed me out. In the living room I asked her if there was anything I could do for her. She stood near the door, not inviting me to sit down and blurted out, "I hope she dies soon! This has gone on too long now. No, there isn't a thing you can do for me either."

I left feeling sad and useless.

July 25 call from Hospice

Lucille died at 10:00 yesterday. I wasn't surprised and imagined that Eleanor and Ann must be relieved. Lucille was ready to die, and they were ready to let her go.

Lucille's nephew has insisted upon an autopsy, which will cost nine hundred dollars and not show anything except what was obvious, that Lucille wasted away from cancer. Lucille would have been horrified at the thought of an autopsy. Ann called demanding that City Hospice remove the hospital bed and other equipment immediately. The anxiety of dealing with death turns some families into rather difficult people, which makes it quite unlikely that anyone can help them in their time of distress. Barbara said she will follow up with Eleanor.

Perhaps Lucille wasn't as crazy as we'd thought not to entrust her family with arrangements for her will.

8

Elizabeth

Elizabeth was perhaps the most contented person I've ever known. Her life looked barren and dismal, but to Elizabeth, life was one small joyous miracle after another. It's true, she was probably somewhat senile, but it was not unpleasant for her, or for those around her. It was as if her mind were washed clean of excess memories, and she was left in her last days with just her favorite memories. Many patients I visited were in the grips of depression and could see nothing good in life; Elizabeth saw only good and was a delight to visit although there was never much for me to do.

The Journal

November 12
When I called, she sounded so shaky, I half expected her to expire before I got there. When I arrived, the door to her room was unlocked and Elizabeth called out for me to enter. "I've been feeling kind of weak and dizzy," she told me. She lives in a second-floor room with a bay window in an older, but securely maintained residential hotel downtown. She has a bathroom, but no cooking facilities beyond a miniature refrigerator and a hot plate. Everything in the room except the television is worn and shabby, but I felt immediately at ease in Elizabeth's cozy home.

Fondling the worn wood of her cane, she told me, "I got this in 1975 when my legs first started feeling weak, and I've used it ever since. It's my right arm. I wouldn't be without it." A walker stood unused by the window. I encouraged her to try it out, but she showed no interest. "Someone put that in here," she told me, as if this mysterious item had nothing to do with her.

Several times, like a child with a new toy, she demonstrated the wonders of her new remote-control television. She seemed happy to have a visitor, and treated me to stories of her life, her favorites told more than once.

"Did you know I'm ninety years old? And I've never been sick before this," she told me with pride. "Don't know why I got sick now."

Over and over she told me, her face lighting up with delight, "In the mornin', first thing I see is Paul—he's my son—coming through the door with scrambled eggs for my breakfast."

"Sounds tasty," I replied. "And how lucky to have such a good son."

"Oh, yes, my Paul's a good son. He's the one got me to move out here from Massachusetts in '73. 'Mama,' he said to me, 'You're gettin' too old to cut grass and shovel snow.' Been here ever since. Got everything I need, right here," she said gesturing around the small shabby room as if it were a luxury condominium.

"My grandmother lived near Boston," I told Elizabeth. "What town did you live in?"

"Nine ninety five North River Street," she told me proudly, like a child who has recently learned her address. She couldn't seem to recall the town.

Her frail life is now anchored to her devoted son's daily visits, and the forthcoming visit of her daughter "at the end of the month." Will she live until then? I wondered.

"They're twins, you know: Paul and Pauline," she informed me proudly as if they were three-year-olds in matching outfits. The thought of her daughter makes her eyes sparkle. Pauline likes to travel and was in Germany when Elizabeth got sick in April. "They sent word to her that your mama is sick, and she came right away, all the way from Germany. That's when I got this," she reported patting the colostomy bag resting on her abdomen. "No one said anything. I just woke up and there it was."

Elizabeth has many joys and delights in her small life. The Catholic lady brings milk on Thursdays. "I told them I wasn't Catholic, but she said it was okay. I gave her a donation one time." Just as when she demonstrated her television, this is reported as if it were the most miraculous and wonderful thing imaginable: milk on Thursdays.

She sat in her worn, vinyl-covered easy chair as if it were a throne. "I've had this chair for years. It's a good one. And then someone figured out this," she pointed to her footstool that consisted of a small cushion perched on a cardboard carton. "It really works," she said with delight.

She treated the homemaker aide from a city program, who arrived to change the bed and do the laundry, a bit like the walker. Her sheets are the oldest, grayest ones I've ever seen. The sight of her tattered nightie neatly folded under the pillow along with a used tissue, brought a smile to my lips. Just like when we were kids, I thought, feeling a warm sense of order and tradition. I could almost hear my own grandmother calling to me, "Here now, get your bed made, and fold your nightgown before you put it under your pillow."

I promised to visit her again next week. She was obviously pleased with my visit, but untroubled by my departure. Senility and a contented heart allow her to live almost totally in the present, untroubled by any concerns beyond her small room with the bay window overlooking what has become a demolition site. An old building is being dismantled and destroyed directly across the street, but even the noise of the heavy machinery does not perturb her.

I took her hand when I said good-bye. Her grip was strong like her full rich laugh. A strong and contented spirit, loosely connected to a weak and unsteady body! Despite the lack of any teeth, a colostomy, and what appears to be abject poverty, she has a beautiful smile and doesn't notice that she's poor. What a dear, sweet, lady!

Over the next several weeks I visited Elizabeth every week, and she continued to tell me her stories, repeating her favorites every time, and gradually, in response to my questions, telling me more of her life.

Her husband died suddenly of heart failure in the forties, and she had two fourteen-year-olds to cope with by herself. Without much feeling and sounding disconnected from her earlier life, she said she'd missed her husband. Her remembered life seems to begin with her arrival here twelve years ago, with only hazy memories of a home in Massachusetts. I asked her if she had grown up in Massachusetts and she nodded her head in a way that made me wonder whether she could remember her girlhood. (I later found out she was born in Ireland and came to this country as a young woman.) The real people in her life are her children. The rest of us are vague and interchangeable players, whom she enjoys like television shows while we are with her.

One day she said, "I guess there's not much hope for me." I agreed that she was pretty sick, but assured her we would keep her comfortable and well cared for. Even to her fear, she was only vaguely and incidentally connected. Feeling weak and short of breath was disconcerting and frightening to her, and she didn't understand why she should feel this way.

December 3

Elizabeth was in bed when I arrived, but she sat up when I brought her some milk, and perked up a little. She showed little interest in the wheelchair that I brought, other than to note that it was "not the kind you can run by yourself." Ever the independent woman!

She wasn't sure how long Pauline was staying. When I asked whether she came every day, she "couldn't say." Days were not that clear anymore. "Is it Thursday? Oh, they bring milk." A man brought her ice cream and she was delighted. She expects nothing so lives in a continual state of delight at all that life brings her. She told me, "Life is what you make it."

Paul arrived. He's a hefty, graying man wearing coveralls and with grease under his fingernails, who obviously loves his mother very much. "Oh, thanks for bringing the wheelchair. My sister and I are taking her out on Sunday."

She wore a brand new flannel nightgown, which seemed to dwarf her diminutive body with its prominent, lace-edged neckline and cuffs. Pauline had gone out and bought her all new night gowns and a bathrobe, and thrown out all the old things. Pointing to the old dresser, Elizabeth confided with obvious pride in her daughter, "Everything in there is new, and all the old things are gone."

December 10

She now has one attendant from 11:00 to 3:00, plus another from 7:00 to 11:00 in the evening. It had taken some time before Elizabeth would agree to accept a hospice attendant in addition to the homemaker's aide from the city program. She was in bed when I arrived shortly after 3:00 with a small spider plant for her.

"I took a spill," she told me. She was dismayed that she had fallen while going just the short distance between the chair and the bed. "Why does it happen to me? Down I go!"

"How awful that must be to suddenly find yourself on the floor. You should let the attendant help you, and when she's not here, use the walker," I told her. "It gives you more to lean on than your cane."

She still resisted the idea of the walker, but seemed to consider it. Very firmly, and with determination in her voice, she said, "I don't want to fall anymore. Could you do something for me?"

"Certainly," I replied eagerly. I felt honored that this very independent lady was at last asking me to do something.

"Fetch the green bottle of ointment and rub some on my back. It's right over there." I couldn't find it at first and she seemed annoyed with me. At last I located the green bottle and she sat up slightly and told me, "Put some on my tailbone. That's where I landed."

I suggested that she lie on her side, but she said the colostomy prevented that. Her skin hung in soft folds and was warm to my touch. She wanted some of the ointment put on her right shoulder, too. She sighed with relief as I applied it.

After she was tucked back in bed, I said, "I hear you went out for a ride on Sunday. Where did you go?"

"Oh, *every*where!" Pauline and Paul had taken Elizabeth out for a ride in a rented car, and her eyes sparkled as she told me about the excursion. The wheelchair was another miracle to her.

"They put me in the wheelchair and wheeled me right down to the car!" After the ride, they put her back in the chair and wheeled her back to her room. "I never had to walk at all!" she told me incredulously.

After a while, she drifted off to sleep, her breathing quiet and shallow. Every little while, she raised her eyelid just a slit: she was checking to see if I were still there. I sat there for a while soaking in the ninety years of her strength and contentment. A remarkable woman.

"Why did I live longer than the rest of the family?" she asked me. I told her she was stronger than the rest, but she shook her head with pursed lips and said, "No, it's because I never smoked, drank or took any dope."

December 17

Katie, her Hospice attendant, was sitting in the straight-back chair by the open door, writing a letter, and Elizabeth was in her easy chair, her feet propped up on her cardboard-box footstool, reading the newspaper. She looked like a new person compared to the small, wan soul I'd seen last week. She's been going downstairs to the mailbox every day using the cane, or the walker, with Katie helping her. She obviously likes Katie and Katie is already fond of her, too. I only stayed a few minutes.

December 24

When I entered the hotel lobby I was surprised to find Elizabeth sitting in a wing chair in the lobby. She recognized me at once, and smiled broadly, extending her small bony hand to me. "You should see your plant. It's doing real good." I had not thought she remembered me from one time to the next.

While we talked she pointed out people in the lobby. "See that old man? He plays the piano on Thursdays when everyone comes downstairs for the free soup." As I was leaving, a man with a deformed mouth told me Elizabeth was mad at him and wouldn't let him bring her ice cream anymore. Elizabeth was obviously a favorite in the hotel and the social atmosphere of the lobby was good for her.

I brought her a Christmas ornament, which she took in her hand and studied as a child would. "But I have nothing for you!"

I assured her I wanted only one of her lovely smiles. She beamed and told me, "You have a lovely smile, too." So we smiled at one another.

I asked her if I could give her a Christmas kiss and, very formally, she nodded, yes. I brushed my lips over the soft and warm skin of her sunken cheeks.

December 31
I brought her some *Reader's Digests* that she seemed to like. She immediately pointed to the spider plant. She had for the moment decided Katie was a nuisance, sitting there all day long. I thought she was joking when she said, "I pay the rent here. She should find a room of her own. I can manage perfectly well on my own. I've no use for her." Elizabeth uses the walker now. I never thought she'd give up the cane. Maybe she has to resist Katie in order to acquiesce to the walker. Some days Katie actually has to leave, but when she returns in the morning, Elizabeth forgets she doesn't need her!

January 7
I arrived to find Elizabeth in bed feeling weak and nauseous, with Katie hovering nearby with concern. We've both seen her pop back from these weak spells, so we told each other she'd be feeling better soon. As I heard our cheery "get well" voices in that small dim room, I thought, one day she won't pop back; she'll slip quietly away during a weak spell. I touched her arm and she withdrew from my cold fingers.

January 21
Elizabeth was sitting up in her chair under a blanket, watching television, with Katie stationed nearby. She pointed to "my" plant, and greeted me with a big smile. She's been feeling weak and hasn't gone downstairs in several days. I tried to convince her to allow Katie to take her downstairs in the wheelchair, but now that she had progressed from cane to walker, she resisted the wheelchair. "Oh, that. That was for when Pauline was here." With that she dismissed the chair, as if that precluded any further use of the chair.

February 5
She fell last night. "The phone rang and down I go!" Someone came and pulled her back up. She reached for my hand and placed it on her scalp so I could feel the knot there, where she'd hit her head.

I remarked on the new hospital bed. "I don't like it," she reported bluntly. She seemed to appreciate my understanding why she liked her old bed, how one gets attached to the old and familiar.

She still smiles and laughs and tells her stories. At some humorous remark of mine, she laughed and said, "You're cute!"

"You're cute, too." I told her. Elizabeth and I now have an established dialogue that pleases her. The stories are always the same, but over the weeks, she has accepted me, and my plant. "I look forward to your visits," Elizabeth told me. I feel honored to be in this woman's life, even in this small way.

February 19
She was sitting in her chair under a new electric blanket, received just today from Pauline. She smiled as I entered, pointing to my plant. She continues to insist it has never been watered and is getting more leaves. I hold my breath and hope it will live as long as she does; it shows signs of being overwatered and with the shades drawn most of the day, it probably doesn't get enough light. It looks smaller each week. Tactfully, I suggested to Katie that she let it dry out between waterings.

Elizabeth told me her usual stories, which seemed to constitute the totality of her memory now. Her past was becoming increasingly muddled.

Elizabeth and I connect on a simple and direct level that touches off a warm joy in me. I hear her gentle Irish brogue and think of my Scottish grandmother, who has been dead many years. Elizabeth is a dear.

March 10
Elizabeth barely spoke today. She understood what I said, but it was as if she were conserving energy and did not deem my questions worth a reply.

Katie was getting Elizabeth dressed when I arrived. Elizabeth was now so thin her skin hung on her bones like some sort of dead white material.

The exterior of the hotel was being painted, and Elizabeth showed mild curiosity when a painter appeared on the fire escape outside her window. In Elizabeth's world of miracles, a painter on the fire escape was no less remarkable than wheelchairs and walkers that appeared in the corner.

I don't think she will live much longer.

March 30
Elizabeth was in bed, looking small and weak. Her hand was black-and-blue: the ravages of a few days in the hospital. She had vomited a little in the middle of the night, and had called the hotel desk who, despite all of the careful instructions, called "911," rather than City Hospice. The emergency crews are part of the medical establishment and are prepared to start failed hearts and to transport people to the hospital. Frequently, patients like Elizabeth who live alone and want to die at home, get confused in the night and when they call for help, find themselves in the hospital.

Because of Elizabeth's increasing tendency to fall, the hospice nurse has recommended admitting Elizabeth to an inpatient unit or beginning around-the-clock attendant care, but Paul has resisted either option. Elizabeth looked worried and very vulnerable. Katie stood nervously to one side.

"I'll find you," I assured Elizabeth, "no matter where you are, and I'll visit you just the same."

She shook her head firmly. "No, I'll be leaving here this evening." I repeated my promise to visit her, and she shook her head even more emphatically. Finally, I wished her a pleasant journey and she smiled and thanked me.

April 6
Pauline flew in this weekend and Elizabeth was finally admitted to an in-patient unit Monday. This hospice in-patient unit* has an

---

*An extended care facility with which City Hospice contracted for inpatient care.

old-fashioned coziness: hand cranked beds, colorful bedspreads, and patterned sheets. Rooms are double, but most have only one patient, which gives a spacious feeling to the whole place.

Elizabeth was sleeping while a stylishly dressed woman read in the chair beside the bed. It was Pauline. How good it felt to meet the woman who made Elizabeth's eyes glow. She would be here until next Friday and was spending every afternoon with Elizabeth. She was in good spirits and was pleased with the care Elizabeth was getting. Elizabeth looked comfortable, which was probably due to Pauline's presence.

"I've tried for years to spend money on my mother, but she has always refused. Since she's been sick I've just bought whatever I thought she needed without consulting her," Pauline told me.

I left my number and told her to call any time, for anything. She made one sizable donation to City Hospice at Christmas and wanted to make another.

April 12

Elizabeth was alert, confused, and quite agitated. She kept wanting to get up and it was difficult to understand her words. Soon after I arrived, she began hollering loudly and anxiously, "Help!" She informed the nurse who arrived, "You had no business leaving me in bed like this! I want to get up now." She pointed at the commode, but the nurse reminded her that she had just used the commode. Firmly, she told the nurse, "Well, I'll be sitting up there," and pointed to the commode. I told the nurse that I would keep Elizabeth company for a while; she left with a visible look of relief on her face.

Elizabeth had a lot of congestion in her chest and coughed too weakly to relieve the congestion, but she did not appear to be in any pain. I seemed vaguely familiar to her.

Her hands were cold, so I held them between my own; she took my hands and held them firmly, looking at them with interest. I fed her two spoonfuls of ice cream that had been left melting in a small dish on the bedside table. She told me, "Now, you help yourself."

I asked her about the small teddy bear on the table. She took the bear from me with a smile and told me, "I bought this little bear twenty-four years ago. I've given him to other people several times, but he always comes back to me." She directed me to put the bear back on the table.

I asked her whether Pauline had gone back to Massachusetts; she told me she had, but in a few minutes, in walked Pauline. Elizabeth looked at her with some surprise and asked her, "How did you find me here?" She seemed to have no recollection of the past two weeks of Pauline's daily visits.

Pauline followed me out into the hallway, and whispered to me that she and Paul had cleaned out Elizabeth's room today. "It was a difficult thing to do, but doing it together made it easier. Mom had change and even dollar bills tucked away, here and there." She was going home Friday. "I can't stand anymore sitting, reading, sewing, and waiting." Also the incessant rains of the past two weeks have pulled her spirits down.

Last week I felt certain Elizabeth would die while Pauline was here, but this week she seemed so feisty and stubborn, I thought she might hang on for a while longer. In her life of miracles, Elizabeth has become a miracle herself. Has she discovered the key to eternal life?

April 15
I found Elizabeth in the hallway, right by the nurses' station. She was confused and restless, so the nurses had brought her out of her room.

The basic problem was that Elizabeth did not like being sick and away from home. At first she thought I was coming to take her someplace and asked me anxiously, "Can I spend a few days at your place?"

She had no idea who I was, but seemed to like to have me sit beside her bed. Her toes were cold, so I put the afghan on her feet, but she directed me to pull it all the way up. I tucked her cold hands under the blankets.

Pauline has gone back to Massachusetts and although Elizabeth did not mention Pauline, I knew she was feeling lost and abandoned. "Try to relax," I told her. "Just rest and don't worry."

"That's easier said than done, you know," she replied. I agreed and she smiled. "I've just been lying here until you came along to cheer me up."

Her speech was now soft and mumbly, so it was difficult to understand what she tried to tell me. What words I could make out made no sense.

April 20, call from Barbara

Because the inpatient facility will be closing down shortly, Hospice has been helping patients and families make decisions about other care facilities. At Pauline's request, Elizabeth will be transferred Monday to a skilled nursing facility in a very posh retirement complex. The cost will be about $2,400 a month, but Pauline will pay for it and Barbara said Elizabeth will have excellent care. How ironic that this little lady who has lived all those years in a shabby hotel room with gray sheets and raggedy clothes will die in first-class surroundings.

April 20

Elizabeth was asleep sitting up with her glasses on a cord around her neck resting on her chest. Congestion still rattled in her chest. I called her name and she awoke easily but was not interested in seeing me. "I'm going to take a nap, " she informed me. I asked her if she wanted me to remove her glasses. She shook her head and brought her lips into a firm negative expression. I knew she didn't see well without her glasses, so she may have felt more in control with her glasses accessible even when she was asleep.

I asked her if Paul had been by and she replied, "Oh, he comes everyday." After a pause, she continued, "Well, that's that and I'm going to close my eyes now." I was dismissed.

April 26

After the intimate homeyness of the Hospice unit, Elizabeth's new quarters were imposing: elaborate lobby, a security desk, then a sleek, high-speed elevator to the floor where I was greeted by a sign telling me visiting hours had just ended. Since I had come that far, I decided to pretend I hadn't seen the sign and I proceeded to the nurses' station where a stocky man in grubby work clothes leaned on the counter conversing with a gray-haired nurse with a bored, distant expression on her face. When I told her I was there to visit Elizabeth, the stocky man turned and I saw that it was Paul. Carrying a glass of juice, he led me down to Elizabeth's room.

Elizabeth was the only patient in a large room designed for four patients. She looked smaller than ever. Paul offered her some juice and told her I was there to see her. She made an effort to look at me, but she had little awareness of the world beyond her own body. I stood beside the bed and feeling strangely nervous spoke louder than necessary, "Elizabeth, I'll be gone for a few weeks, and as soon as I get back, I'll come see you." I heard my loud voice speaking the improbability of seeing Elizabeth alive again. I knew she was going to die before I could return. Elizabeth stared at me for a minute and then closed her eyes again.

Mid-May
A postcard from Barbara: Elizabeth died May 12.

The news was not surprising, but I felt a sense of loss that did surprise me. Each visit to Elizabeth was so brief and so ordinary that I'm not quite sure how I ended up feeling so connected to this frail, stubborn woman. I had witnessed a very strong spirit preparing to depart from a weak and wobbly body. Now that she had finally departed and I would see her no more, I knew that I would miss her.

9

Soo Ying

Soo Ying spoke excellent English and was equally at home in both the Chinese and English speaking communities. For Soo Ying, the issues were the familiar ones of pain control, maintaining her independence, and coping with depression and frustration. She had explored both traditional Chinese medical treatments and the latest American techniques. She took the pain medications prescribed by her physician, but she also relied on a Chinese ointment to relieve her pain.

Beyond the cultural differences I found an intelligent woman, who having been independent and self-sufficient all her life, had a difficult time coping with the loss of physical mobility. Although initially brusque with me, she quickly relaxed and accepted me.

The Journal

October 20
Barbara and I drove south on the freeway and exited just before leaving the city limits. We drove down a bleak, treeless street that paralleled the freeway, and eventually turned onto a short street that dead-ended into a sort of no-man's-land along the freeway. The houses were of no particular style, but the owners of some had

invested effort and pride in improving their investments. The house next door was little more than a glorified shack, surrounded by a short chain-link fence, behind which a mongrel dog barked. In contrast, Mrs. Ying's house might have been transported from a suburban neighborhood: it was a large, square edifice built over a two-car garage.

Mrs. Ying, a totally bald, very thin lady, was sitting in a wheelchair at the kitchen table when Barbara and I were shown in, and Flora the attendant was tending several large pots on the stove. Flora is a rather dull-witted woman with limited nursing skills, who speaks little English, and no Chinese.

A plate heaped high with fried chicken sat on the table; several times Mrs. Ying asked us if we would please have some chicken. She smiled only occasionally and then without enthusiasm. Her English was good, but she communicated in a brusque style. Since I learned that Chinese verbs have no tense, I've been less taken aback by the abrupt, declaratory English sentences many Chinese-Americans use.

Barbara showed Mrs. Ying a cassette tape player she'd brought for her to use at night when she cannot sleep. "I don't want it. Too many wires." Despite Barbara's enthusiastic encouragement, she would not agree to try the tape machine. Barbara later told me that on her last visit, Mrs. Ying had been very enthusiastic about trying music.

The physical therapist had come this morning to help her with exercises. She reported that it helped "a little." Pain medication helped "a little," also the Chinese balm rubbed on her arms and legs helped "a little." Each "a little" was begrudgingly emitted from between her thin lips.

She had many complaints and little enthusiasm for any suggestions for improving her situation. Flora had been hired by the family as a twenty-four hour, live-in attendant, but needed time off because Mrs. Ying was very demanding day and night, and she could get no rest. Alice, a hospice attendant, came from 10:00 to 1:00 seven days a week to give Flora a break.

Mrs. Ying's biggest enthusiasm during our visit was for the pink booties we brought her. Her feet get cold and regular slippers fall off. I think she liked having a present, too.

Flora was cooking under Mrs. Ying's direction. Mrs. Ying had been a good cook and was exacting in her directions. She's a bit hard-of-hearing and Flora's minimal English combined to make it a trying procedure for both of them.

Barbara said that Mrs. Ying has talked of taking her own life and that I should try to get her to talk about it. Now that her pain is under better control, the idea may no longer be compelling or appealing to her. She likes to be in control so is determined to walk again, although this prospect is doubtful. Perhaps suicide is more a control issue for her than a serious wish for escape.

Her son Dennis, who is an accountant, lives in a nearby city and would like to have her move into his home, but she resists this and wants to stay in her own home. He calls her daily and visits when he can. Her ex-husband is in a convalescent home and other relatives live in the area.

October 23

She was eating oxtail and boiled potatoes at the kitchen table when I arrived. She complained to Flora that it was too fatty and criticized her for where she had bought the oxtail.

She told me, "Something good is on TV tonight: 'The Thornbirds.' " She directed Flora to fetch a crumpled television schedule from the living room, but I could not find the movie listed, because it was the guide for last week. I explained this to her, but she seemed to have trouble grasping the concept of last week although she was quite clear that today was Thursday.

She has been wakeful at night and always calls Flora in a panic. Flora imitated her calling in the night, "Hurry, I am dying. Come quick," and told me how she was kept running all night long.

Mrs. Ying seemed embarrassed by Flora's remarks. "Things often feel worse at night, don't they?" I asked her. She nodded. "How easy it is to become thoroughly frightened when you're awake in the middle of the night." I asked Mrs. Ying again whether she would like to try listening to music at night, but she firmly refused.

Very soon she directed Flora to put her in bed because she was sleepy. She called for me to help. "Lady," she directed, "help

Flora! The wheelchair always gets stuck on the carpet! What should she do about that?" By then Flora had the chair past the carpet edge and was ready to transfer her to the bed. Mrs. Ying's legs were uncontrollable and quite useless. She had only one good arm and not much ability to move on her own at all. She was afraid that transferring her was too hard for Flora. Flora, though short, was strong in a stocky way. She accomplished the transfer well. They looked like two small dolls with Flora's short arms around Mrs. Ying's thin chest. I assured Mrs. Ying that Flora was very capable, and to try not to be nervous when she was being transferred.

Just as Flora had placed her on the edge of the bed and her limp, rag-doll legs still dangled off the edge, the telephone rang, so I lifted her legs onto the bed and tucked her in while Flora answered the telephone.

October 30
Another fragmented visit, but with more feeling of connection. Mrs. Ying was eating a snack in bed when I arrived. I had to ring the bell three times before Flora heard it in the bedroom.

Flora rubbed a medicated Chinese balm on her bony back. At that moment Barbara arrived to discuss hours with Flora. They went into the kitchen to talk and Mrs. Ying took the opportunity to tell me about wanting to end her life. She wanted to know how much time she had left and hoped it was very short.

Flora lacks tact and sensitivity at times and needs a lot of praise and appreciation. She cruelly "teases" Mrs. Ying, saying she will abandon her, or that she will call back a former attendant Mrs. Ying really disliked. I have suggested to Flora that her teasing is inappropriate and only increases Mrs. Ying's anxiety, but Flora is not the sort to respond to gentle hints. Barbara has spoken to Dennis about Flora's behavior, but since Flora was hired by the family, there is not much more that City Hospice can do.

Mrs. Ying talked about her pain, and of how she calls Alice or Flora and how they ignore her. Flora insists she answers right away and comes as quickly as she can, but that Mrs. Ying is hard-of-hearing and does not hear her. I told Mrs. Ying that Hospice would speak to her doctor about having her pain medication changed.

No wonder Mrs. Ying has become a difficult patient! Were I confined to bed, in pain, with no one who understood my needs, I too, might yell and demand what I could from the paid help, and, like Mrs. Ying, I might contemplate suicide.

A young Chinese woman came into the bedroom with soup and a noodle dish. My God, this skinny woman eats all the time! They spoke in Chinese, but it was clear that the soup displeased her and the noodles were only marginally acceptable. Bringing food to the sick seems to be the custom in almost every culture. When so much is out of control, food becomes the one concrete offering a loving friend or relative can make. Mrs. Ying appreciated her friend's visit, but did not hesitate to complain about the food.

Next a social worker from the Cancer Society came in to discuss paying for relief hours on the weekend. Mrs. Ying felt confused and wanted to have someone write down exactly what was being arranged. She told me she was concerned about finances, but I think the main worry was of being at the mercy of a series of strangers who might abandon her, or ignore her cries for help.

After I left Mrs. Ying, I stopped by City Hospice and talked to the nurse about having Mrs. Ying's medication changed. The nurse had already talked to her doctor, who had refused to change her pain medication because he said she would complain anyway! The nurse had appealed to the Hospice medical director for assistance in communicating with Mrs. Ying's physician.

November 6

As usual, Flora was feeding Mrs. Ying when I arrived. Incredible appetite for a dying person. There seems to be no hour of the day that I can visit and not arrive during a meal. I wonder whether she eats because she does not know what she wants and food is the one thing she can demand with reasonable assurance of getting from the attendants; and they in turn, no doubt use food much as the mother of a cranky, teething toddler might.

I brought flowers that Flora plunked into a vase without any attempt to arrange them. Mrs. Ying thanked me profusely several times.

Flora pulled up a chair and the three of us talked. Both were feeling more rested: Flora because of the new weekend relief, and Mrs. Ying because she was sleeping "a little better." Mrs. Ying still does not like Alice, who is there most of the time Flora is off. "Alice is rough, and she scolds me. She's lazy, too. You should come when Alice is here so you can see exactly what I have to put up with." I had already spoken with Barbara about Mrs. Ying's complaints about Alice. Although Barbara is continuing to monitor the situation, it appears that Mrs. Ying's complaints are unfounded; Alice is an experienced attendant, well thought of by patients and families.

The medication change was finally made, which has certainly improved Mrs. Ying's disposition. Her face looked calmer and her voice has lost its strident, painful quality.

Flora still teases her, threatening jokingly to leave, or to quit. I told her again, more forcefully, "Flora, please don't tease Mrs. Ying. It's upsetting and unfair." She paid no attention to me and in a few minutes she started teasing again. Can she really be unaware of the anxiety she causes with her remarks, or is this her way of controlling a difficult patient? Or of getting Mrs. Ying to tell her how wonderful she is and begging her to stay?

After a while I told Flora I would keep Mrs. Ying company while she took care of other things. Flora liked to hear everything that was going on, but I knew Mrs. Ying did not feel as free to discuss what was on her mind with her there. Flora went into the kitchen to begin fixing dinner. Periodically, Mrs. Ying would interrupt our conversation with a look of anxiety on her face to ask whether Flora had gone home, or whether "the other girl" was going to come. The thought of being abandoned terrified her.

Mrs. Ying told me she had seen a movie about a woman who took an overdose of sleeping pills, and we talked again about her wish to end her life. I suggested that this might not be the "easy way" she imagined. "Think about those who would be left behind."

Bluntly, she replied, "I've thought of them enough and I can't think about them now. I get so frustrated with the pain and the worries. Often I feel like throwing myself out the window!"

I didn't point out that she could not turn herself in bed, much less cross the room and throw herself out the window. Instead I remarked lightly, "Since the ground is only one floor down, you'd be unlikely to kill yourself that way and you'd probably only end up with bruises and broken bones to add to your pain."

She sighed, "You're probably right. An overdose of sleeping pills would be better," she added, but I could tell she wasn't really considering this. "I get so frustrated, and bored."

"Being stuck in bed is difficult," I agreed, "but try not to dwell on things you can't really change. You can use this time to reflect upon all your happy memories."

"Happy memories?" She looked at me with surprise. "I don't have any."

My suggestion must have stirred something for she began to tell me how she had had a dress factory in the Chinese district. "But it was hard work." I thought of all the times I've walked through that area and peered into the cramped little factories, with rows of small Chinese ladies sitting hunched over sewing machines. These factories have no names and some are below ground, extending under the sidewalks where crowds throng overhead. I could easily imagine Mrs. Ying directing her workers sewing away at piecework rates.

Her husband had been an antique dealer in the same district, so they had both commuted all the way downtown everyday for years and years. They have been divorced for over ten years now and she said, "He spent all my life savings!" The divorce was hard on Mrs. Ying. She didn't say whose choice it had been, but I saw sadness and loss in her eyes.

"Will you rub my back with this Chinese balm?" Whether the various ointments patients use offer intrinsic relief or not, I'm not sure, but the opportunity they provide for human touching is a boon to both patients and care givers. Mrs. Ying is terribly thin and although she can scarcely move, her back felt surprisingly strong under my fingers. While I was rubbing the balm on her back, she told me, "I've given away dozens of bottles of this balm, but now I have no more and no one will give them back!" She spoke with bitterness in her voice. "I've taken care of other people all my life."

She seemed generally afraid. Of dying? Of suffering? Of losing control? Maybe all these and more.

While we talked, the telephone rang and Flora answered it in the kitchen and then came into the bedroom to find a number on the list by the bedroom extension. A doctor was trying to reach Dennis, and seemed impatient with Flora, with Mrs. Ying, and with me because we all had only one telephone number for Dennis, and apparently Dennis was not answering his phone this afternoon. Mrs. Ying didn't know who the doctor was; she thought he might be her ex-husband's physician.

Mrs. Ying has finally figured out who I am and has even remembered my name. "When will you be back?" It may be time to visit her more often.

She asked me to bring her a nail file, "a steel one." The request seemed innocuous at the time, but later I wondered whether she was looking for a weapon to hurt herself.

November 11
Mrs. Ying has taken a dramatic downturn. Barbara arrived on a routine visit to find her barely able to breathe and in terrific pain. Flora didn't seem to realize the severity of the situation, and had not called Hospice. Barbara called the nurse, who came out at once. Roxanall, a morphine medication, and oxygen have been started. Twenty-four-hour nursing care has been begun and Flora will no longer be needed.

Mrs. Ying's ex-husband died Thursday, which is why the doctor wanted to reach Dennis so urgently last week. Although Barbara suggested to Dennis that it would be best to tell his mother, he decided not to tell her. Mrs. Ying has had visitors and telephone calls every day, so Barbara suspected that someone else may have told her. The news of her ex-husband's death could account for the sudden downturn in her condition.

November 12
Both Meredith, the new practical nurse, and Flora greeted me at the door. Flora had come to pick up some of her belongings and had stayed to visit. Meredith was very matter-of-fact and had an old-fashioned sturdiness to her manner. She wore a nurse's white pantsuit and looked as if she had just walked off the floor of a major hospital. Two Chinese women were in the bedroom with Mrs. Ying, keeping a kind of bedside vigil. A tube ran across the hallway from the oxygen tank in the next room to Mrs. Ying.

Meredith informed me that Mrs. Ying was not incontinent, but she was keeping her in a diaper anyway, so she was grateful for the supply I brought from Hospice. "She finally voided today:

120 cc's, very concentrated," Meredith continued her report. "I am trying to get liquids into her. She is more alert today and taking small quantities of juice."

I went in to see Mrs. Ying, who was half awake and moaning, while one Chinese woman stroked her leg and Flora and the other Chinese woman stood at the end of the bed and watched. Seeing little point in adding my presence to the watchers, I told Mrs. Ying I would return another day.

As I left, Meredith told me, "I didn't give the Roxanall at 1:00 because Mrs. Ying was sleeping and I didn't want to wake her." At 1:30 Mrs. Ying awoke crying in discomfort, so she gave it then. With an official nurselike efficiency, she raised her wrist, looked at her watch and announced, "The Roxanall should be taking effect soon." This didn't sound like good pain control to me. Roxanall is a liquid that is so easy to give that even a sleeping patient is little disturbed by the intrusion. It is crucial to the establishment of good pain control to maintain a regular schedule of medication, so that the pain has no chance to reoccur. If medication is only given "as needed," the patient experiences a roller coaster of pain and relief, and the body has no chance to adjust to the medication. Meredith had been hired from an agency by Dennis; apparently she was unfamiliar with hospice pain control procedures. I called the hospice nurse to alert her to the situation.

November 18
Mrs. Ying died peacefully last night. Roxanall and oxygen kept her fairly comfortable for the last few days of her life.

I never met Dennis, but when I heard the news, I thought of the grief he must be experiencing at the loss of both his parents within ten days. It was overwhelming to contemplate. It was good to know that the Hospice bereavement program would be available to him during this difficult time.

10

Diana

Sometimes it's not the patient who needs hospice as much as a family member does. Because Diana was the daughter of a patient, I was introduced to a new kind of assignment. After working closely with a series of elderly women, all dying, it was with a sense of relief and readiness for a change that I met Diana, a woman not much older than I am who was facing, not her own death, but her mother's.

Barbara told me, "Rita is now mostly unconscious, full of tubes, and beyond our help, but her daughter is having a rough time and needs support. She's been caring for her mother with the help of a part-time hospice attendant, who stays with Rita while Diana goes to work at a hospital on an early morning shift. She's a very nervous and lonely woman around fifty. Although she has three grown children I get the feeling she's never really left home. She's responded well to my visits, but I feel she needs more time to talk, and more support than I can provide, so I want you to get involved."

The Journal

September 15 nonvisit to Diana
I arrived right on schedule to meet Barbara at Diana's home, but there was no answer when I rang the bell. Just as I was about to

leave, a muscular, young man in a tank shirt came up the steps and let me in.

"Oh, that hospice woman's already gone, but she said you'd be coming. She left a note for you." He ushered me into a room off the kitchen where his grandmother lay in bed with her tubes protruding, and a black-and-white cat snuggled beside her. He gave me the note from Barbara. "I'll go see if my mother's awake." He left me there, and disappeared into another part of the house. It was rare to see a hospice patient with tubes of any kind other than oxygen used for comfort. Apparently, Diana had insisted that the hospital insert the feeding tube when her mother stopped eating.

Rita's eyes were open, but stared straight ahead unseeing, yet I had the impression she was aware of my presence. Before I could decide what, if anything, I should say to Rita, the young man returned to say his mother was still asleep. I introduced myself and said I would be back another time. He let me out without responding to my introduction.

September 22 call from Barbara
Rita has pulled out the feeding tube: an incredible feat for a nearly comatose woman. Diana called Hospice, frantic to have the tube reinserted, but when the nurse went out, she helped Diana see that her mother was trying to tell her she was ready to die. Diana was still struggling to assimilate all this.

September 22
A good first visit. Diana is a nervous, high-strung woman with long graying blond hair, pulled tautly back from her face. She wore jeans and an oversize man's shirt. She invited me in and somewhat awkwardly offered me coffee. "Do you want coffee? I'll put the water on. Instant's on the table." We sat at a small Formica table in the kitchen, only a few steps from where Rita lay in bed. The kitchen was the only room in the house that was not a bedroom; when the upstairs had been converted to a separate apartment years before, Rita had apparently seen no need for a living room. While we talked, Diana stayed attentive to any change in Rita's breathing, and kept her voice low because she didn't want her mother to hear us talking about her. From what I'd read I knew that hearing

is usually the last sense to go, so Rita probably heard much of what was said even from the next room.

I felt Diana's inner wheels of expression, process, and growth turning and gathering momentum. So many things came up today, but over and over the one conclusion: she knows she should take care of herself, but she's not doing it. "I drove by the lake today," she told me, "but I couldn't get out of the car. I couldn't even fully look at the water. It was like I was afraid to enjoy it." We talked about her back pain and how the tension added to it. She didn't sleep at all last night. Her mother was awake all night, but most nights since she pulled the tube out, she has been sleeping well.

"I'm worried about how it will be . . . afterwards," she said, swallowing hard with anxiety. "Already, I feel a loss every time I turn the corner to come down our block." She faced the hard work of caring for her mother matter-of-factly. She dealt with tubes and medications, bowel movements and catheters, superbly, and with inspiring zeal and love, but I could see she really was apprehensive about how she'd react when Rita died.

"Because you're dealing with your feelings now, you'll continue to be able to deal with them later," I assured her. Anticipating how you'll feel later may be worse than anything you'll actually feel." I pointed out "afterwards" would be easier if she started taking care of herself now.

As Diana talked, I realized that Diana and her mother had been very close friends through all the years they'd lived together. Although Diana had married young, the marriage had not lasted, and Rita had welcomed Diana back home with her small son. Diana had married again and had had two more children, but it was clear that marriage had not been a big part of Diana's life, and that she and her mother had raised her three children here in this same house where Diana had grown up.

Diana talked animatedly of their life together. "Oh, my mother knew how to have fun. We always had such a good time together, and she could always see the funny side of things. We sure laughed a lot. And there's not a thing I couldn't discuss with my mother. I never felt the need to have a best girlfriend to confide in, because Mom was always there and I told her just everything." Her brothers and sisters had gone their own ways, leaving Rita and Diana to the confines of their intimacy.

When Rita became ill, their relationship became even closer, and Diana neglected even the few casual friends she had, and spent all of her time with her mother. A stroke left Rita unable to speak, so they developed a fingertip code to communicate. "One tap meant yes," Diana explained, "two meant no, and three strokes meant, . . . 'I love you.' Even now, it's on her mind: that she loves me. The other day she must have known how tired I was, and she tapped out one, two, three. It gave me the strength to continue even though I was exhausted." There were tears in Diana's eyes, and I could feel how much she loved her mother.

"I try not to cry in front of Mom, but I'll be there taking care of her, and the tears will start to come. I hold the tears in and then go into the bathroom to cry." I wasn't sure what to say. Hiding tears, holding them in, doesn't seem healthy, but I wasn't sure what Barbara would say, whether by this time, there were too many tears for her to cry with her mother.

With my prompting, she agreed she would begin this week to take a little time for herself each day, and next Thursday we'd talk about what she'd done. "I don't know why, but I'm really afraid to take time for myself, even though I know I should."

I suggested that she *give* the time, but she must see that. She's holding on so tightly that it's hard for her to let go, even for a moment.

She told me about her uncle's death seven years ago. "He was in terrible pain and wasted away to ninety pounds with colon cancer. It was awful, but he died peacefully, in the hospital, with me and Mom right there. When he took his last breath, I was the first one out of the room. I was so scared!" He was the first dead person she'd ever seen.

We'd talked almost an hour and a half when her son came in.

September 26, call from Hospice
Rita died this morning. The on-call nurse went out.

September 28 call to Diana
Diana was glad to hear from me and to be able to tell me how her mother died.

She had sensed the end was near. That night she had last checked her mother at 1:00 a.m., and since she was sleeping peacefully, she had gone to bed herself and slept for several hours. "I awoke at 5:00 a.m., and I just knew something had happened. My feet felt like lead! And it took forever to get from my room to Mom's room."

"I'm sorry now that I went to sleep and left Mom alone. I wish I could have been with her until the very end." I heard a painful twinge of guilt in Diana's voice. Or was it the "if only" that is the disbelieving reaction to the first news of death?

"Your mother might have waited for this time alone," I told her. "It might have been too difficult for her to slip out of life with you, her daughter whom she loved so much, right there. Frequently patients die when the person caring for them happens to be out of the room, even if for only a few minutes."

"Well, maybe so, but I still wish I could've been with her at the end. As soon as I discovered that Mom had died, I called Hospice and the nurse came out. I don't know what I'd have done without Lia to help me dress and wrap Mom's body. And she was right there with me when Mom's doctor came to pronounce her dead." She'd been afraid of touching her mother's body, but during the wrapping, the body rolled toward her, and she found herself holding her mother's body in her arms. "I'm amazed that I could do that!"

"Diana, you have much greater strength and ability to cope than you're aware of on a conscious level," I suggested.

She kept her mother's body at home until 2:00 that afternoon, so that everyone had a chance to come by. "All of the children and grandchildren came. And friends, too, and the priest from our church."

The burial was Tuesday in the cemetery where her father, who died in 1970, was also buried. Her son and her daughter stayed with her at the funeral and have supported her throughout the time since then.

She was using sleeping pills prescribed by her own doctor to sleep, and didn't feel quite comfortable taking them. I suggested she stay in touch with her doctor, and reminded her of the importance of taking care of herself, which included getting rest. I pointed out that she had not allowed herself to sleep deeply in so long that her body was now trained to wake frequently and to sleep only fitfully.

Diana wanted to get out of town for a few days and planned to take a trip with her son. "I can't bear to be here in the house without her. I haven't gone into her room since they took her body away. I'll do it soon, but not yet." I told her not to rush herself, to take her time.

October 3 call to Diana
Diana was back from Mexico. She'd had a great time: she'd conquered her fear of flying with a few beers, and her back had started feeling better in Mexico.

"I miss Mom terribly, but I'm doing okay, I guess. I still talk to her, and I haven't moved anything out of the room yet," she confided. "When we got back from Mexico, it was like finding out all over again."

She returns to work Monday. Probate hearing is scheduled for October 15, and her oldest son will be going with her, because her brother might contest the will, which left the house entirely to Diana. Diana was apprehensive, but she'd hired an attorney who told her not to worry.

She told me again everything that had happened the night and morning her mother died. There was both comfort and pain in the retelling of the last details, the reliving of the final moments.

October 23 call to Diana
She said she'd been meaning to call me. "I know I should be getting out, but I've done little besides going to work." She was very lonely and more grief was now coming up. "I can't bear to see anyone, or do anything. I just want to sleep and be left alone." She's been unplugging the telephone, which is why I hadn't been able to reach her. She sounded glad, even relieved, to hear from me, and agreed to meet tomorrow.

October 24
She opened the door looking rumpled and weary, dressed in a wrinkled shirt and baggy pants. Apologetically, she told me, "This is how I dress every day at home, and when I don't have to go to work I even stay in bed." She shrugged her shoulders and, moving as if it were a great effort, turned on the gas under the tea kettle. "All I have is instant coffee. I hope that's okay."

"I wish I knew why I was so tired," she said, easing into the vinyl kitchen chair. Pain flashed across her face. "And my back has been killing me."

I suggested treating herself to a massage. "Diana, it's not surprising that you feel tired. You've lost your mother and your best friend, all at once, and look at all the months you went never getting a full night's sleep. Of course, you're tired."

"The funny thing is that, tired as I am, I have a hard time sleeping at night. I just toss and turn."

"You trained yourself to stay alert while you were taking care of your mother. Your body may take a little while to realize it's okay to sleep soundly now. Also, you have suffered a major loss and it's a natural grief reaction to have trouble sleeping."

"Oh, it is? I thought it was just me." Relief was in her voice. "Is that why I can't concentrate on anything, not even my mother's medical insurance billings?"

"Certainly," I reassured her. "Grief can affect you in many ways. Give yourself time." She hates going any place, but she enjoyed her daughter's visit last weekend.

She was feeling very lonely; no one wanted to listen to her. Her son didn't want to hear about it anymore; "Aren't you relieved that it's over?" Her boyfriend John thought she should get out of the house and stop thinking about her mother. "I've put him on the back burner, and only see him on Sundays." She saw an old friend this week, but it was difficult to call and she almost canceled at the last moment. Afterwards, she was glad she went, and had renewed contact with her friend.

Her brother was contesting the will, alleging that her mother had been out of her mind when the will was made. Diana was worried about losing her home, but the lawyer told her she can't be kicked out. She was feeling hurt by the way her brother was treating her, and the whole thing worried her, and added to her deeper feelings of grief and loss.

She was grateful for my reassurances that her grief was normal and appreciated the books about grief I had brought. Because of the attitude of her son and her boyfriend, she'd hidden her feelings of grief and loss, so our conversation was the first opportunity she'd had to express all that she was feeling. She was relieved to hear that there was nothing wrong with her for feeling this way.

She seemed interested in the hospice bereavement social and didn't seem alarmed when I suggested the possibility of short-term, professional counseling.

She recognized that her relationship with her mother was more than a mother-daughter relationship. I suspected that relationship had been the only close relationship she'd ever experienced. She had avoided seeing people during the long months of her mother's illness, so the few casual, mostly work-related, friends she had, she'd deliberately shut out. Her relationship with John was a long-term one (ten years she reported), but he was unsupportive now, and she seemed disinterested in the relationship. Perhaps it was a relationship more of habit than substance. I wondered whether she would be able to form close relationships in the future, and I thought some kind of counseling or support during the grieving process was essential in preventing her withdrawal into herself.

She'd expected the actual death of her mother to be extremely traumatic, but she'd surprised herself by surviving that quite well. She'd even been able to relax and enjoy the week in Mexico, but now she was surprised to feel terrific grief and loneliness. "I feel so lonely, and I miss her terribly," she told me with tears running down her cheeks. "I don't understand how I could feel so good in Mexico, and now this. . ."

"It's normal to experience ups and downs," I assured her. "You'll continue to experience changes in your feelings as you accept the loss of your mother on deeper levels."

Sometimes she forgets that her mother is dead; then is startled again with the painful reminder that she's gone. She admitted that she goes into her mother's room and weeps. It sounded on purpose, but since she's had no one to talk to about her grief, and she spent the final months before her mother died struggling not to cry in her mother's presence, it may not be such a bad thing; she certainly needed some outlet for the tears.

I spent nearly two hours with her and she hugged me warmly when I left. Driving home, I felt a warm glow of satisfaction: I had really helped Diana today. I thought about all the ways I would help Diana as she worked through her grief. This was a real opportunity for her to change her life, and I was ready to help her do it.

November 1

She had tried to call me to cancel, but then was glad I came anyway. She has had strep throat and was not feeling well. She has such mixed feelings about being with people, that from the moment she agrees to see someone, I think she is planning to cancel.

Emotionally, she was doing much better this week. She had read one of the books about grief and wanted to copy out some parts. She had tried reading some passages to John to explain what she was going through, but he wouldn't listen, and actually walked out of the house when she persisted. He derided her for "just following along with what those books say." Neither would her son discuss anything or listen to her. My visit last week really helped a lot, she said.

"I still talk to Mom and I feel her strength helping me." She needed more reassurance that she was doing the right thing.

I mentioned how illness makes us vulnerable, and how her feelings may be more volatile while she was sick with strep throat. I suggested that she may have memories of her mother caring for her when she was sick. Her face lit up with the joy of remembering, and she eagerly told me how her mother used to bring her cups of hot tea and tuck blankets around her when she was sick.

All the while we talked, her son kept marching through the room, making phone calls, and noisily opening and closing doors, getting ready to go out. I sensed he was uncomfortable with my visit. He'd been out of work for several days and had been driving Diana crazy. After several false departures, he finally left. During all that time our conversation was difficult, but there was a closeness in our having to converse around the intrusions.

Diana has agreed to attend the hospice bereavement social next Thursday. She seemed very open to new experiences now, and I hoped she'd also join the ongoing bereavement support group. I pictured her exploring her feelings in the company of other bereaved people and receiving the support that she can't get at home. Perhaps losing her mother would end up being the positive kind of experience that would lead her to make new relationships and expand her limited life beyond her job and her home. I felt very excited to be a part of all this.

November 7 taking Diana to the Hospice bereavement social
When I called to confirm picking her up for the bereavement social, she said she wanted to cancel because she'd been up all night
worrying about what the attorney had told her. She was teary
voiced, and I heard the whine of a little girl who'd been abandoned
by her mother. She'd visited her attorney the day before and had
found him impatient and unwilling to answer her questions. She
had called him back this morning to clarify what he had said and
he'd yelled at her.

She did not seem to know how to handle the situation, so I
suggested she needed a new attorney, that she should not put up
with such treatment. "I don't think you should worry about doing
anything else until next week. Try to just forget about it for a few
days. You know, Diana, if you would take a nice afternoon nap,
you might feel better about the whole situation if you do go to the
social."

At first she said, "Maybe," and she would have to call me,
but when I told her I would have to call her, she said she would
definitely go. It was a habit with her to set things up so she could
cancel, but I guess when she realized that I would not leave her
with her "maybe" and would be calling her back, she acquiesced.

When I picked her up at 5:45, she apologized for not making
a hot dish, and only bringing cold drinks. I assured her that
drinks were necessary, too, and I was just glad she'd come. Diana
was nervous and awkward. Jana, the hospice nurse who had
helped Diana the day Rita had pulled the tube out, greeted her
warmly. I saw Diana come alive as she relived with Jana the time
of caring for her mother. It was an important connection for her,
and she told me she wished Lia, the nurse who had helped her
the day of her mother's death, would come. Seeing and talking
to those who were involved with her mother's care revived her as
if she herself had ceased to live and breathe the day her mother
had died.

Barbara greeted Diana with a hug. I mentioned the attorney
problems Diana was dealing with. She assured Diana that a letter from her mother's doctor would serve to refute the claims that
her mother was out of her mind, and that she should try to pay
no attention to her brother's noise, and that she would prevail in
the end.

Diana stuck by my side throughout the social period before the food was served, and then followed closely behind me with her plate of food, and sat beside me while we ate. She talked to no one other than the hospice staff who spoke to her. After we finished eating, she seemed anxious to return home, as if being away from where she had last been with her mother was too painful to endure for very long.

I dropped Diana off at home and she hugged me and thanked me for bringing her. I wondered if she would ever go again without my bringing her. Not likely. She really needed some kind of support during this difficult time. Maybe if she joined the bereavement support group, she would feel more comfortable coming to the social.

November 21 call to Diana
She said she was doing fine. She still cries sometimes. Her daughter found a new attorney for her and has been very supportive and helpful. John has called every day but she hasn't felt like going out much. She had no interest in the coming holidays and wanted to avoid having a Thanksgiving dinner. I suggested she could avoid the work of a holiday dinner, but she could get together with her children for support. She was mildly interested in the bereavement group and agreed to meet the social worker who ran the group.

December 4 call to Diana
She was sick with a cough and on antibiotics. The meeting with the social worker somehow never happened. Diana actually sounded more interested, or at least less resistant, now than last week. I must follow up before her interest wanes.

She had a good Thanksgiving with all three children. "I said the grace, which was something Mom always did. It made me cry, but just for a minute." She missed her mother over the holiday, but said she was feeling much better than she had been a few weeks ago. She was still not seeing or calling friends and wanted to avoid Christmas.

December 5
Diana must have had her telephone unplugged today, for she never answered.

December 11 call to Diana

She still had a cough, but she sounded less glum this week. She has been to the park by herself and to Rita's grave every Saturday.

"I was awakened in the night by a visit from Mom. I just know she was there. She didn't say anything, but I could feel her there beside me. And later my daughter told me she saw Nana by the dresser on the same night." The experiences seemed to comfort Diana, but she needed acknowledgment from me that such things were possible, and "normal."

The ability to identify with a person can be a valuable skill in working with patients and families; however, it can also set up expectations that are not helpful to either the person or the care giver. The superficial similarities Diana and I shared had made it easy from the beginning for me to identify with her and to provide compassionate and sensitive support to her as she coped with her mother's death. It was about now that I realized that Diana and I were very different, and that the solutions I saw as appropriate were not suited to Diana. Could someone more experienced than I have helped Diana more effectively? I don't know, but perhaps an experienced social worker might have identified the task at hand more realistically than I did.

Death comes not only to mature, self-aware, fully functioning people; it comes to everyone, in every kind of family situation. When I first began working with families I assumed that whatever anxiety, depression, fear, or strange behavior I saw in people was directly related to the approaching death. Eventually, I realized that people arrive at death with whatever problems and ways of coping they have developed over a lifetime, and it's not realistic to expect lifetime habits to change during a short term hospice intervention.

Long before Diana's mother became ill, she had accepted as normal, and even happy, a life that, had it been mine, I would have found depressing, boring, and unsatisfying. I'd have done anything I could to bring about change, and I would probably have seen the experience as an opportunity to make major life changes. Diana, however, was not interested in changing her life. She was grateful for whatever Hospice could do to help her cope with her mother's death, but only within the context of her life.

December 19 call to Diana

She had agreed to attend the bereavement support group, but on the night she was to go, she didn't feel well and set out in her typical ready-to-cancel mood.

"I said I'd go, so I drove over there, but I couldn't find a parking place." So she went on home. She admitted that she'd been looking for an excuse not to attend, that she'd been against the idea from the beginning. I wanted to urge her to attend the group another time, but this time I saw that no matter what a good opportunity the group was for many people, it was not for Diana. What I really had to learn was to set aside my own ideas and opinions and to see Diana exactly as she was, without the cloud of my own judgments and expectations.

Still swallowing my disappointment, I told her, "Only you know the best way to cope with your grief. The group was only a suggestion. If you change your mind, you can always call Hospice later on. How's your cold doing?"

"Better," she replied, relieved that the subject of the group had been dropped. She told me that she and her son will go to her daughter's for Christmas. She sounded depressed in a low-level way, but she didn't seem interested in doing anything about it. "Oh, I'm doing fine."

After I hung up the phone, I found myself thinking about Edith, who had also been very close to her mother, and who had never formed any close relationships after her mother died. True, Diana had her children and John whereas Edith had no one else, but still there was something reminiscent of Edith in Diana's attachment to her mother. I wondered whether there was anything Diana could do to avoid the long, lonely years that Edith had endured. And I wondered whether it was the degree of closeness in the relationship, or the fact that it was an unusual closeness for a mother-daughter relationship, or the absence of other relationships, that led to a life so filled with grief and mourning that no new relationships could grow.

11

Evelyn

The institution of the family is the fascinating subject of much sociological research; however, most of the academic interest is focused on young families: mothers and fathers raising young children. I've had a chance to see how the relationships developed in childhood endure into old age.

When her sister became ill, Evelyn as a matter of course moved into her home and took care of her. She was tired, but she devoted herself to Clara's care with determination and sometimes stubbornness. Although I never met Clara, I got a feeling of the family relationships when I met Evelyn and Clara's niece Alice. When I heard Alice complain that Evelyn would criticize her no matter what she did, I saw her for a moment as a stand-in for her mother, Clara's older sister, who had died nine years before. This was a close family, who never hesitated to take care of their own, but they were also feisty and used to contending with each other's idiosyncrasies.

Evelyn was part of a family that coped and she coped well with her sister's illness and death. Though there may be no siblings left to care for Evelyn if she becomes ill, the family has already produced the next generation of people who care and who can cope.

The Journal

December 4, conversation with Barbara
Barbara had just returned from a visit to two sisters: Clara, who

was dying, was ninety-three and Evelyn, who was caring for Clara, was eighty-eight. Clara was eating a large bowl of ice cream, but told Barbara with great certainty that she had only three days to live. Barbara thought she might live quite a while if she kept eating ice cream, but she was concerned about the "well one," Evelyn, who looked awfully tired. Evelyn was in the habit of taking the bus to the store as well as traipsing back and forth from her house to Clara's house, so Barbara asked me to take Evelyn shopping.

December 5 call to Evelyn
I called to set a time to stop by to get acquainted so that I might sometime help out by taking her shopping. Right away she mentioned that she needed to go to the market today so I agreed to pick her up at 3:00.

December 5 shopping with Evelyn
I arrived to find her sitting at the window with her coat on. I never met Clara, who was sleeping when I arrived. Evelyn has been taking care of Clara with the help of part-time hospice attendants. She is a small, chubby, determined lady with a great sense of humor. We left the sleeping Clara with Wanda, the hospice attendant, and set off for the store.

Evelyn relaxed with me at once. I pushed the cart at the market as she chose her groceries. She looked around and remarked, "There's a whole different crowd here in the afternoon. I usually arrive when the store opens." She's so short, I thought the butchers would overlook her standing patiently at the high meat counter, but after a long time, she was waited on. Lamb stew meat was on sale so she was planning a lamb stew for dinner. No wonder she was tired, making dinners like lamb stew!

On the way back to Clara's, we stopped at Evelyn's house that is nearby, so she could pick up her mail. When we arrived at Clara's, I brought in the groceries. Evelyn sent Wanda home early and put on the kettle; we had coffee and cookies, and talked. She kept pressing me to have more cookies.

She was tired. Caring for Clara was hard, and she has been doing it for quite a while, and "this is not the first time either. I'm getting ready to call my niece in Sacramento and holler, 'Help!' "

She had been hoping that her niece would volunteer without being called.

She was tired of being away from home, and she missed her own bed, her own pots and pans and nice sharp knives. She does not sleep soundly and wakes every time Clara does.

I left her my number and told her to call if she needed anything and to plan on going shopping again next Thursday.

December 13 call to Evelyn
I called to ask if 3:00 would be a good time to bring by some supplies. She replied, "That would be just fine, but I do not intend to be here. My niece is arriving this morning and just as soon as she gets here, I'm going home." This last was spoken with determination, and then she added, "I'm awfully tired." She sighed and told me she did not sleep well last night because although the hospice attendant was there, she awoke to the smell of gas; according to Evelyn the attendant had not turned the stove off properly. I assured her that a house as old as Clara's was probably leaky enough that there was no danger from the gas, but I sympathized with her worry. I also silently sympathized with any attendant who could work under Evelyn's scrutiny. Barbara and the attendant coordinator were aware of the friction between Evelyn and the attendants, who were all quite competent.

Clara has been catheterized and hates it, but urine was getting to be a real problem since she has a cough and, "with every cough, urine flows." Evelyn told me the whole story of the morning attendant, who put Clara on the commode against her explicit directions. Barbara had already told me Evelyn had fired the morning attendant, and been having difficulties with the night attendant as well. Evelyn is a strong woman who insists on being in control of everything. Evelyn confided, "Between you and me, I was looking for a reason to fire her all along. I never liked her." Why? "She was too familiar and she rubbed me the wrong way."

Now Evelyn was managing with just Wanda in the afternoon and the night attendant. I told her a replacement could be arranged, but she replied, "Oh, that will be up to my niece. I'm going home." She made it sound as if she lived across the country and would be permanently gone. I asked her how long her niece would be staying. "Oh, until close to Christmas," which was only about ten days off. I hoped Evelyn would feel rested and ready to come back to Clara's by then.

Seeing her sister deteriorate was very hard on Evelyn. Clara was sometimes confused about where she was and other times, she was "as sane as you or I." Evelyn said she had so much to do at home, and had done no shopping at all. "I might just write checks this year." I agreed that might be a good idea because she should rest so she doesn't get sick herself. She said, "That's what everyone's worried about, but I'm a tough old bird." I told her even tough old birds could get sick.

December 13 visit to Evelyn and Alice
Evelyn was standing in the doorway with her coat on when I rang the bell. She was getting ready to take the bus home and was grateful for my offer of a ride. (I wondered if she had held off going home, knowing I would offer a ride.)

I brought in the supplies and she introduced me to her niece, Alice, a woman in perhaps her late fifties, who looked quite dazed and disoriented. I told her Barbara would come by Monday and could arrange extra help if she needed it and, in the meantime, to call Hospice any time day or night. I pointed out the sticker on the telephone with the City Hospice number. Evelyn had not mentioned Hospice so Alice seemed relieved to hear that a nurse was on call twenty-four hours a day. I also told her she could call me.

While Evelyn was fussing about, Alice haltingly asked me, "What should I do . . . who do I call, if she . . . passes."

"All you have to do is call Hospice," I told her. "The nurse will help you make any other calls."

"Oh, that's good to know. Do you think I should call Evelyn if . . . it . . . happens during the night? You know I asked her, but she said she didn't want to think about anything like that. What do you think I should do?"

"That's a hard question," I told her. "You'll have to play it by ear, but if it were near morning, I might be tempted to wait until morning to call Evelyn." I told her I would call her tomorrow to see how everything was going and she seemed relieved and pleased.

Since she was getting a ride, Evelyn added a few things to her already-bulging bags. She was tired and anxious to get home. While I was talking to Alice, she picked up her bags to show how cumbersome they were and declared, "Oh, how glad I am not to have to take the bus!"

She reminded me of an impatient child interrupting an adult conversation, so I directed her in a parental voice, "Evelyn, put those bags down! We'll be ready to go in just a minute."

Evelyn's step was much slower this week, and her ankles more swollen. In the car on the way to her house she told me, "Alice just doesn't understand what I've been through and why I'm so tired." I sympathized and told her it was easy to see why she was tired.

She said Clara had declared that what she (Clara) needed was "an old-fashioned cocktail."

"Evelyn, you're the one who should have a cocktail and put your feet up." That reminded Evelyn that she'd forgotten the wine at Clara's house and had none at home.

"When my husband was alive, we always had wine with dinner." So we stopped at a market and I offered to buy the wine. She thrust a twenty-dollar bill into my hand, and told me to buy a half gallon of Hearty Burgundy. I ran in to buy the wine while poor, tired Evelyn waited impatiently in the car.

When we arrived at her house, I carried the bags and the wine while she fumbled in her purse looking for her keys. She had a terrible time with the two locks on the door and insisted her son must have been there and locked a lock she never locks. Finally, I took the keys and she stood by, relieved to have someone else handling the problem. The door was sticky from the rain; with a gentle push it opened and Evelyn headed up the stairs, groaning with difficulty at every step. She was truly exhausted. She pointed out the dirty dishes in the kitchen and I suggested she leave them be and just rest. I asked if there were anything I could do while I was there. "Not a thing," she replied. Now that she was home, she was anxious to be rid of me.

December 14 call to Alice
Alice is sixty-nine years old! Nine years ago her mother (Clara's older sister) died and she cared for her until three days before she died when she was hospitalized. She has company coming the 21st, so she will have to leave on the 20th. She felt Evelyn would criticize whatever she did. She said there was no "reason" for Evelyn

to complain about not having Christmas cards, being so tired, etc. Alice said there was plenty of help and not much to do anyway. "The hospice attendants are wonderful," she reported. I tried to point out Evelyn's stress and worry about Clara might come out in indirect complaints and worries. Since Evelyn tended to be critical, I suggested that Alice use her own best judgment rather than worrying about trying to please Evelyn.

Alice and her sister had been up before and she thought the fired attendant was wonderful, but she knew that Evelyn did not like her.

Clara woke only twice in the night and has eaten only small amounts of pureed foods and liquids. She does not always know where she is and who Alice is.

"I told my husband if I ever become ill, not to try to take care of me at home. He should either get twenty-four hour help or put me in a rest home." This preference for herself comes out in unspoken resentment at being asked to help care for Clara.

December 20 news from Hospice
Clara died today at 10:30. Alice had called Evelyn and she had arrived just before Clara died. The hospice nurse was there, too. Alice must return home today. Such timing!

December 22 call to Evelyn
She had just returned from a trip to Clara's house to let the equipment be picked up. Her feet and ankles were better now because she had taken her diuretic. She was going to her son's for Christmas and intends to rest.

She sounded tired and relieved. She was leaving the rest of the decisions about the house until after the holidays. She was not sure whether to sell the house as is or to fix it up and then sell. Clara left her estate to various people "in percents," so Evelyn thought she might need my help to figure all that out.

As I hung up the telephone, I wondered how long Evelyn herself would live, now that her sister was gone. Someone from the Hospice bereavement program would be calling her shortly. She would certainly be lonely, and without the responsibility of looking after Clara, how would she fill her days? And who would eat the lamb stew?

12

Peach Dumplings

I stand before the mound of fresh peaches at the roadside fruit stand. In a daze I let my fingers stroke the soft, furry skin of a peach. Mesmerized by the pungent peachy smell in the warm air of the August afternoon, I reach for a basket of peaches and head for the cashier.

It isn't until I'm back in the car that I wonder why I've bought a whole basket of peaches. A dozen large ripe peaches is too many for someone who lives alone. I feel rather foolish as I drive home from the country, but the smell of warm peaches filling the car makes me feel warm and content, and strangely excited.

Dumplings! That's why I bought this large basket of peaches. My head swims with visions of hot, sweet dumplings, oozing peach juice mingled with drawn butter and crunchy granules of cinnamon sugar. I breathe in deeply as if I could smell those heady smells even in the car.

I cannot think of peach dumplings without thinking of my grandmother, and now that she is dead, the thought of dumplings evokes a flood of memories. I yearn for the sweet, rich dumplings as if I could make her live again, embrace her one more time, if only I can make the dumplings as she did when I was little.

I spent most of my childhood unsuccessfully trying to escape being scolded by my mother. Even if I managed to complete all my assigned chores, I might get chided for how I'd done them, how late I was in accomplishing them or for being generally messy and disorganized.

What a contrast Gramma was! No matter what I did or didn't do, she had nothing but smiles and loving praises for me. At the time I didn't have the words to describe her style of loving, but I see now that it was the truest example of unconditional love I have ever experienced, before or since.

Gramma didn't live with us, but she spent long periods of time visiting us each year, between Thanksgiving and New Year's, and whenever my mother's bursitis acted up, and sometimes for our birthdays: hers and mine were only a week apart at the end of June. I loved Gramma's visits, the more extended the better. Sometimes I'd come home to find that she'd done all my ironing, or hemmed my new skirt, or made a special Czechoslovakian dessert, maybe *buchty*, the little pastries filled with prune butter.

I loved to come home from school and find Gramma home alone. She always greeted me as if she were delighted to see me and hear whatever small child news I brought from school. I can see Gramma now, leaning over the gray Formica table in my mother's kitchen, a well-worn cotton-print apron around her grandmotherly figure, over an equally well-worn cotton housedress, with her soft cloud of thin, nearly white hair, and her sparkling eyes. How I loved it when Gramma smiled upon me!

"Oooh! Gramma, what are you making? Can I help?" I'd cry. My mother was an efficient cook who allowed only limited opportunities for helping that always seemed to end in my failure. But Gramma always found some way for my small clumsy hands to help. And I felt less clumsy with Gramma than with my mother.

"Well, with all these nice looking peaches, I thought I'd better make some dumplings."

"Oooooh! Dumplings! Dumplings! I love peach dumplings! Can we have them for dinner? Is Daddy gone?" I knew that we never had dumplings for dinner if Daddy were home. Such decadence: a dinner of such dessertlike character filled me with excitement. My father required meals of meat, potato, and vegetable, arranged on the plate in unvarying New England supper fashion. Compared to the usual fare of boiled potatoes, pot roasts, and boiled vegetables, peach dumplings were my ambrosia.

And she'd chuckle with barely contained merriment at my excitement. "Your daddy's gone and won't be back until Wednesday. Your mother's playing bridge, so I thought you and I could get dinner ready before she gets home. Go change your dress and then you can help with the dumplings."

It was unheard of to wear school clothes at home (or Sunday clothes to school), so I'd rush upstairs to take off my dress and put on a polo shirt and a pair of slacks. Then Gramma would tie an apron around my waist.

Arriving home from the country with my basket of peaches, hurriedly I climb the three flights of stairs to my apartment. Filled with anticipation and breathless from the stairs, I balance the basket of peaches on one hip as I grope for my door key. Once inside, I wonder where the dumplings recipe is. Gramma needed no recipe; she just scooped out flour and mixed in eggs and shortening with a deftness cultivated in the hundreds of times she'd made dumplings. I sort through a box of recipes and find a card headed "Peach Dumplings," but it's in my daughter's handwriting when she was much younger and I don't trust it. (One year for Mother's Day, she copied all my recipes on three-by-five cards and presented them to me in a plastic box labeled "Food File." Unfortunately, many teaspoons became tablespoons and other details of preparation were lost in the copying.)

I sort a little further and there it is: a limp folded paper, barely legible, the ink faded and obscured by butter stains, but it's the dumpling recipe in Gramma's own handwriting.

Childish excitement fills me as I measure out the two cups of flour and remember how when I was too small to be trusted with the flour I'd watched Gramma scoop out the dusty white flour. What kind of shortening did she use? I squint at the faded page but all it says is: one-quarter cup shortening, melted. I guess at the stiff white kind in the round can; if she meant butter, she would have said so. Two eggs and one-quarter cup milk; this is easier. Now one-half teaspoon of salt and one teaspoon of baking powder.

Mix flour, salt, and baking powder. Add melted shortening. Beat eggs lightly. Add milk. Add to flour mixture. Dough has to be firm enough to handle, not too hard and not too soft.

Reading her instructions, I'm swept back to the gray Formica table covered with flour and to the memory of the soft, pliable dough between my fingers. How could anything this much fun actually turn into dinner? I'm sure I held my breath the whole time I handled the dough; I wasn't often allowed such intimate proximity to anything this messy. The idea was to cover the peach with a smooth even layer of dough, but no matter how hard I tried some little bit of the peach would show through, and more dough would cling to my fingers than to the peach.

"There, there, you did fine! It's almost covered. Smooth the dough over this way just a little more. Oh, these will taste good!" No matter my results, she always encouraged me and applauded my efforts. Meanwhile, she would have neatly covered the rest of the peaches and have them piled like snowballs on a plate.

Have water boiling in a large-enough pot to hold at least four dumplings. Give them room. Drop one by one, cover and let boil twenty minutes. Watch them for they like to boil over.

Then squeezed at the bottom of the page, as if I could forget: "Serve with melted butter and sugar and cinnamon."

"Can I shake the cinnamon, Gramma?"

"Well, sure you can. Here, I'll put the sugar in the jar. You can add the cinnamon." She would watch as I added the cinnamon to the sugar, knowing that my sweet tooth would keep me from adding too much cinnamon. "One more shake. There now, that's enough. Here's the lid. Put it on tight so the sugar won't fly out when you shake."

Inanimate objects often took on a life of their own in Gramma's instructions. With my mother, I was messy and uncoordinated, but with Gramma the sugar was unruly and tended to fly out of the jar, and the dumplings liked to boil over.

Oh, Gramma, I think with warm, moist tears of memory in my eyes as I mold the dough around my peaches: it was your loving encouragement that allowed me to grow up ready to try new things. I believed you whenever you assured me that I could manage some small task, and I got used to thinking I was smart enough to keep unruly sugar from flying out of the jar, and alert enough to keep those dumplings under control. And maybe my answer was worth raising my hand in class. And perhaps I was big enough to babysit for the neighbor's children. And sure, I could probably get a real job. And have boyfriends. And go away to college. And have children of my own.

I grew up to her litany: you'll do just fine. Oh, you look so pretty! What a smart girl you are. I'm so proud of you. You always work so hard. I'm sure you did your best; that's all anyone can ask.

The water is boiling and I ease my dumplings in. Each one sinks, then bobs to the surface. I notice that a sizable piece of dough has escaped from a dumpling and bobs loose in the water. As I watch the dumplings in the swirling water, I can practically hear the clatter of dishes and silverware being set on the gray Formica table.

"Here comes your mother! Just in time. You better get the table set and call your brother and sister." And Gramma would bustle about, hovering over the kettle of dumplings boiling on the stove, steam covering her glasses, while I continued to shake the cinnamon sugar, long after it was homogenized. These were the fifties, when people ate supper in the kitchen on a bare Formica table. Clatter and clang and I would have the table set.

The smell of the peaches wafting on the steam would go right to my head. "Dumplings! Dumplings! We're having dumplings for supper!" I never missed an opportunity to tease my younger sister and brother. "You better get your hands washed or I'll get all the cinnamon before you get to the table! And I got to help Gramma make the dumplings!"

I set out a bowl, melt the butter, and mix the sugar and cinnamon. Not exactly sure how to tell when the dumplings are done, gingerly, I lift one from the pot. I cut it open. Juice oozes out and steam rises from my bowl. I pour on a generous portion of melted butter and liberally sprinkle on cinnamon-sugar. The rich, sweet smell fills my head and loosens a few tears in my eyes. I feel warm and happy. And loved. Oh, Gramma, thank you for dumplings and for loving me and for helping me keep the sugar from flying out of the jar. I love you, Gramma, and every time I think of you, I have to remember that you died and I'll never hear your voice again. I'll never get used to your being gone. I miss you terribly.

Oh, what a heavenly taste! My dough is a bit mushy, but it doesn't matter: I am utterly content as I leisurely eat the first dumpling. It's almost like having Gramma back for a brief moment. With every sweet bite, I see her face and hear her voice. I feel her smile inside of me.

When I was grown and had children of my own, I asked Gramma to send me the recipe. When it arrived, I enlisted my young daughter's help in the kitchen. She loved the sticky feel of the dough, and she listened enthralled as I told her how Gramma had first taught me to make peach dumplings long ago and far away when I was just a little girl. Her small fingers were no more apt at smoothing the dough over the peaches than mine at her age. She oohed and aahed as I slid the dumplings into the kettle of boiling water. I melted the butter and she shook the sugar and cinnamon in a jar.

Watching my daughter slurp her way through her first peach dumpling filled me with a sense of family and home that I don't often feel. After dinner we called Gramma and my daughter, who is Gramma's first born great-grandchild, told her, "Gramma, we made dumplings!" I heard Gramma chuckle with the familiar sound of delight and approval. The joy of dumplings had now been transmitted to the next generation.

Gramma began to grow old. She still spent several months each winter with my mother, but she no longer drove so my parents now had to pick her up, and she had to wait until someone had time to take her home. The loss of independence saddened her, I know. She and I talked by telephone and sent cards to each other on holidays.

Each birthday she was surprised to find herself still alive. She lost her interest in oil painting, and I gave up trying to convince her to visit me. Arthritis stiffened her fingers and sciatica settled in her hip joint, making walking a slow, painful prospect. Still she never complained. I don't think she made dumplings any more. I lived three thousand miles away and all the others were counting calories or watching cholesterol.

As I put the leftover peach dumplings in the refrigerator, I relive for the thousandth time the news of her death. She was ninety and quite ready to die. I guess I should have been prepared, too, but how can anyone ever be prepared to give up that much love and caring?

And, once more, I feel the disappointment of not having been with her when she was dying, but filled as I am tonight with her presence and her love, I realize that it is because of Gramma and how she loved me that I've been able to be with other people's grandmothers when they were dying, like Elizabeth. And with those who never got to be anyone's grandmother, like Edith and like Anna.

13

Tom

Outwardly Tom and I had nothing in common, and at the time I was introduced to Tom, several other volunteers were already involved. I was the only woman assigned to Tom and I was apprehensive whether Tom, a gay man in his late forties, would accept me.

From the first, however, Tom and I had an easy rapport and before long I found myself growing very fond of him. Throughout the eight months I knew Tom, I reminded myself that Tom was dying and that I must not become too attached to him. When I first realized how fond of Tom I had become and how quickly I would have to say good-bye to him, I railed against the fate that had not let me know Tom before he became sick. It was later that I realized that we had met at exactly the right time.

On a less personal note, the journal of my experiences with Tom is interesting as an example of the variety of changing arrangements that must be made to accommodate a patient's shifting condition. All of this was coordinated by the City Hospice social worker, using every available community resource. Several agencies and organizations participated in Tom's care and numerous individuals assisted in paid and unpaid roles. And they all loved him. He was a uniquely likable person, who made everyone glad to help him, even though his care was often difficult.

The Journal

March 19, telephone call
Tom's friend Bill, who lives nearby has been taking care of him,

and he needs relief. Two volunteers are currently staying with Tom, one evening each; I am to give a third evening of relief.

Speaking in rapid-fire, as if he has had to say these same things many times, Bill told me how he and Tom have been friends for twenty years. Tom originally worked as a barber, but more recently he has worked at an office job. His job was very stressful and Bill says Tom will never be able to return to that work, but he might be able to return to cutting hair. "Tom has always been fiercely independent and the lack of control he now feels is very difficult for him."

Tom's problems, Bill said, began in the fall and became serious toward the end of January. He had anxiety attacks, difficulty driving, and then problems handling his checkbook. A seizure put him in the hospital for a month, where he had numerous tests and X rays, and the tumors were finally discovered. A brain biopsy, which was scary for both of them, disclosed that the tumors were inoperable, and radiation was prescribed. He has lost his short-term memory and tends to become confused and anxious when left alone.

While Bill and I spoke, Tom interrupted to comment that he felt like he had just been discovered naked in Macy's window! Actually, he interrupted twice to tell Bill the same thing, which is, I guess, the sign of how poor his short-term memory is and why it is so wearing for Bill to be with him now. Bill said his short-term memory, of a few minutes ago to several months ago, is terrible; however, his long-term memory seems unaffected. Writing notes seems to help and being able to refer to notes gives him some sense of continuity.

Bill sees Tom every morning, then Claudia, an attendant from the Cancer Society comes daily for six hours, and after work, Bill brings Tom dinner and spends the evening with him, unless there is a volunteer. And weekends he spends most of the time with Tom. I mentioned the need for him to take care of himself and he said, "I know Tom would have done the same thing for me and I'm glad to be able to help him."

I will meet them both Monday evening.

March 22
I skipped the old fashioned elevator and climbed two flights of stairs in the older high rise. Tom greeted me at the door. He is a

tall, handsome, robust man; only his total lack of hair betrays his illness. As he turned to usher me into the small apartment, I noticed the huge scar on the side of his head, where the biopsy had been performed.

Bill was close behind in greeting me. I thought he would leave as soon as I arrived, but he hovered over Tom and me until Tom commented, "You know, Bill, you can go now and we can converse by ourselves."

Tom's apartment consisted of a bed-sitting-room plus a small separate kitchen and an eating area, which had been turned into a barber station, complete with swivel chair and scissors and combs all laid out on a long table in front of a vast mirror covering most of the wall. The apartment is tastefully decorated with lavish paintings on every wall and exotic sculptures and fancy lamps on ornate tables. Despite the small space and the large number of furnishings and decorations, the room felt comfortable and didn't feel crowded.

At last Bill left and Tom and I talked. He was full of positive-thinking sayings and philosophies. "As my father always told me, when you're feeling low, try thinking about someone else rather than yourself. He was a wonderful man—my father—and I had a really wonderful childhood. We weren't wealthy, but my brother and I always knew we were loved and cared for. I've always felt I was very, very fortunate to have such loving parents. Love is the most valuable treasure on earth. I see so many unhappy people, and I think that if only they knew that by helping someone else, they would end their own unhappiness. My father had a way of always making people feel good about themselves."

The tumors caused much repetition. He asked me a zillion times, "Tell me, Joan, how did you come to be a Hospice volunteer?" And he told me over and over, "When this illness is behind me, I'd like to be a volunteer, too."

Does all that positive thinking cover up doubts and fears? He alluded to vague unhappiness despite all the talk of how lucky he was and what a wonderful life he'd had. I suggested that he could use Hospice volunteers to express any fears or worries or other unhappy feelings.

On a deep level, how much Tom's litany was like Edith's! Hers was all gloom and suffering; his was all love and helping others, and neither expressed the heart. Edith did when she stopped talking. I wondered what would lead Tom to express his true feelings.

March 30
Tom seemed much the same this week: he still looks healthy and hale, yet cannot remember what he said or did from one moment to the next.

"Well, my illness was caused by my own foolishness," Tom informed me. "Drugs. So foolish." I expressed disbelief and he told me about taking drugs in the sixties. I pursued it a little further and he admitted that the doctor had only said drugs might possibly have contributed to the tumors, not that they caused them.

"Don't be too hard on yourself, Tom. The sixties are long gone and there's no point in blaming yourself. It's more likely that the illness came unrelated to anything in the past." He was unconvinced.

"And have I told you that I've lived many years as a homosexual?" he inquired in much the tone one might use to mention a stamp-collecting hobby. "It seems like another world now and I'm glad to be out of it." We talked of relationships and the difficulties, alluding to sexuality rather than actually discussing it.

Over and over he asked, "How was your day?" and, "Is there too much cold on you from the window?" and then with greater and greater frequency, whether I was tired. "I could just go to bed if you're tired. You don't have to worry about me." Bill had asked me to stay until 11:00 so I didn't know whether I should leave early or not. I asked Tom if he wanted me to leave and he said, "Oh, no!" A little after 10:30 he admitted he wanted to go to sleep so I called Bill who seemed relieved to hear Tom was sleepy.

Tom was entirely upbeat, never voicing a moment's doubt or despair. I've heard that he cried for days when his hair fell out; yet he maintained tonight that it had not bothered him in the least. I made numerous suggestions about difficult feelings one just might have in his situation, hoping he might take the opportunity to divulge some fears or worries.

April 5
Bill called me late afternoon to say he and Tom had had a rough day. "We went out for a meal and some shopping, and we got into

a discussion about selling Tom's truck. We each dug our heels in and said things we didn't mean." Bill needed to get away and didn't want to leave Tom alone. I agreed to come over at 7:30.

Tom greeted me enthusiastically in the hallway as I came up the stairs. Over and over he complimented me, "You're looking terrific today. That sweater suits you perfectly." He was his usual cheerful self and never brought up the subject of the truck or mentioned any disagreement with Bill, but he seemed very glad to see me. "Could I kiss you on the cheek? You're such a wonderful person!"

I'm certain I blushed, but `I was flattered and charmed. Of course, I obliged. How good that Tom can reach out for affection, especially when he and Bill are at odds.

Conversation seemed less disconnected tonight. We talked of relationships, guilt, happiness, marriage, children. He told me that he feels stupid when he cannot remember things. Last week this was "no problem," so little by little he is letting me in on the true picture.

Before I left, I showed Tom where the bran muffins I had brought were, so he could have them in the morning. Even as I spoke, I realized that by morning he would have no recollection of how the muffins had appeared in his kitchen.

April 7

As usual we watched television. Tom knows all the old movie stars. He kept saying, "Can you imagine what it must be like to be a star and have such an exciting time to look back on? They were so creative. And you know they had so much fun making these movies. It wasn't just a job." He told me about the famous people whose hair he had done.

As the evening progressed, Tom seemed concerned about me. "Are you comfortable there? Do you want a pillow? Please make yourself at home, Joan."

"Tom, you're worrying over me like Bill worries over you," I teased him.

He smiled, but his concern continued to punctuate the conversation. "Is it warm enough in here for you? Is there a draft on you?"

"I'm just fine," I protested over and over. Finally he pulled himself out of his easy chair and disappeared into the large walk-in closet. I heard him rummaging around, obviously looking for something. In a few minutes he emerged from the closet carrying a folded blanket. Smiling, he opened the blanket and spread it over me. I was overcome with emotion. I was supposed to be the one taking care of Tom, and here was Tom taking care of me.

Curled up under the blanket, I found a lump in my throat as I listened to Tom talk again about, "when I get better and go back to work." I remembered with a jolt that Tom is dying. How easy it is to forget. I hope there are months and months of these warm, lovely evenings, and that Tom stays healthy for a very long time.

April 14

Tom greeted me enthusiastically, "I'm so glad you're here! So good just to see another human being."

"Have you been lonely?" I asked him.

"Yes, I guess I was. I have all these notes here to tell me what is going to happen, but I wasn't sure. . . ." He handed me two pieces of paper. One said: Bill will be here with dinner at 7:00. The other said that I was arriving at 7:30.

"Well, of course you're confused," I told him. "These notes have proven false, since Bill hasn't arrived yet and I'm late, too. Are you hungry?"

"No, I'm just glad you're here." He said "glad" but I heard something more like "relieved" in his voice.

I had brought a small bunch of yellow daisies that Tom arranged in a very large crystal vase. Tom said, "It's been a wild week," but he couldn't remember exactly what had happened.

It was after 8:00 when Bill arrived, breathless, and with more flowers, sent by friends in the flower business! I arranged flowers while Bill put dinner in the oven and ran around giving Tom and me instructions.

"And your disability income has been nipped in the bud, and we have no money!" Tom's doctor had gone to Europe and left a report with the disability office that Tom was back to work April 1! Bill was a wreck trying to straighten it out, but Tom seemed unconcerned, as if it were happening to someone else.

Bill showed me how to use the new VCR and finally left in a flurry. We watched a movie and chatted off and on.

Tom asked me if I could suggest anything he could do to ease the burden on Bill. "Well, Tom," I said, "You're doing the best you can. Just cooperate as much as you can, but you still must speak your mind when you need to. Even though it's necessary for you to depend on Bill for almost everything, of course you want to make what decisions you can."

Later in the evening, he began asking if Bill would be returning. When I asked, "Do you want him to?" he said, "Oh, no," but still he kept asking, so when I got ready to leave, I suggested that he call Bill, which he did. Despite his protestations, I think he needed reassurance that Bill was there for him.

April 25

When I arrived Tom was alone fixing coffee. I helped him find the tea and he got out a cup for me. Just then, Bill burst in with a TV dinner for Tom and dismissed Tom from the kitchen. "Now you just go sit down. I've got to get your dinner in the oven and Joan will fix your coffee." Tom looked embarrassed, but with only minor hesitation, he sat down in the other room while Bill bustled about giving me directions for the TV dinner, as if it were a complicated soufflé.

Tom looked a shade less robust and was now having trouble with one leg. Bill protects him like a mother hen. Sadly Tom told me, "Bill has always been a nervous type, somewhat compulsive. Taking care of me has been really hard on him, so I try to be understanding. I truly appreciate everything he does for me. If only he could learn to relax a little."

"You're more patient than I'd be in your position," I told Tom.

"Well, I can bear Bill's overprotectiveness most of the time because I'm certain everything will come out all right and I'll be able to control my own life again. The doctors will be sending me back to work before long." I told him I hoped so. Will he be as accepting of Bill's role if he sees no possibility of regaining control?

I asked if he had any other friends coming over and he said, "No, they kind of fell by the wayside."

"Oh, how sad!" I burst out, amazed that anyone could abandon this sweet man, just when he needed friends the most.

"Yes, that really surprised and disappointed me, but I understand how my situation might be hard for some people." I detected no bitterness in his voice.

April 31

I arrived home past the time I was due at Tom's so I called Tom to say I would be there as soon as I could. He was there alone so he was very glad to hear from me, and ready to meet me downstairs to make sure I got in all right. In his anxiety, he wanted me, someone, anyone, there right now.

I rushed over and was greeted enthusiastically by an anxious Tom. His leg was giving him trouble in spite of increased medication. He said he's had no pain. "I'm only afraid that I'll go to stand one day and the leg will give way entirely."

After Bill left, we watched pieces of movies. A little after 9:00 Tom took his regular medication, which Bill had left for him. "It's the Decatron caper," Tom chuckled, the joke still fresh to him since he couldn't recall the prior repetitions. "Sounds like a grade B spy thriller, doesn't it?"

When I went into the kitchen to dish out the ice cream, Tom followed me in and sat down in the barber chair in the dinette. "I don't know what this medication—the Decatron caper—is supposed to do. Will I just wake up one morning and this noodle will just click into place, and I'll get ready to go to work and just lead an ordinary life again?" It was a real question, not just rhetorical wondering, and I had the feeling that he had asked others the same question and wanted my answer.

I had been told by the hospice nurse that it was probably impossible for his memory to return, but that seemed too harsh and hopeless a statement to make to Tom. I spoke slowly, hoping the right words would come to me, "Well, no one knows exactly what will happen . . . but probably nothing all at once." That sounded evasive even to me, so I continued, haltingly, "Perhaps your memory won't ever come back, so you'll have to find other ways to remember things, like writing notes."

"I think I will get better. I really do. So many people are helping me. And the radiation is helping, I know it is." Facing the truth, no matter how awful, is important to how I live my life so Tom's buoyant confidence troubled me, but I also heard in his voice the strength and hope that enabled him to cope with a truth that I'm not sure I'd be able to face, were it the truth for my life. Should I try to temper Tom's confidence in getting better? I felt suddenly without answers, without any ideas of the right way to die, or how I could help Tom. I looked at Tom and I saw in his eyes that he did see the truth *and* he had genuine hope. To have hope when the prognosis is good is easy. Tom was showing me a whole new dimension of hope. Whether he died or recovered was almost beside the point; Tom's hope would guide him through whatever was to come.

"Tom, I truly hope you will get better, but no matter what, you can count on me, and the others at Hospice, to help you however we can." Inspired by Tom's hope, I wanted to give him something.

Then he said, "You know, I've always considered myself an intelligent person, but lately I feel so, well, stupid."

"You're still intelligent," I told him. "Loss of memory is not loss of intelligence. And I can imagine how awful it must feel to give over control of your life to someone else."

"Oh, I'm so glad you understand!" and with that he gave me a grateful hug and we returned to the other room to eat ice cream.

Shortly after the ice cream, Tom said he was tired and would I mind if he crawled under the covers. He didn't want me to go so I agreed to stay until the movie was over. It felt very companionable to sit on the couch and talk to him in his bed across the room.

At 11:00 I turned out the lights, drew the shade and said good night. I reached down and touched his shoulder, but later as I thought of the several weeks that I would be out of town, I wished that I had kissed him good night. I hope he stays all right while I'm away. The thought that he could deteriorate rapidly made me sad.

May 23

Tom was glad to see me after my trip. I thought of him often while I was gone. The postcard I sent Tom was propped up on the table, but Tom, of course, had no idea where it had come from.

Tom is having more difficulty walking now. Ever the gracious host, he asked if I wanted more cola and then rose unsteadily from his chair. He headed first toward the bathroom, then realizing his error, he maneuvered toward the kitchen with halting steps. Walking takes much concentration, sometimes more than he has.

To make better use of the limited attendant hours Tom's insurance pays for, Barbara, after conferring with Bill, has arranged for Tom to spend days at an adult day health center and has shifted the attendant hours to the evening. Since Claudia could not work the evening shift, a new hospice attendant has been assigned to Tom. Tom misses Claudia and doesn't care for the new arrangement.

"Those people at the center are in pretty bad shape," Tom told me. "I don't like going there, but I want to cooperate with anything that might help get me back on my feet." This possibility was voiced with less conviction now than before I went away.

May 27

I stopped in to see Tom at the center. He was delighted to see me. His walking was very unsteady, much worse even since the other day. I suggested a cane might be nice and he agreed, but said he was being careful. I said even though he was careful, his brain was not able to give good directions to his legs. "Oh, is that what's happening?" He seemed genuinely relieved to hear this explanation. We talked again of all the radiation therapy and medication he has had, whether it will "work." I heard the anxiety and fear in his voice. He told me about a friend who had been shot in the head and how he had been brought back to normal despite severe brain damage so "this is not impossible."

When the social worker for the center came over, Tom beamed and put his arm around me and said, "Doug, I want you to meet. . ." He fumbled frantically for my name and failing, burst forth with, ". . .the most wonderful woman in the world!" What a superb recovery!

Greg, the night attendant, is quiet, but Tom said, "He's a nice kid." He was glad to have someone there, even a "silent Sam." Being alone is hard: such anxiety. He said sometimes he wakes up after a lonely night and has a hard time waiting until Bill arrives. Barbara sent games home with Tom, to give Greg and Tom something to do at night. A nice idea, but I don't think Tom's concentration is sufficient for games and Greg does not sound like much of a game player.

May 30

Tom and Bill had (by separate reports from each) a terrible day. There had been a mishap and Bill had "blown a fuse." I first heard the story from Bill on the phone: "Well, did I ever have a mess to clean up this morning. Tom decided to fix himself a cup of coffee and got instant coffee and creamer all over the whole kitchen!" Tom's kitchen is too small to merit such excessive language, yet Bill continued, "I was a good hour cleaning up that mess. So we couldn't go to see the parade after all. Well, I guess I'll have to hide the instant coffee where Tom can't get at it." I suggested putting everything in small containers, so that if there were a spill it would be small, but Bill was in no mood for easy answers. The strain of caring for Tom was starting to show on him.

Tom told me his version after Bill had nervously departed. "Bill has been in a state of high anxiety all day. Joan, he has been just ridiculous! I think I spilled a little instant coffee and he really blew a fuse. You would have thought I had committed a terrible crime, the way he carried on. There was nothing I could say or do after that. I just sat here and kept my mouth shut while he went into a rage. I worry about Bill: he's going to make himself sick. I may end up having to take care of him someday."

He still talked of "when I get better . . . can return to work . . . drive my truck," etc., but late tonight he finally talked about "going to sleep and not waking up."

"You know, Joan, I'm not afraid of dying. We all have to die and I guess it must be peaceful. I think we go where we were before we were born. I believe in God. I just hope it won't be too hideously painful." I told him that most pain can be controlled with medication, and that Hospice would see that he was given whatever medication he needed.

Tom still dislikes going to the center. He hates the van ride there and he hates being there. "Those people are in terrible shape." I kept pointing out the center's role in keeping him at home as long as possible, as a best option. Althought many of the others at the center are older than Tom, most are in no worse shape than he is; interesting that he sees them as so much sicker than he is.

He seemed less sick at home today than when I saw him at the center (probably because he stays pretty much in the easy chair at home and relaxes here), but he still walks very badly.

June 14

Tom's left hand is not much use anymore. I looked just in time to see the bowl of ice cream sliding onto his shirt front. His leg is very weak, too. He refused my proffered hand out of the chair, but it was difficult for him to stand up unassisted.

We watched *Gas Light*, an old Ingrid Bergman movie that Tom had seen long ago; he remembered some scenes, which he kept telling me. This part of his memory was impeccable.

Tom is tired of being sick, and would like to see improvement. "I'm keeping depression at bay, but I wish I knew what was going to happen." He still talks about going back to work, of how great it would be to tell Bill, "Okay, Bill, give me the keys to my truck now." He looked so confident, that I could almost visualize the scene.

June 17

More new arrangements for Tom: a night attendant so Tom won't have to be alone at night and Bill won't have to get Tom ready in the morning. And Nora will replace Greg in the afternoon. Piecing together these arrangements was a continual struggle for Barbara. To cover around-the-clock care for Tom, she utilized Tom's private insurance, Medi-Cal, the Cancer Society, a gay community group, and special City Hospice funds.

June 21

Tom was, according to Bill, "indisposed," and Bill was as Tom would say, "in a state of high anxiety." Soon after I arrived, Tom came teetering and tottering out of the bathroom, holding his pants up with his good hand and trying to steady himself on the furniture and walls with the same hand. Bill caught sight of Tom, whirled him around, and exclaimed, "Well, just a minute now! Let's get ourselves a little more together first," and proceeded to zip and button and tuck Tom as if he were a negligent five-year-old. Embarrassed for Tom, I tried to ignore the whole scene. Caring for Tom, day in, day out, was probably a lot like caring for an oversize five-year-old and was definitely wearing on Bill.

There was now a loose, rough quality to Tom's skin. As his brain exerted less definite control over his muscles, his whole body sagged and he seemed to be aging very quickly. His attention was still excellent and except for the memory loss and repetition, he was coherent. Events were not always properly placed in time: he said Bill helped him make a will "today," but I knew this happened some time ago. He was worried about his disability checks and whether Bill was handling everything properly.

"How difficult it must be to have to give up control of even your own checkbook!"

"If Bill were sick, I would gladly take care of him," Tom told me. Then we had fun imagining what a rotten patient Bill would be. As Tom laughed, I felt his worry dissipate, at least for the moment.

July 4

Tom had somehow garnered two cigarettes, which he delighted in smoking soon after Bill left. He admitted, "Smoking cigarettes has become a little game I play with Bill." His last available rebellion. How self-aware Tom is.

His gait grows ever more unsteady. A wheelchair to transport him to the center has arrived. He was nervous about using it, and wondering whether he would be able to maneuver it. With his nearly useless left hand, I doubted he would be able to propel it at all. I assured him someone else would worry about pushing the chair. He also mentioned concern about how he would be able to maneuver it through tight spaces in the apartment, although no one has mentioned using the chair at home. For all of his talk of getting better, he seems to have an inner perspective on his inevitable decline that shows itself in moments like this. I told him we could always move things around to make more room.

We watched a romantic Cary Grant movie that was just reaching the conclusion when Larry, the night attendant, arrived. The old fashioned romance of the movie put both of us in good spirits, and when I left, Tom impulsively gave me one of the lilies from the vase on the table. I went home feeling very lucky to be in Tom's life.

July 8

I took Tom to his doctor today via the Medi-Van, jouncing across town with the metal lift clanging away, the two-way radio squawking of lost wheelchairs and even a lost driver, and Tom telling me over and over about how hard the seats in the van are. He was now in a wheelchair all day, so he no longer had to endure the hard van seats. The driver bolted Tom's wheelchair in place for the ride, and I perched on one of the "cement" seats.

Traveling by wheelchair may have been easy for Tom, but I was a bundle of nerves maneuvering the chair through doors, in and out of elevators, around furniture and through narrow passage ways. Entering the doctor's waiting room was a carnival. I propped open the self-closing door with my foot and attempted to back the chair into the room, but first I had to rearrange the furniture in the small waiting room. Once inside the room, it took me several tries, and more furniture rearranging, to turn the wheelchair in the thick pile carpeting. I never noticed before that the world is this full of tight places, unnecessary doors, and doorjambs that jam everything.

Getting Tom standing upright on the scale and back down without both of us ending in a heap on the floor was a challenge. Everyone at the doctor's office was about five feet tall and looked to me to maneuver Tom, who is well over six feet tall. Dr. Rollins, a clean-cut young doctor, was sympathetic and concerned about Tom's condition.

After the brief office visit, Tom and I waited in the lobby for the van to return. By the time we reached Tom's apartment, both Tom and I were exhausted. Tom dozed and I nearly did too, while we waited for Nora, the attendant, to arrive. What a luxury it seemed when I left Tom's apartment and headed home: just to walk without maneuvering the wheelchair around obstacles!

July 11

"The only thing I can do is to be patient. There's really nothing else to do right now." Tom has said this sort of thing before in relation to getting well again. That connotation was still there, but today I heard acceptance in his voice, acceptance and patience for whatever is next. He acknowledged that there was no way to know the full effect of the radiation treatments. I commended him on his patience, and I wondered if he were aware of the signs of deterioration. Changes along the way like adding a night attendant, and now the wheelchair, did not seem to alarm him. Once he realized that someone would push him, he relaxed and accepted the wheelchair as merely a device to make life easier. Equanimity: that's what Tom exhibits. I hope I can learn it from him.

August 1
Bill called me at 5:00 to see if I could come early. "Tom fell yesterday and today his foot just would not work properly and he's had some stomach pain, so I need to get out to get his dinner." When I arrived at 6:00, Tom was in his chair, looking tired. Tom had no injuries and could scarcely recall his fall. Bill bustled about, then left to get dinner. Tom said he wanted to lie down because his stomach was bothering him, so I helped him onto the bed. He was very unsteady tonight. He felt better after a few agonized belches and dozed off for nearly and hour.

When Bill returned, Tom slept on while Bill heated his dinner and talked to me. "You know, Joan, Tom's illness has been a humbling experience for me. It's frightening to think that this could happen to . . . really anyone."

"Yes," I agreed. "And it's frightening to realize how quickly everything changes, and how fragile health is." I sat down in the barber chair and looked at my reflection in the mirror. For a brief moment, I could imagine Tom standing behind me, scissors in hand, discussing what to do with my hair. Knowing that Tom would never cut hair again, I felt tears welling in my eyes, and quickly turned the barber chair away from the mirror and toward Bill, who continued talking in the kitchen.

" 'Type A' that I am, I could easily have a heart attack. I've been thinking about that a lot lately," Bill said with a catch in his voice. He paused for a moment and when he began to speak again, his voice was firmer and the catch was gone. "For Tom's sake, I try to maintain the routines: pizza on Fridays, movies on the VCR on Saturday night, and dinner out on Sunday afternoons."

"You need to be ready to alter routines as Tom's condition changes. I know Tom appreciates all you've done, but week by week and day by day, he's changing, so what's worked well all these months may need to be altered." Later, he volunteered that perhaps he should keep food in the house for Sundays, in case he can't take Tom out.

I watched as Bill got Tom to sit up, stand, then directed him, "Put your good hand on my shoulder." Slowly they progressed to the chair. "Okay, good, Tom. Just a little further." As soon as Tom was seated and I had pushed the table close to his knees, he said he had to pee, so off they went to the bathroom, Tom's hand on Bill's shoulder, and then back to the chair once more. It was an ordeal for Tom, but amazingly he navigated quite well like this. Watching the two men: Tom, tall and robust, though now awkward and near crippled, and Bill, shorter, compact and sturdy, I felt the accumulation of the years between them, of the years of being friends, of lending a hand, a shoulder, an encouraging word.

Seated again, Tom wolfed his dinner as if he had a train to catch. Eventually, Bill left, and soon Tom was in pain again. (According to Tom's doctor, the pain was indigestion.) I gave him one of the antacid tablets Bill left for Tom. Tom asked for help removing his jeans: he has put on weight and the jeans exert too much pressure on his stomach. For a few minutes he sat in his underwear, but the pain continued, so he wanted to lie down.

Following Bill's example, I offered my shoulder. Tom put his hand on my shoulder, but his feet did not cooperate. With great difficulty, we got as far as the end of the bed, and, fearing Tom would crumple at any moment, I suggested, "Tom, maybe you can get on the bed from here. Just lean forward now and you'll be on the bed." But Tom was totally lacking in coordination and ended up half on and half off the bed, looking like he would descend momentarily to the floor.

Tom mumbled, "Maybe I should start over."

Seeing that he was slipping backwards and down, I held him from behind, keeping him on the bed, while I tried to figure out how I could possibly get him the rest of the way on the bed. "No, Tom, don't go backwards! We have to figure out how to go forwards."

I first tried to get him to push up with his good leg, but with despair in his voice, he said, "It's no good, I'm too weak." We were both only a breath away from tears. What on earth could I do? Tom outweighed me and I could feel gravity multiplying every ounce of his flesh by ten.

But in the next moment, dragging his entire weight with just his one good hand, white-knuckled, grasping the edge of the bed, he pulled himself onto the bed. He lay exhausted, on his stomach, still crosswise, but safely on the bed with his legs extending awkwardly off the edge. I heaved a sigh of relief and sat down next to him on the bed, and rubbed his back until the stomach pain subsided. After a while, I helped him move, very cautiously, with more awkward rollings and heavings, toward the head of the bed. I felt as if we had scaled Everest together.

He lay quietly a while, then asked me to put an opera on. It took quite a while for me to locate the records; Tom could not recall where they were kept. Finally, in a closet I discovered two shelves filled with records, mostly operas. I never did find the one he asked for, but ended up with *Tosca*, which he loved. He told me the story of the opera and about all of the "fabulous" prima donnas he had seen, the gorgeous sets, and costumes. He told me how he had first learned to love opera as a boy. "Every Saturday I listened to radio broadcasts from the Met. I waited all week long for that. And we had a neighbor who was a retired opera star, who let me listen to her records and showed me pictures of her in all her costumes. She was so glamorous and when she told me the stories of the operas she'd sung in, opera came alive for me." Tom lay propped up in bed and I sat in his usual easy chair and we listened to the opera. We were now just two friends enjoying the music. What a contrast to our earlier misadventure.

"One reason for these stomach pains might be worrying about what's going to happen next, and where all this will end," Tom offered while the opera played.

"Yes, that certainly could be. Please try not to worry. I know that's hard," I replied, knowing that if I were in his place I would be a nervous wreck with worry.

"Bill keeps talking about 'dire consequences' like losing my truck, or even my apartment. Do you think that will happen?" he asked me.

"Here we are enjoying opera in your apartment. Try to enjoy this now without worrying about the future. I really don't know what will happen next." But I did know that Barbara was trying to arrange for Tom to be admitted to an inpatient unit. Caring for Tom at home was becoming more and more of an ordeal as he lost ability to walk and required more attention. I couldn't bear to tell him how soon he would indeed lose his apartment, but I brought up the idea of the inpatient unit as not such a terrible place. "There are lots of volunteers, plus it's close enough for Bill to visit frequently, and me, too."

"Are all the patients old people?" he asked me. I told him, no, that there were people with AIDS and other young patients.

"But in the meantime, Hospice is going to do everything possible to keep you at home as long as possible." Tom was reassured, at least for the moment.

August 8
A quiet evening with Tom. He was hungry and could not remember having had dinner. "Are you sure I had dinner, Bill? It must have been pretty small."

"Yes, yes, you ate. Don't you remember that nice Swiss steak, with the potatoes and gravy?" But of course, Tom remembered nothing of the nice Swiss steak and he was convinced he was starving.

Bill was concerned that rich foods might cause the stomach pain. Tom had a voracious appetite and little memory of the pains when they were not present.

We watched an AIDS special on television, then "Masterpiece Theatre." Tom got sleepy during the AIDS special, but woke up for several hours, then got sleepy again around 10:00. He wanted to go to the bathroom and seemed to be walking better this week, but I didn't want to take the chance of a bathroom fall, so I suggested that he use the urinal, and discreetly retreated to the kitchen. Soon he curled up in bed and fell asleep.

August 22
Tom's dinner was in the oven when I arrived, and Bill was still running in circles. Claudia and her children had been by to visit and had brought pictures from Tom's birthday dinner at her house. I looked at the Tom in the pictures and was shocked to see how much he had deteriorated since then, but all I said was, "How your hair has grown since then!" He now has nearly a full head of a peculiar fuzz.

Tom seems to have relinquished his sense of modesty. When he uses the urinal, which is frequently, I leave the room, but this may not be necessary anymore. Bill told me, "To Tom, you're like an old shoe." Not a very flattering simile!

He got sleepy a little after 9:00, and I helped him to bed. I could feel him shaking as he steadied himself on my shoulder. Walking was a huge effort for him, and I held my breath the entire time he was on his feet.

He made no mention of the impending admission to the inpatient unit September 1. His truck has not yet been sold and it was still an issue with him. "If there's a miracle, I want my truck." The truck symbolized his normal, independent life, and understandably he resisted letting it go. Bill, on the other hand, has been struggling to keep up the payments out of Tom's meager disability checks and was anxious to sell the truck.

August 25

Hospice got a call from Tom at 4:00: he'd been dropped off by the van at home and Nora hadn't arrived yet. Barbara was out of the office so they called me. I called Tom and told him to stay seated, not to walk around, and I would be there as quickly as I could. He sounded anxious, but at least he had remembered to call Hospice for help.

When I arrived, he was still alone and greeted me still in jacket and cap, with his fly open. "Oh, am I glad to see you! My legs are just like rubber, and I was afraid I'd fall."

I helped him out of his jacket and guided him to his chair. Walking was a tremendous effort and when he collapsed into the chair, I hugged him. "Okay, Tom, you can relax now."

"Thank you, thank you for coming over! Thank God you're here."

I put water on for tea and stowed the wheelchair in the closet. "Here, let's get your shoes off." The doorbell rang; it was Nora.

"Well, I see they dropped you off early!" she accused Tom. "I have told them and told them! They are supposed to call me. Barbara told me to come at 4:30 instead of 4:00. The other day I was on the street corner until 5:30! And they changed the color of the van on me, too!" She gestured angrily, alternately at me and then Tom; we were both silent as she continued her tirade. "I refuse to stand on the corner anymore!" She was ranting and raving. I suggested she talk to Hospice, and she snarled, "I'm done talking to them. September 1, I'm gone, so I really don't care anymore."

Then she ordered Tom, "Take off your socks, Tom!" I reached to help him, and Nora barked. "He can do things himself! Oh, look at that swollen ankle! Must get you into bed. Stand up, Tom! Now, lift, lift, come on!" Poor tired Tom fell back into the chair once, but with a supreme effort he arose and "lifted" his poor rubbery legs on command.

When he got onto the bed, I leaned over and kissed his cheek, and told him, without much conviction, that I would leave him "in Nora's good hands."

Schedules are crucial in caring for someone like Tom. I was horrified at Nora's outburst. Poor Tom was devastated by his experience and she seemed oblivious to his exhaustion and concerned only with her own inconvenience. As soon as I got home I called Barbara. She was disturbed to hear what I reported about Nora's behavior, and told me she would report the incident to the attendant coordinator and also speak to Nora herself.

August 29, last weekend at home
There was a final incident with Nora on Thursday. Hospice moved quickly and terminated her. Claudia, Tom's favorite attendant, was filling in until the first. I guess Tom couldn't take the orders and demands anymore and spoke up to Nora. Good for him!

Tootsie was on television but Tom was too sleepy to see much of it. I first helped him to the bathroom, then back to the chair, then when he repeatedly dozed in the chair, on to the bed. He still does remarkably well moving about the apartment despite enormous difficulties with his virtually useless left leg and arm.

Tom didn't mention tomorrow's move to the inpatient unit. I kept wondering whether I should bring it up to give him a chance to talk about it, but in the end, I didn't because I couldn't bear to mar this last evening at home. After the many months of pleasant evenings spent here with Tom, I was sad beyond words to know that he would no longer be able to sit in his favorite easy chair, watch television in his own home, sleep in his own bed, and live here among all of his familiar belongings. Sometimes I forget that Tom will die and I will never see him again; this move reminds me with a start of the inevitable conclusion that I must be prepared for.

When Larry arrived we talked for a few minutes. I was touched by his concern for Tom. He thought Tom would go downhill rapidly in the inpatient unit. "This is his *home!*"

"Oh, I hope not!" I replied. Tom's condition had deteriorated to the point where it was becoming too difficult to care for him at home anymore. Tom could scarcely walk now and could do very little for himself. Bill was exhausted with the daily effort and worry of caring for Tom. An inpatient unit seemed to be a good choice, but it was a sad reminder that Tom was going to die.

I said good-bye to Larry, and realizing I wouldn't be seeing him anymore, I felt even sadder. The end of an era, and the new era didn't look promising.

September 2, first visit to Tom in the rehab unit
Because there were no openings in the hospice unit, Tom was admitted to the rehab unit for patients recouperating from major surgery. Tom greeted me enthusiastically when I entered the patient lounge, where he was sitting in his wheelchair, wearing a huge bib spattered with remnants of lunch. "Oh, Joan!" He was smoking a cigarette given to him by a "nice lady" named Mary, whom he introduced me to twice in the first two minutes I was there.

"Oh, everyone here is very nice. It's great here," he told me, but anxiety was evident in his voice and in a tightness about his eyes. He liked the hearty meals, trips down to the garden, and sessions with a physical therapist. The anxiety and confusion about being here have shortened Tom's already-brief memory. Only a few minutes after I gave him a pack of cigarettes, he forgot they existed and was surprised when I pulled the pack from his shirt pocket. "You know, I only smoke one or two cigarettes a day, just to calm my nerves." He smoked four or five in the short time I was there.

"Do you know what has become of my watch and ring?" He was sure the expensive watch and ring were lost, despite my reassurances that Bill had put them away for safekeeping because the rehab unit did not like people to bring expensive jewelry. Also his finger was too swollen to wear a ring anymore.

News of an earthquake evoked concern for his mother. First he told me he should call her; later he told me he had, and she and his father were fine. (His father has been dead many years.)

September 10

It was midafternoon when I arrived to find Tom in the lounge smoking. "How's it going, Tom?"

He said he was "feeling better." (I later found out he had had a seizure.) His leg was still swollen and was elevated on a pillow. His arm was bruised from getting stuck between the bed and the bed rail. He has lost all sensation in his left arm; it gets caught wherever it flops and he can't feel it.

"Well, I think it's working. I have more energy every day and I'm looking forward to getting back to normal. And to being myself." Tom's hope continued strong, but what else could he do? "You know, Joan, I think conniving to get cigarettes keeps me mentally alert. By the way, do you have any cigarettes, dear?"

I pulled a pack from my purse, and Tom beamed. "Oh, thank you, thank you! Oh, let me give you a kiss. You are so wonderful to me!" I brought cigarettes to Tom because I didn't know what else to bring him and his appreciation told me cigarettes were probably the one vestige of a normal life I could give him.

When I left he lifted his cheek for my kiss. All at once I noticed how vulnerable and sad he looked. I wished I could scoop him up in my arms like a small child, and keep him safe from pain, from fear and anxiety. And from death.

September 17

There was a birthday celebration for a hundred-year-old lady at the center Tom used to attend, so Barbara arranged for Tom to be transported to the center for several hours. I popped in to see him while he was at the party. He looked exhausted and bewildered, but seemed to be enjoying himself. The center staff fluttered nervously around Tom.

Someone took Polaroid photos of Tom and one of his old "smoking buddies" at the center. Although someone was careful to see that a photo was slipped into Tom's pocket, I had the feeling the staff at the center were trying to catch a last fleeting glimpse of Tom.

September 21

"Well, you're looking lovely today. Is that a new blouse? And is everything copacetic in your life?" Tom's customary greeting, though it does not vary much from day to day, always warms my heart.

A frantic patient in a wheelchair called out to me repeatedly. "Miss! Miss, now you come here!" Patients saw my Hospice name badge and assumed I was someone new to answer their bidding. I took her bib off and reassured her that the nurse would return.

With a smile Tom said, "They're going to enlist you here."

September 30

I approached Tom from the right rear, as I've realized that his peripheral vision on the left side is going or gone. One day he couldn't see an ashtray just to his left. "Hello, dear. Is everything copacetic with you? By any chance do you happen to have any cigarettes?"

Tom was anxious, confused, and sad tonight. When I asked him what was wrong, he said, "To tell you the truth, Joan, I've been feeling a bit depressed."

"What's getting you down? Anything in particular?" I asked.

"I'm tired of being sick and wondering when I'm going to get well." Even in depression, his hope continued.

"This has been a long ordeal, hasn't it?" I replied, not knowing how to reassure him.

He was uncomfortable from so much sitting in the wheelchair. I worked at readjusting the various pillows stuck in behind and under him, and braced the chair while he attempted to scoot back up using his one good leg. He complained of a headache and after a long wait, a nurse brought him aspirin. I wondered if the tumors were acting up, or whether the headache was caused by the reading glasses, which make indentations on his head, and which he has taken to wearing all the time, peering over the tops to watch television in a smoke-filled room. I think he likes the glasses because he has so few personal items left.

He talked again of getting better and, very gently, I tried a new tack. "Tom, at this point, you know recovery may be . . . unlikely."

He responded speaking strongly and sincerely, "I honestly think I will get better. After all the radiation therapy and the De-catron caper, I do feel better. I think I'll survive this."

What could I say? "That would be wonderful. I truly hope you'll get better, but no matter where you are or what happens, you can count on me coming to visit you." Tom knew he was dy-ing, but despite Barbara's efforts and mine to get him to talk about dying, he rarely wanted to talk about it. I didn't think he was denying the reality of his decline; his way of coping with the unthinkable was to emphasize hope.

September 31
I called Bill to see how he was doing. An hour! He talked on and on, repeating everything four times over. The truck has been sold but the sale was still being finalized. "I could settle peace in the Middle East faster," he told me several times, pleased with his clever phrase. He has also sold a few pieces of Tom's furniture, but was basically keeping the apartment intact because Tom's mother and brother may arrive any day, and he didn't want them to tell Tom the apartment was bare. He's been expecting Tom's family every day since Monday and has alerted the hospital to call him if they show up. "Tom's brother makes me nervous with his fanatical religious talk. That man is nuts!" I told him to call me if I could intervene in any way. They called Tom on Friday but no one knows what day they told Tom they were coming and of course he cannot recall.

Several times Bill referred to Tom's "final weeks" and seemed to think the headaches were a sign of "the end." Although Bill has been relieved of Tom's physical care, there was no way to relieve him of his anxiety for Tom.

October 1
I arrived at 5:15 to find the patient lounge empty. Where was Tom? In bed, the nurse reported.

Tom was lying crooked in bed on his back, with his left arm dangling through the bars, awake and staring into space. I asked him what he was doing in bed. He replied, "To tell you the truth, I'm bored." I told him it was about time for dinner, and then I asked the nurse for someone to help me get him up. Tom is now more unwieldy than ever, so I was afraid to tackle the transfer from bed to wheelchair by myself. A male nurse came to helped Tom up. His pants were quite wet, but he seemed as unaware of it, as he is of his swollen leg. I talked with Mary in the lounge while Tom was taken to the bathroom for cleanup and change. She told me Tom did watercolors today. He never remembers these activities. He no longer has any of the simple joy of reflecting upon the pleasantries of the day. No wonder he was feeling bored.

At length he was brought out for dinner and I sat with him at the table. As usual he loved the cigarettes I brought and he smoked several after dinner. He's no longer eating every last morsel on his plate, but his appetite remains hearty.

Arrived home to find a message from Bill on my answering machine. His truck was in the shop for major repairs and he wanted a ride to the hospital to see Tom on Sunday evening.

October 3

I picked Bill up at 7:30 and he insisted on stopping at the ice cream parlor. By the time we arrived, laden with ice cream for Tom and all the patient regulars, I feared we would find Tom already in bed, but he was in the lounge with his leg propped up on a chair, looking terribly uncomfortable. His left leg was twice the size of the right. Bill hunted down the egg-crate cushion and together we got Tom up, the cushion inserted beneath him, and then back in the wheelchair, with cushions tucked here and there for protection and comfort. The fact is, he's too big for the wheelchair and has less and less control over his body, which makes matters worse.

Bill, like a social director, distributed the ice cream. Tom ate his rapidly but with difficulty. Tom was more interested in cigarettes than ice cream, and smoked several in quick succession, managing to light the filter end of one.

Bill hardly sat down the whole time we were there: running here and there, to find the cushion, then for cigarettes, out to the nurses' station innumerable times, back and forth, up and down. The strain of the past year threatens to push Bill over the edge. How much more can he endure?

At 9:00 we got ready to leave and pushed Tom's chair closer to the television, but he'd slipped down again and was uncomfortable. I could see where his shoulder was pressing into the metal of the chair back, so I insisted we help him readjust. I loosened the strap and put the brakes on; Bill moved Tom's foot off the chair and told him to lean forward so I could readjust the cushions. The next thing I knew, Tom was slipping forward and down, off the chair and right to the floor. Bill ran to find a nurse while I stayed with Tom to reassure him. Not a nurse was to be found, so Bill said we'd have to get Tom back up ourselves. Seeing Tom in a heavy looking heap on the floor, I didn't have much hope we could do this, but somehow we eased him back into the chair, just as the nurse belatedly arrived. Tom was grateful for the new position and immediately forgot the catastrophe. Lack of memory can at times be a blessing.

On the way home, Bill told me, "Tom keeps asking about Stan, our friend who died of AIDS. Over and over I've told Tom that Stan passed away, but, you know, I think Stan's spirit is not yet at rest and lingers near to help Tom pass over."

"It might be Tom's way of dealing with his own approaching death to talk about Stan," I suggested.

"Maybe so, maybe so." Bill was quiet for a few minutes, and then he continued. "I try to spend quality time with Tom, to make his last weeks as nice as possible. I try to bring ice cream or something I know he used to like, but, it's getting harder and harder for me to be with him. It seems so hopeless. Tom doesn't even remember my visits anymore. I'm not sure I'm doing enough, but what else can I do?"

"Although on a conscious level Tom forgets visits almost immediately, I think, on another level, he remembers and appreciates everything. What you've done for Tom is important, and it is enough; it's all you can do."

Earlier this week, I felt Tom would live for a long time; tonight, I'm not so sure.

October 7

Tom is now in bed for seventy-two hours bed rest for his leg. He looked surprisingly relaxed and comfortable in bed even with his leg elevated. He was just lying there, not sleeping, television on too low to be heard. He couldn't locate the television control, and when I found it hooked to the bed rail, it seemed unfamiliar to him. He asked if he could have a cigarette, and assured me he'd been allowed to smoke in the room. It sounded plausible, but it was fortunate I checked at the desk: "Absolutely not!" the nurse informed me. Tom said no one had been to see him, but I knew that meant nothing.

He seemed in good spirits, and asked several more times about having a cigarette. "When the seventy-two hours are up," I told him, "the nurse will wheel you to the lounge, where you can have a cigarette."

"Oh," he replied, "I can walk down there whenever I want to." Tom has not been able to walk any place in sometime; his confusion may provide a comforting illusion of mobility.

October 9
Saturday evening, rainy and dark. Arrived to find Tom in bed with a piece of equipment (something for his leg) plus the phone receiver dumped on top of him with water from the equipment all over the floor. Tom was unaware and unconcerned. A nurse came in and removed the equipment and wiped up the water.

"Does it hurt?" I inquired, running my fingers across the taut skin of his extremely swollen leg.

"No, not at all." His speech was a bit slurred.

He asked for his glasses to read the paper. I gave him the glasses, but then I read the paper to him because having only one usable hand made manipulating the paper impossible. I held out the paper to show him a picture and he had difficulty seeing the picture even though my finger was pointing to it.

October 12
Tom was still confined to bed, and the bed was now sloped down at the head with the feet elevated, so Tom appeared to be sliding headfirst into the headboard. There was a large handwritten notice taped to the foot of the bed warning that Tom must be left in this "Trendelenberg" position at all times, except for meals. He was dozing when I arrived, but roused easily when I called his name.

"Oh, am I glad to see you!" he greeted me. "You're looking lovely. Have you done something new to your hair? It's very becoming."

"No new hairdo, but thanks for your compliments. You always make me feel so good, Tom."

"Well, you make me feel good. I'm so glad you're here." His speech was badly slurred now, but his leg was not as swollen.

From that scrunched down, upside-down position, he assured me, "I feel like I'm really getting well very quickly now." What incredible optimism.

He was only allowed out of bed for fifteen minutes at a time so he was becoming confused about what time of day it was. "Well, it's almost time for breakfast." He greeted the man in the bed opposite with a hearty, "Good morning to you, sir! Did you sleep well?"

How strange it is to think about the changes going on in Tom's brain as the tumor grows. It must exert uneven pressure on his brain, resulting in sudden lapses and confusions, then other times, brief interludes of relief and clarity.

He seems to be losing ground daily. Dear, sweet Tom. I cannot bear to think of losing him. Not yet.

October 15
Call from Bill. Tom had a terrible time last night with pain in his leg. The nurse gave him the maximum medication currently prescribed, but it didn't help much.

"One night I was talking with Tom when suddenly he seemed to forget who I was," Bill told me with anxiety in his voice. "He said, 'You know Bill, my friend with the crew cut, don't you?' I was speechless! I haven't had a crew cut in years. I tried telling him that I was Bill, but he didn't seem to believe me." This was hard on Bill.

He wants to let the apartment go November 1 and will call me next week to arrange a time for me to come over and help him pack up.

October 15
Tom was asleep in Trendelenberg position. I called his name and he came immediately awake saying, "I've been hollering for a pee

bottle and causing all kinds of trouble." Two urinals hung on the railing. I gave him one, which he put in place and worked at for a while with no result. When he started to shiver, I suggested he forget the pee bottle. He agreed and when I pulled the covers up, he sighed his thanks.

"Joan, will I survive this?"

"I don't know, Tom. Maybe not. It's hard to say what will happen next, but you'll be kept comfortable."

Before I could say any more, he wanted to know, "Is everything intact at my apartment?" I told him I hadn't been over there, but I was sure that Bill was taking good care of everything.

"I had a dream, Joan. I dreamed that I woke up under crystal, like a bird, with my feet sticking up in the air. It was the oddest experience." What a perfect image!

Tom gestured toward the man across the room who sleeps soundly day and night and never stirs. "I hope it's at least a year before I'm in that shape."

"He looks very peaceful and comfortable, so I wouldn't say he was in such terrible shape," I replied.

Even though he doesn't remember anything for five minutes, Tom remains affably social, chuckling in response to funny bits I read from the newspaper and commenting on the sounds coming from the hallway. Sliding head down in Trendelenberg position, he called unheeded greetings to the little man in the next bed who hobbled out into the hall with his cane.

Dinner arrived and he was rolled up into a more or less upright position. A nurse brought him a cupful of pills and before long he was having trouble staying awake to eat. His mouth didn't work well anymore, and sometimes food got stuck on the left side of his lip. As he got sleepier, he had more and more trouble coordinating fork, food, and mouth, and would raise an upside-down, empty fork to his mouth. He dozed, so I asked him if he were through; he said, yes, he was stuffed, but only moments after I removed the tray, he was reaching in the air, surprised that the tray was not there. Several times I moved it back, he took a few more bites, then dozed off again.

He never finished his dinner. Sleep was too powerful. I tucked him in again as the nurse came in to roll the bed back down into Trendelenberg. "His leg's much better so he'll be let up Monday.

You know, Tom's one sweet man." The nurse glowed when she said his name; Tom charmed everyone who took care of him.

October 17
When I arrived, a gray-haired nurse was holding a cup to Tom's lips. I greeted him, and he looked at me as though from behind a thick cloud. I saw recognition on his face, but also a puzzled look that told me he couldn't recall exactly who I was. He tried valiantly to introduce me to the nurse, telling her effusively what a fantastic "nurse" I was. The nurse told me he'd been making no sense at all, and she was grateful for my offer to help him with dinner.

"Isn't that sad that she's leaving us?" he said as she heaved a sigh of relief and left the room. I assured him we would manage quite well and proceeded to cut up his meat. His good hand was shaking and he still seemed to be behind the cloud. I fed him several forkfuls of meat, which he took without question.

After several minutes, he suddenly said, "Oh, is this dinner here? Well, I think I'll have some," and he reached for the fork. The cloud had lifted. With only minimal assistance and guidance, he ate his dinner, and conversed amiably with me. He was coherent and perceptive.

When I commented that he now had a private room (both other patients having disappeared since my last visit), he looked at me with a twinkle in his eye and said, "Well, they tell me I'm getting a new roommate, a beautiful young woman named Joan Taylor."

He was full of questions. "Do I still have an apartment?" he inquired. I assured him that he did and that Bill was taking care of all that. And, "Has anyone heard from my brother or my mother?"

"No, I don't think so. Would you like to see them?"

"Yes, I would, especially my mother. I'd like to give her a great big hug and tell her how much I love her."

The conversation became philosophical. Tom said how he noticed that worry did no good and whenever he saw someone worrying he tried to put his arm around their shoulders to comfort and reassure. I commented how graciously he accepted being taken care of by so many people and he replied, "Well, I can see that they want to help me, that it makes them happy, so I just cooperate. It makes me happy to make other people happy."

On my way out, I spoke with Mary. Tom had been gotten up for lunch but had had some pain, a feeling like his leg was broken. She was so glad to see him. She'd been reluctant to go see him in his room. "In his weakened condition, I was afraid of passing germs and I'd feel terrible if I was the cause of . . . anything." I assured her that was not a problem and that I really appreciated the time she spent with Tom.

October 18
Barbara talked to Tom's brother. "They came here two or three weeks ago and got as far as the intersection near the hospital, and got confused with traffic, so they just continued on out of town and back home! Can you imagine? The brother's words were, 'And never again!' "

Bill and Hospice are Tom's only family after all.

I called Bill to tell him about Barbara's call to Tom's brother. "Perhaps we should just tell Tom bad weather has prevented their visit," I suggested.

He spent a couple hours with Tom last evening, having arrived right after I left. The hospital administration wanted to know about funeral arrangements and Bill wanted to know about Veteran's benefits, and whether Barbara has talked to Dr. Rollins (Tom's personal physician). Also, what about donating organs per Tom's request on his driver's license?

I again suggested that he talk to Dr. Rollins himself. A few minutes later he called me back, having been lucky enough to catch Dr. Rollins. He was aware of the "phantom" pains Tom has had, and told Bill that he had changed the medication order. He's been checking Tom once a week, and was pleased with the progress of his leg.

Bill said, "I asked him the sixty-four dollar question: how much time left?" Dr. Rollins said that considering the pattern of plateaus and considering the leg improvement, Tom could go on for from three or four weeks to four or five months. He might be comatose within a few weeks.

Bill has been visiting every other day (the routine since Tom was admitted) and he seemed startled when I mentioned that I'd been going nearly every day. Now feels like the time to be with Tom as much as possible.

October 19

I arrived to find a nurse shoveling food down Tom's throat. She was happy to leave Tom's feeding to me. Tom couldn't exactly feed himself anymore, but if I loaded up the fork and put it in his hand, he could lift it to his mouth. From time to time he would reach the fork toward the plate and try manipulating it. I'd let him try for a bit, then ask him if he wanted me to reload the fork. Each time he would say, "Oh, yes, please," as if it were a new and wonderful idea.

At one point he told me, "Joan Taylor is the sweetest, kindest person." When I told him that I was Joan, he said, "Oh, I could say the same about you, too, dear." But a short time later, he was again using my name, "Thank you, Joan," "It's so good to see you, Joan," etc.

He's been moved across the hall and now has more talkative roommates, but they are out of his view. The nurse came in and in a loud voice spoke to the man in the corner, "Did you wet your pants, Mr. Ramirez?" Tom and I cringed for poor Mr. Ramirez, and agreed the nurse could have been more tactful. Tom's sensitivity for others continues despite his own decline.

"I think they're getting ready to kick me out and set me loose on my own." Does this image of getting better and back to "normal" keep his spirits up?

October 20

Tom has a catheter now. Although he was sleeping when I arrived, as I talked to him, he awoke gradually. He didn't know about the catheter and said he had to pee. I told him he could just relax and let go. He was worried about making a "wet spot" so I explained the mechanics of the catheter, the tube and the bag hanging below his view. He said, "Can you see anything happening now?" I looked and, sure enough, urine gurgled through the tube as a look of relief spread across his face. We both grinned at the wonder of the catheter. He felt better having peed and not had any "wet spots." He didn't understand why he was peeing so much, so I told him about the diuretics they were giving him to prevent his leg from swelling. He always appreciates my explanations, although I'm sure someone more informed has already told him these things.

I read Tom bits and pieces from the paper. He was struck by a story of a Vietnamese welfare recipient with a wife and three children who'd won two million dollars in the lottery. He was concerned with how it would affect someone's life to suddenly have so much money.

I looked at the picture on his bedside table: a photo of colleagues from work at a Christmas gathering, and realized for the first time that the smiling man on the right was Tom. I recognized only the mustache and the watch and signet ring. How I wished I could have known him then! What a good-looking man Tom had been. It was shocking to realize that less than one year could so entirely change a person's life. When I had shown Tom the photo a few days ago, he'd been vague and thought the people were "some volunteers who are helping me." I showed Tom the picture today and he recognized the people, and I could see happy memories flit briefly across his mind. He confirmed that the handsome, smiling fellow was indeed himself.

October 22
Tom was already eating when I arrived, green peas rolling every which way. He seemed to list to the left despite my repeated efforts to center him. The catheter was unhooked and lying on the floor.

Tom asked about his mother and father several times. I told him his mother was praying for him, and, gently, I told him that his father had died a long time ago. "Oh, really?" he said, sadly and with surprise, "When did that happen? My father was such a wonderful man."

He also asked about money and expenses several times in various ways, ranging from worrying about whether he's been fair to Bill, to wanting to budget to make sure his niece is provided for, to concern about the hospital expenses, to worry about his apartment. He needed all the reassurance I could summon.

An addition to our after-dinner routine: I fetch his toothbrush so he can brush his teeth, which he does with great vigor. Then I read him the newspaper. I try to hit the highlights of the news, the funny stories, and anything about AIDS or local news.

"I've been watching a little boy over there," he told me gesturing toward the end of the bed.

"Did you make him up?" I asked tentatively.

"Oh, no," he replied with surprise.

"Well, then why can't I see this little boy?"

"Maybe the bedpost is in the way." After a pause he said, "You know, this isn't the first time this has happened to me."

"What? The first time for what?" I prodded.

"Seeing people just appear here." He didn't seem frightened or worried, only matter-of-fact.

"Tom, just enjoy whoever shows up, whatever appears. I wish I could see the little boy, too."

He got sleepy soon after eating so I rolled the bed back down and gave him a good-night kiss. What he really wanted was a cigarette, but he settled for a hug.

October 23
Bill called with good news: Tom's niece Cynthia had just found out that Tom was sick and she was coming up for several days.

October 25
When I arrived Tom was sitting before his tray, but not touching anything. "I've been desperately waiting for someone to eat with," he greeted me. When I directed his attention to the food, he fed himself quite well.

A large bouquet of red roses and white carnations was on the nightstand. Who brought these? "I don't know." Did your niece bring them? "Oh, yes."

He enjoyed seeing Cynthia, but the visit has triggered a round of worry and what sounds like guilt. He kept asking me if his niece's children needed anything, and whether my children needed anything. "I just don't want them to be without anything. If there's anything I can do, please let me know." Had he done enough? "How I wish I had lots of money to give to my niece and her children." Confusion aggravated the worry.

How strange that Cynthia's visit has triggered this much anxiety in Tom. According to Bill, they haven't been close in many years but were always fond of one another. Does he wish he'd devoted more time and money to relatives like his niece? Does he feel badly about how he's spent his money? Or his life? I reassured him over and over that he was a very generous person and that Cynthia was happy to have his love and affection and doesn't need any money. Still he fretted on and on.

Part way through dinner he became agitated and wanted to disconnect the catheter. Several times his head nodded to his chest. Does the medication cause this sleepiness? He receives his medication each night just as dinner is beginning and always gets sleepy soon after.

October 26, call from Bill
Bill called to tell me all about Cynthia's visit, which he thought went very well.

Cynthia spent a great deal of time with Tom, brought flowers for him, and for the nurses, too. "She was just wonderful with Tom," Bill reported excitedly. "She brought the family album so he was able to relive old times, with pictures from years ago." Tom's long term memory is intact, so what a treat it must have been for him to leave the confusing present for a little while and enjoy the clarity of old, happy memories. "Tom did Cynthia's hair for her wedding and he enjoyed her children when they were small, so although they hadn't seen each other frequently in recent years, Tom has always been very fond of Cynthia. And she was very upset that no one had let her know how sick Tom has been." Seeing his niece got Tom worrying about his mother so Cynthia arranged a phone call, and Tom talked to both his mother and his brother.

Cynthia and her husband stayed in Tom's apartment. When they departed, she left notes to Tom and to Bill, which, with tears in his voice, he read to me over the phone. He was so touched by the extent of her caring for Tom. Cynthia left two hundred dollars with instructions that Tom should have all the cigarettes, candies, fruits, or whatever he wanted, that he should want for nothing.

October 27
Barbara had come to see Tom at lunch and had brought him a box of hard candies. Unfortunately, Tom must have tried to help himself because most of the candies were on the floor when I arrived. Oblivious to the sticky, crunchy mess under foot, he greeted me

effusively, "Oh, you're looking terrific today, Joan. That color really suits you."

He was only half way rolled up and trying to eat a dinner of spaghetti and green peas, most of which was landing on his chest. No one had bothered to put a bib on him either. Once again I wished I could be with Tom every night for dinner, plus lunches and breakfasts as well. I rolled the bed up higher so he was more or less sitting upright and put a bib on him. I cut the spaghetti. The person who plans a menu of long stringy spaghetti and round rolling peas for people who have to eat in bed must have a streak of sadism, or never have had to struggle with such difficult fare in bed.

Tom was in good spirits and full of witticisms. The strange man across the room was deep into conversation with himself that sounded like very bad (and loud) TV show dialogue. "It really is funny when you think about it." When the man said something about jewels, Tom told him, "You're a jewel, my friend, one of a kind!" We had lots of giggles and hugs and kisses.

Just as I got ready to leave, Tom said, "If you see him, tell him I love him." Who? I asked. "My Dad," he replied looking suddenly very sad and lonely. I reminded him that his dad had died many years ago. He seemed surprised and grief-stricken. "My father was a wonderful man, Joan. Everyone liked him because he really knew how to make people feel good. He had something nice to say to everyone, and he liked and respected people even if they were pretty difficult to be around." Whenever Tom described his father, it always sounded like he was describing himself.

Tom's grief reminded me of how Edith reexperienced the loss of her mother near the end. Is the loss of a beloved parent a metaphor for the loss of one's self? A metaphor so powerful that reality and past events are changed, and the loss is not just remembered but relived?

October 29
Tom's voice rattled softly someplace deep in his throat, and most of what he said was unintelligible. An occasional phrase was quite clear, but most of what he said was lost. His head inclined severely

to the left and his whole body slumped leftward, despite my repeated attempts to drag him more nearly upright.

Although his general confusion has deepened, he used my name immediately when I arrived and throughout the two hours I spent with him, most of it helping him to eat. He fed himself a little, but soon his eyes closed and I fed him. Chewing was difficult and sometimes he'd forget to swallow. He gave several violent sneezes, and coughed a few times. I think his throat is not working right anymore; the left side of his mouth hasn't been functioning for some time now.

He continues to see visions of children and other people and tells me about them. Tonight he saw something about knee level beside the bed and tried intently to reach it. "Tom, what you see is in your mind. It seems clear and real, but it's not there and it can't be touched," I told him, hoping to ease the frustration on his face. "What is it that you see?"

After several garbled attempts to explain, he said sadly, "I wish I could tell you, Joan."

There was a card from his brother. I showed Tom the enclosed photo of his mother and father taken in 1970. "Oh, yes, that's Mother and Dad. How are they?" Again, I had to tell Tom that his father had died. "Oh, yes, I forgot. I was closer to my father than anyone else in the family. A wonderful man." He still worried about his mother, but not as frantically as earlier this week.

After he'd eaten, I rolled the bed back down. Sitting up was an effort that exhausted him, and he was relieved to lie down. He dozed off and I noticed with alarm how irregularly he was breathing. First he'd breathe loudly, raspingly, rapidly; then suddenly he'd stop breathing for a frightening number of seconds, then restart with a noisy, sucking in-breath. I put my hand on his arm and whispered to him, "Breathe easy," and "Don't forget to breathe."

He seemed to be fading fast and though I knew death would be a release for him, and for all of us who have been taking care of him, I resisted letting go of him. I wanted to stay there day and night to make sure he kept breathing, and I found myself wanting to holler for the nurse to come and make him breathe!

October 30

I spent nearly five hours with Bill at Tom's apartment. I sorted and packed the kitchen, the bathroom, and several drawers in the living room. Bill nervously ran hither and yon throughout the small apartment, inspecting various items I unearthed.

I decided to buy a dresser of Tom's. The tall, heavy dresser with its deep drawers reminds me of Tom and I'll enjoy having it in my home. Bill insisted I take a lovely glass candlestick.

In going through a drawer, I found photos of Tom's French designer lover, who took him to Europe twice. Bill showed me photos of Tom taken years ago; one taken on the beach in San Diego, showed Tom looking tanned, virile, and handsome back when Bill first met him.

Getting the apartment cleared out was necessary, but Bill also needed to talk. After we'd packed almost everything, Bill sat in Tom's easy chair and directed me to sit down. "Barbara arranged for me to see a grief counselor," he told me, "but, I don't know, I'm just not the kind of person who can talk to just anyone about these things. I realize I've leaned on you a lot emotionally."

"This is the time to lean on someone," I assured him.

"You know, Joan, I awake in the night and sit bolt upright, wondering what to do with Tom's ashes or some such concern."

Both Bill and I think the end may be near. Such changes over the past week. Thank God Cynthia came last week! I suggested now was the time to visit Tom and that he would have lots of time later for sorting and selling belongings. He repeated this back to me several times, as a good idea. "Visits are hard though. To see him like this. . ."

November 1

Tom was sound asleep when I arrived and it took a few minutes to rouse him, but once he was awake, he was much more alert than he's been in some time. His speech was clear and he managed his dinner slowly but quite well. He was in marvelous spirits, very affectionate, full of witticisms and compliments, and very aware of everything going on in the room.

With happiness making his eyes twinkle, he told me stories from his childhood of two aunts of whom he was very fond. All of his worries had evaporated and we floated through the evening on what felt like a wave of his happiest memories.

The nurses all like Tom very much. I had to call them when Mr. Ramirez started moving the tray table of the man who is kept strapped into his wheelchair. Tom got a kick out of the commotion of three nurses all trying to disentangle a sheet from the wheel of Mr. Ramirez's wheelchair. I referred to the spectacle as a floor show, which amused Tom and later on he referred to "the floor show" as one of the pleasant events of his day. How good it was to see Tom smiling and laughing, and generally coherent. Interestingly, he lost all coherence when a nurse came over and we were both teasing him. A slight stress like that now interferes with his mental functioning.

Off and on throughout the evening he mentioned French people, France, Paris, Charles de Gaulle, etc., until I noted his preoccupation. "Have you ever been to France, Tom?"

At first he said no, but immediately he corrected himself and said, "Yes, one time." His features became very soft and a look of contentment spread across his face. I remembered the photos of the handsome French designer. After a few minutes, he turned to me with his eyes sparkling and a small smile playing about his mouth and said, "Joan, all your fantasies will come true at the Eiffel Tower!"

We joked and giggled all the while I fed him. I was standing across from him leaning over his dinner tray, a spoon in my hand, when he asked me, "When is some lucky man going to marry you?"

"Oh, Tom, I don't intend to ever marry again," and perhaps remembering some movie I'd seen, I told him with a grin, "I'm not the marrying kind."

He beamed at me and said, "I just love the way you look, standing there saying that, 'not the marrying kind'!" And I loved the way he looked across the tray at me.

As I fed him the next spoonful, I teasingly said, "Well, you're not the marrying kind either, are you?" He blushed, and chuckled his agreement with my assessment. We grinned at each other like two flirting teenagers, who have just admitted how much they like each other.

After his dinner I held his good hand in both of mine because it was so cold, and because I was filled to bursting with love for him. We sat there for a long time holding hands, not speaking, just sitting there in a glow of intimacy, that was probably as inexplicable and unexpected to Tom as it was to me. There were no words. He gently intertwined his fingers with mine, and I breathed in at the sudden rush of knowing that much more than our fingers were connected.

What a crazy world this is! At no other time in Tom's life or mine, under no normal circumstances, would we ever have sat holding hands, been this close, and felt this enormous affection. Out there in ordinary life, Tom and I might have passed on a neighborhood street, and he would have had not the slightest interest in me, nor I in him. But here, on the soft boundary between life and death, our positions and roles fell away and we were together.

When I got ready to leave, he was still awake, but beginning to doze. I told him Bill would be arriving shortly, and he replied, "If you see Bill, please tell him that I'm ensconced in a French dream!" I pulled the blanket up over his shoulders, and for a moment a worried look played across his face and he dipped briefly into the anxieties of a few days earlier. "If you know of anyone who needs any help, please let me know." The anxiety was now brief and vague; no names now, just "anyone." My departure sometimes triggers these small flights of worry, reminding me of when my children were small and how when I'd kiss them good night, they'd remember some worry they just had to tell me right then. I leaned down and kissed Tom's cheek, and he smiled up at me with the trusting look of a contented child.

Driving home, I shivered in the cold and thought of Tom tucked in his warm bed. I realized that I'm now always thinking of Tom, in the background of whatever else is on my mind, and that part of me never leaves his bedside. I look at the rain and I think of Tom in his bed in that room without windows; I eat lunch and I think of Tom being fed by a nurse; I go to bed and I think of Tom sleeping and I wonder whether he will slip away in the night.

November 2
What a shock to see how Tom had slipped since yesterday! He was sleeping very deeply and it was nearly impossible to rouse him. Bill's phone call to Tom's doctor worked wonders because an egg

crate mattress was now in place and the change to a soft diet has been made.

Tom was very weak now and would never have been able to manage regular food tonight. He never fully awoke, and he took only small amounts of food, each mouthful an effort. I'd been feeding him morsels of meat, carrots and pea soup, when his very tentative appetite seemed to fade, so I offered him strawberry pie instead. A look of interest flickered across his face; he nodded, still with closed eyes, yes, he'd like some pie. I smiled: Tom's sweet tooth was still alive and well. After a few mouthfuls, when I asked him if he wanted more, he shook his head, no, and managed to say, "I got pretty much satiated on pie before all this began."

Off and on throughout feeding him, he would try to say something, but his voice had once again fallen deep into his throat and most of what he said was unintelligible.

While I was feeding Tom, morsel by morsel, making sure that he completely chewed and swallowed everything, and all the while stroking and caressing his arm, a doctor came in to visit the elderly man at the other end of the room. The old man told the doctor how terrible he felt; he had a myriad of complaints: pain in his stomach, shortness of breath, chest pain. The doctor was sympathetic and explored each complaint, but it appeared that nothing was seriously wrong and that he was progressing as expected. Finally the doctor told the old man that he would order new medication to ease his pain. With that, the doctor was gone. If the old man had had someone to sit with him, I wondered whether he would have had so many complaints, and if the doctor had had more time to spend there, whether he would have ordered new medication. After the doctor left, the old man was agitated and grouchy with the nurse, who offered to bring him the new medication. I could hear in his voice that this was a poor substitute for what he cried out for. He glared at me and stuck his tongue out; he no doubt envied Tom all his visitors.

How peacefully Tom was resting when I left. My good-night kiss startled him a little, but he acknowledged my departure with a nod and a muffled good night.

Later I called Bill to let him know how Tom had slipped, and that the doctor's orders were in place. He sounded a little calmer than the last time I talked to him. As Tom lets go, I think Bill is letting go, too.

November 3

When I arrived a thin nurse I'd never seen before was taking Tom's blood pressure. She said she had been unable to rouse him, and asked me whether I was planning to feed him. I said that if he wanted to eat, I would feed him, so she left. I sat down beside Tom, and rubbed his arm, calling his name. After a few moments, he responded. I told him it was dinnertime and asked him whether he was hungry. He said yes, so I raised the head of the bed and moved the tray into place.

He ate very little, and could no longer suck the straw hard enough to bring liquid into his mouth. For each spoonful, I asked him whether he wanted some meat, some vegetable, some soup. Each time he'd slowly nod his head, yes, but I was not sure whether he really wanted to eat or whether he was just being nice, so I told him, "Tom, you don't have to eat anymore than you want, but I'll keep feeding you just as long as you want to eat. You just need to let me know what you want."

He nodded slowly and said, "Okay." Since he couldn't drink with a straw, I fed him milk with a spoon, which worked quite well. I complimented us on our mastery of the milk-with-a-spoon routine and he gave a small smile. Several times while I was feeding him, he gave forth with immense wide, loud yawns. I remembered how Edith did that too, in the days just before she died. At a time of such low energy, the forcefulness of the yawn is startling.

Looking at his face, I found it difficult to believe he was sick. Although his eyes were closed all the time now, his color was good and he had a robust, sturdy look that reminded me of the photograph Bill showed me of Tom on the beach. Unlike many dying patients, Tom has lost no weight, has suffered little pain, and seems genuinely at peace. I wondered whether meals and medications were an unwarranted intrusion now. As I fed him each spoonful of food, I wondered whether I was just giving his poor weak body more work to do and prolonging the dying process. But if I didn't feed him, what did I have to offer him? It felt so concrete and connecting to feed him. I realized that I fed Tom now more for me than for him.

Bursting with my feelings for Tom and the excruciating awareness of how little time he had left, impulsively I told him, "Tom, you are a wonderful friend! I feel so lucky to know you." He tried to respond and I could tell by the look on his face that he wanted to tell me I was a good friend to him, too.

The tall nurse, who was especially fond of Tom, came in to talk to me and to see how Tom was doing. She turned toward Tom, who appeared to be already deeply asleep, and said, "He can hear every word we say, can't you, Tom?" He nodded, yes. The sleep of the dying is strange, very deep, yet it was true Tom could hear my voice even when I spoke very softly.

How much longer will this go on? I want Tom to die easily and soon, but I don't ever want to let him go. Some hospice volunteer I am!

November 5
I arrived just as the dinner trays were being distributed, as I often have. The curtain was drawn around Tom's bed, and even before I pulled back the curtain, I could see through the space at the end of the curtain: his face was the ashen gray color of death. My heart pounded wildly and my throat closed. Shock! For the eight months I've known Tom, I've known he was going to die, and for the past few weeks, I've realized the end was near. Yet tonight when I walked in and saw his ashen face, I reeled with shock and disbelief.

Doug, the social worker from the center, who had continued to visit Tom, came up behind me, but then left me alone with Tom. Tom looked peaceful, his mouth slightly open, and one eyelid raised just enough to reveal his eye. I stood above him and swore I could hear him breathing. I leaned down so that my ear was near his mouth, but there was no stirring of air. I touched his cheek with my hand and was surprised to find it warm; more hope: maybe he wasn't really dead . . . but I knew he was. There is such a certainty to the look of death that I knew it was only my heart wanting to hold onto Tom that played tricks and saw life where there was only death.

I was glad for those few private moments with Tom. Through the crack in the door, I could see Doug pacing back and forth in the hallway, so I went out to talk with him. He told me Tom had died this afternoon about 1:00, and that Bill and Barbara were coming over at 6:00. After a few minutes Barbara arrived, and in a few more minutes Lee, another volunteer who had visited Tom when he was still at home, arrived. We all went in and sat around Tom's bed behind the drawn curtain, and waited for Bill. How natural it seemed to sit there, with Tom, talking of our times with him and how much we cared for him. I half expected him to join in the conversation.

It was nearly 7:00 when Bill arrived, looking calmer than I expected, carrying his black vinyl portfolio. I moved out of my chair, which was nearest Tom's head, and gestured to Bill to sit down. Without really looking at Tom, he sat down and started rifling through the portfolio, looking for a paper. Barbara told him to forget the paperwork for the time being and to just relax. It was a few minutes before Bill really looked at Tom. I could feel how hard that was for him. He was surprised to see the dark color of the back of Tom's head; I explained how the blood falls to the bottom, when the heart stops beating.

Before we left Tom's room, I stood over him again and put my hand on his forehead. The final touch left no doubt: the cold raced through my fingers and into my heart, screeching that Tom was dead. Good-bye, Tom, my dear, sweet Tom.

Barbara, Bill, and I went to the coffee shop on the corner. We had pie à la mode to commemorate Tom's sweet tooth, and I told them about Tom's fondness for strawberry pie just the other night. We drank endless cups of coffee and listened to Bill tell stories of Tom.

Driving home, I kept sighing and sighing and sighing as images of Tom flashed across my mind, bringing a smile to my lips and tears to my eyes all at once. I remembered that long ago Sunday evening, when he covered me with the blanket. Yes, that was the moment I fell in love with Tom, and he became much more than a patient to me.

"Is everything copacetic in your life, Joan? You're looking lovely today. Is that a new blouse? You look fantastic in that color." He had this charm and caring, not just for me, but for everyone, even the strangers who took care of him in the end. "Would you happen to have any cigarettes, sweetheart? I don't really smoke, but I like one once in awhile, just to relax."

I came home and listened to Barbara's message on my answering machine. It was like finding out all over again, and this time I cried.

November 20, Tom's funeral
How many times I'd driven by the cemetery without ever imagining I'd one day find myself standing on this hill of military graves to say good-bye to someone dear.

Four honor guards stood on the grass beyond a canopy that had been set up over several rows of folding chairs. All the volunteers who had known Tom were there, and Barbara had brought a camera to take photos for Tom's mother. The air was cold, so everyone stood huddled in small groups on the one short section of sidewalk not yet in shadow, talking quietly and waiting for the service to begin.

Claudia and I, who had never met before, talked of our friend Tom. Meeting her, I felt reconnected to Tom in the memory of all the times he'd told me about Claudia. Bill, whom I'd never seen in anything besides jeans, was all slicked up and nervous in a suit and tie with Tom's friend Bob from Portland in tow.

A few old friends of Tom arrived and joined the clumps of people standing awkwardly in the weak winter sun. Several coworkers from his last job arrived just as the service began. "Where were all these people when we were desperate for people to spend evenings with Tom?" Barbara whispered to me.

A nondescript, dull-witted chaplain, who looked all at once uncomfortable in his uniform and as if he'd panic if he had to appear without the security of his well-ribboned uniform, walked to the front of the canopied area, pressing the requisite Bible to his midriff. Awkwardly he approached the podium and, nervously clearing his throat, he indicated that the service would begin. I shivered as I took my seat next to Barbara in the shadow of the canopy, and I remembered being with her at Anna's funeral: outwardly very different, but beneath the surface, there was the same tightly apprehensive undercurrent of unfamiliar emotions.

The chaplain announced, as if he were imparting secret information he'd just decoded: "We are all going to die." He hadn't bothered to find out anything about Tom, and kept referring to a card and pronouncing Tom's name in a too-loud, too-precise way that made me feel he was intruding. "I never knew Thomas Noren. I never had the opportunity to know . . . Thomas Noren, as you all have known him. We come together today for the purpose of paying our respects to . . . Thomas Noren." Very quickly he ran out of words. "The boy's mother has written a poem that she asked be read here today." He gestured for Bob, Tom's friend, to come forward.

Bob read the poem Tom's mother had written, something about leaving the physical for the reality, and a quote from Revelation. The chaplain then asked if anyone wanted to share any thoughts. No one said a word. The chaplain signaled and the honor guard aimed their rifles at the sky and fired off several rounds of blanks. Each volley startled me and brought tears to my eyes. A lone trumpeter stood a little distance up the hillside, at the edge of the rows and rows of white gravestones extending as far as the eye could see. The sun was already low in the sky and cast a magical light through the eucalyptus trees, silhouetting the trumpeter as he lifted his trumpet and played taps.

One of the young women in the honor guard walked across the grass and toward the canopy, very sprightly in her step, with a clean wholesome look about her. I could almost hear Tom greeting her, "Why, thank you, sweetheart. You certainly look lovely today." She picked up the flag from the podium and presented it to Bill.

The entire service was over in mere minutes and people resumed chatting in small groups, but the air was growing cold, so soon everyone began moving toward the cars. Bill showed us on a map where Tom's ashes would be buried.

How lovely this spot is for Tom's ashes: the long sweep of the peaceful hillside, looking out on the city below, with the winter sun slanting across the rows of sparkling white gravestones. Tom would be pleased.

Dear, sweet Tom, wherever you are, dear heart, I hope everything is copacetic with you.

14

Lauren

During a period when Hospice was unable to accept patients, I had an opportunity to volunteer at a home health agency that provided services to terminally ill patients. Dying patients, whether in a hospice program or not, face many of the same issues, but patients not in a hospice program do not receive the same level of services and support. I had come to take for granted many of the hospice services and procedures: adequate pain control, good communication with the patient's personal physician, supervision of attendants, regular nursing visits, and a twenty-four-hour on-call nurse. The agency that was caring for Lauren provided nursing visits, but not as regularly as hospice would have, a minimal number of social worker visits, and a few visits from a physical therapist. The services she received were good, but not as well-coordinated and not as complete as with the hospice team approach. Had Lauren been a hospice patient, I think she and her family would have had an easier time coping with her illness and death. I often felt helpless and overwhelmed, as I never had with the hospice team to call upon.

The Journal

April 13
I called Lauren late afternoon to see if we could get together on

189

Thursday. She's a young married woman with a husband and a two year old son. "I'd love to," she responded, "but Thursday I'll be in the hospital undergoing chemotherapy. Then I have relatives coming from Wisconsin Saturday, who'll be here most of next week."

"Perhaps we should wait until your relatives leave."

"That's not necessary. They won't be staying here, and I won't be spending all my time with them while they're here, and besides, I'd welcome a new face. My main problem is boredom. I can't drive anymore and I don't feel well enough to do much. I really get bored."

She's certainly articulate and willing to express herself. I told her I'd call Monday to see when we could get together, and to feel free to call me in the meantime.

May 5

After a series of cancellations we've finally met. Lauren met me at the door with her cane and began talking even before she had hobbled back to her chair. She's a small woman with the short curly hair that many chemo patients have. She settled herself into one of the two large blue recliners that sat facing the television in the sparsely decorated living room of the small older home. "Oh, I'm so glad you came. My main problem is boredom, and lack of mobility."

We talked for over three hours, exploring ideas for things we might do together and things she might try on her own. She has a hard time getting comfortable in any position, so cannot concentrate on reading or sewing. She likes visitors but told me sadly how most of her friends tell her they are "too busy." She wants to get out, so we talked about various outings we could take: the art museum, shopping, the park. "My favorite thing is to go out to lunch. Could we do that?" she asked.

I tried to find out what kind of interests she'd had before she got sick, but it seemed that her life had been pretty much limited to her job, her husband and child, and a few friends in their old neighborhood.

They bought this house last summer and she became sick right after they moved in, and she never had a chance to decorate. The walls were mostly bare, and except for the toys strewn about the floor, the house probably looked much as it had the day after they moved in. Lauren didn't seem to have any passionate interests, but she was intelligent, and pressed by the unrelenting boredom, she was willing to try almost anything I suggested.

"I can't cook anymore and my husband isn't a very good cook. I used to love to cook. Now meals are a problem. Sometimes my aunt brings us casseroles, and a friend makes soup."

Her husband does just about all the caring for their son. "Michael's in day care now because it's gotten to the point where I can't take care of him unless someone else is here. When I tell Michael that I'll read him a story, he tells me, 'No, Daddy will do it.' " I heard sadness and loss in her voice. She sighed, "That hurts me terribly. Maybe it shouldn't, but it really does."

"Of course it hurts you. You're Michael's mother and you love him very much. Not to be able to care for him must be very hard on you." Lauren nodded sadly. "Don't forget, though, that most little boys decide at some point that only daddy can do things for them. It's part of growing up, but in your case your illness accentuates the normal lessening of Michael's dependence on you. How does he respond to your being sick?"

"Michael knows that my leg hurts, so sometimes he says his leg hurts. He was two in November and he's still not toilet trained. I worried about it for a long time, but the day-care center says not to worry, and since I really can't do anything about it, I've had to let go of worrying about it." Lauren shrugged her shoulders and shifted uncomfortably in the recliner chair. "I just wish I could get comfortable!"

"Are you taking pain medication?" I asked.

"Oh, none of them work. I've tried them all, but nothing helps. My doctor says what I have isn't pain, that it's pressure." I saw in her face the exhaustion of withstanding a pain that her doctor denied.

"Pain is very personal," I told her sympathetically, "and pressure sounds to me like just another name for pain." Whether her pain can be controlled with medication or not, it seemed wrong to deny its existence by calling it something else. In a hospice program the nurse would have worked with Lauren and her doctor to control her pain, and certainly no one would have told her she didn't have pain.

Fumbling around for some way to help Lauren I asked her, "Have you ever tried visualizations, or pain meditations?"

"No, someone gave me a book about visualization, but to tell you the truth, I never read it. Do you know how to do these things?"

"Some. I have some books, and I've attended workshops, so I could teach you enough to see if you liked it. Visualizations and pain meditations are very helpful to some people, and it certainly can't hurt to try."

"I don't know whether I believe in these things," she admitted, "but I'm willing to think about trying something." I mentioned massage, but she says she can't lie flat comfortably. I told her someone good at massage, used to working with sick people, would be able to massage her in any position.

"I know I'm dying, but I don't know how long I have. Until just a couple of months ago, I was walking around without any problem. I hate being so immobile. And I wonder whether it will get worse." She has been undergoing chemotherapy that does not seem to have much effect. "I think my doctor is going to leave it up to me, whether to have more chemo."

"Lauren, it's really always up to you," I reminded her. She seemed startled. I'm always surprised to see how people follow doctor's orders without questioning; what a shame for an intelligent woman like Lauren to hand over decisions to her doctor, especially now.

She told me about watching a television commercial about hydroelectric power. "I watch the water rushing down and I think about how good it might be . . . to just fall down the waterfall with all that water and just get it over with."

"I can see why you might feel like that some days," I told her. She seemed relieved not to be told she shouldn't think such things.

"My therapist says I think too much about other people," she said, "worrying about my husband and my son instead of myself. She says I must have anger to express." Sounds like pretty standard "professional" advice. Lauren's therapist was a private counselor, not connected with the agency.

"Don't be too hard on yourself," I told her. "It's natural that you're concerned about the two people closest to you."

"I should start talking more about these things with my husband, but it seems easier to talk to you." She feels badly that he must do all the housework and child care on top of working.

"Do you feel close to him right now?" I asked her.

"I feel like we are drifting apart a little," she said sadly. I could imagine her tired and worried husband, never complaining, but never expressing his feelings either.

She calls it boredom, but the predominant quality about Lauren appeared more like depression to me, not deep or chronic, but there's that familiar why-bother-nothing-works air despite her more buoyant personality that expresses itself as well. Getting her out will help, and I think I may be able to get her interested in massage or visualizations, but I wonder how long she will be well enough to do these things.

May 13

When I didn't hear from Lauren to confirm our tentative Friday date for lunch, I called her Friday morning. Her husband Henry answered. Lauren had taken a pill for an at-home chemotherapy treatment last night and was pretty much out of it, so he'd stayed home from work. I offered to come stay with Lauren for a few hours, and I urged him to call me if he needed help. Curtly, with a certain reserve evident in his manner, he thanked me for calling.

May 20

When I arrived to pick Lauren up, Henry answered the door. He brought the wheelchair down the stairs and put it into my car. Lauren made her way down the stairs using a cane, slowly but unassisted.

In contrast to our last visit, Lauren barely spoke. She responded to my questions with brief phrases and appeared to be in discomfort.

I pulled into the bus zone in front of the restaurant and pulled the wheelchair out of the back of the car. Positioning the chair near the car door, I offered to help Lauren out of the car, but she managed on her own. As she lowered herself into the chair, I realized too late that I'd neglected to put on the brakes and the chair moved slightly back as she sat down. I'm afraid wheelchairs make me exceedingly nervous and I always manage to do something foolish. At least no one has ever been hurt.

With a waiter holding the door, I wheeled Lauren into the restaurant and positioned the wheelchair at the table nearest the door. I left her reading the menu and went to park the car.

During lunch Lauren continued taciturn. "You're so quiet. Is something wrong, Lauren?" I inquired gently.

"Just a bad day, I guess. I wish I felt better."

"Is there anything particular making today bad?" I pursued.

"Well, I tried to pay some bills and got all mixed up writing the checks. I got so frustrated." This obviously upset her. "And I don't know why I've been feeling so tired and weak."

"Chemotherapy is exhausting," I reminded her. "Besides that, chronic pain and discomfort are also tiring. When you're feeling like that, paying bills may be too much to ask of yourself. Can Henry take care of that?"

"Sure, but he does so much. I wanted to do at least this one thing, but I couldn't!" Her face was tight and her voice was strained.

"Lauren, are you feeling pain or just tired?"

"Both," she replied. She talked again about the various medications she had tried, none of which gave her much relief. She told me how the nurse had urged her to continue with the pain medication her doctor had prescribed.

"I wish there were a magic pill I could give you that would give you total relief from pain!" I blurted out. And I didn't say it, but how I wished at that moment for a magic pill that would zap the cancer and stop Lauren from dying. I had felt so good about being able to take Lauren out to lunch, as if that would make everything okay. Lunch was not enough, but lunch and foolish wishes were all I had for Lauren.

She smiled, appreciating my wishes, and then gave a small laugh, which sent her into a coughing spasm that obviously caused pain in her abdomen. Even my attempt at lightheartedness hurt Lauren. The despair at the table was no longer Lauren's alone. Despair grabbed at my throat, and I set down my fork. The remains of the lunch on my plate suddenly looked disgusting and I pushed the plate aside.

In the quiet, I noticed that Lauren had recovered from the coughing spasm and had resumed eating with the same tight, pained look on her face. She was going on, not sinking into the despair. I realized that I was barely breathing, and startled, I shook my shoulders and took a deep breath.

"More tea, Lauren?" She nodded and I filled both our cups. Our eyes met for a moment and I continued. "Have you thought any more about the idea of trying visualizations or pain meditations?"

"I can't go on like this, Joan. I have to try something."

"Well, I can bring my book of meditations one day next week . . ."

Immediately she interrupted, "What day can you come?" We agreed on Friday. "It can't hurt," she said.

After lunch it was obvious that she was anxious to get home. She said she enjoyed the lunch and I assured her we would do it again, hopefully on a day she was feeling better.

At her house, she made it up the stairs unassisted, as I followed closely behind her. She sank onto the couch and a look of relief spread across her face. I offered to help her to bed, but she assured me she could manage by herself. "Don't forget about next Friday," she said as I left.

May 27

First she called to cancel and then a little while later she changed her mind and said she wanted me to come after all. "I'm sorry, Joan," she told me, "I get so depressed and the effort of going anyplace or doing anything is so great, that sometimes I don't even want to see anyone. But I do want you to come, if you still can."

She met me at the door in a bathrobe. She'd been lying down on the couch, but she said since I was there she wanted to sit in the recliner chair. Using her cane she headed for the chair. One moment she was awkwardly making her way across the room, the next, without warning, she slipped to the floor. I moved quickly over to help her up, but she said she was okay and managed to get to her feet by herself.

"Lauren, you need a walker," I suggested. "That would give you more to lean on than the cane." She agreed and asked if I could find out if the agency had one she could use. Falling must be happening more frequently because she wasn't alarmed at the fall; it was as if it were something annoying but customary.

We talked a little and Lauren ate an apple. She said she feels weak and tired most of the time, but rarely sleeps for more than an hour or two at a time. The nurse came yesterday and, having talked to Lauren's doctor, encouraged her to try taking the Rox-anall (a morphine medication) he had prescribed . "I tried it once and felt worse so I haven't tried it again," she told me, shrugging her shoulders with the despair that I was now accustomed to seeing in her.

Knowing that Roxanall wasn't the kind of thing you can try once and expect results, I said, "Lauren, I think we should try to reach your nurse. I think she may be able to help you a little more with the Roxanall." I dialed the phone and luckily the nurse was in the office. I told her Lauren's experience with the Roxanall, and she then spoke to Lauren.

When Lauren hung up the phone, she reported, "She says I must take the Roxanall for a while, get a schedule established, and allow my body to adjust. She said not to give up, but I did try Roxanall for a long time another time. It doesn't help. Nothing helps."

"Try not to get discouraged, Lauren. The nurse and your doctor will help you find a way to control the pain."

Changing the subject, she told me they had paid for Michael's day care all the way until next May. "It will be one less thing to worry about if— well, when something happens to me."

"That's hard to think about, isn't it?" I asked her. She nod-ded, but didn't seem inclined to pursue the question.

"Are we going to try a pain meditation today? Did you re-member to bring your book?" she asked briskly. It was clear she wanted to try this today, so after she finished her apple, we went into the bedroom and she lay down on the bed. I covered her with a down comforter.

Although I had copies of Stephen Levine's pain meditations with me, I decided to use my own words rather than read some-thing. I was more than a little nervous. It all sounded easy in the books, but here I was sitting in a chair beside Lauren's bed. Did I really think I could change her pain? She was as willing and open today as she ever would be. Lauren was not the kind of person ready to believe in everything the New Age has to offer, but in her despair she was willing to try almost anything.

The two most important things I wanted to show Lauren were using her breath as a focus and directing her attention intentionally. I started by having her focus on her breath. "Just relax and bring your attention to your breath. Don't breathe any special way; just watch your breath." After a few minutes, I continued, "Now, bring your attention to your feet; notice if there's any tension there. If there is, let it leave on the next out breath." Was she awake? She seemed so still. Was I going too quickly? "Using your attention like a little spotlight, move up your ankles, and notice any tension there." Gradually, I guided her attention from feet to head, periodically redirecting her attention to her breath.

When we had gone through the entire body I asked her to visualize the whole body. "Now allow your attention to come to the area of discomfort." I could feel my own breathing becoming shallow. Was I asking her to do something too hard, maybe even dangerous? Was it appropriate to get right into the pain? Did she even have any pain today? I wanted her to like and see the value of working with these techniques and I didn't want to scare her off by attempting something too hard on the first try.

She didn't stir or show any sign of agitation, so I continued slowly, and tentatively, "Notice the sensations in that area. If there's pain, notice what it's like. Is it warm? Is it tingling? What kind of pain is it? Sharp? Throbbing? Does it spread from a center point? Just notice what's happening. Don't try to change it." Each word plopped out of my mouth and into the air as if coming from a dark place, deep within me. Each word revealed something hidden, something unmentioned, maybe unmentionable. The words continued to emerge like trespassers, but I was breathing more freely now. I watched Lauren: she didn't move, and her breathing was quiet.

"Notice the edges of the area of discomfort. Does the body tense around the edges? Try to soften around the area, letting the discomfort float freely." She seemed to breathe more easily now. Was she softening around the pain, or was she asleep? I was quiet for a few minutes, just watching her breathe. "Now bring your attention back to your breath. Feel how easily, how quietly it flows

. . . in and out . . . rising and falling . . . in and out. Nothing to do. It happens by itself . . . in and out."

In a few minutes, she opened her eyes. "How do you feel now?" I asked softly.

"The pain's the same. No change at all," she told me, bursting my bubble of expectation.

I asked about tension in other parts of her body and she said there hadn't been any, that she was relaxed to begin with, except for the pain. She looked more relaxed to me now. Maybe her despair made it difficult for her to notice or acknowledge any relief that was less than total.

"This was just to show you the technique. To see whether it's going to help, you need to practice. Teaching the mind takes time. You may not notice any change right away, but keep experimenting."

"How many times a day should I do this?" she asked. She seemed glad to be starting on something new, even though it was clear she was pretty skeptical.

"When you wake in the night, you have lots of time, so try it then, or when you lie down to go to sleep. Several times a day would not hurt and might be useful while you're learning how to do it. Experiment. Find what works for you. Work with the breath, but try other images as well."

"I need to have more control," she said. I agreed that learning meditations would give her a more active role in dealing with her illness.

"You know, Joan, I feel like I could really sleep right now. I haven't been able to sleep well in such a long time." I left her all snuggled up under the down comforter, ready to sleep. So I guess she got something out of the meditation after all!

June 2
Having talked to the nurse and gotten a walker for her at the agency, I called her to see when I could bring it out. "Can you come today?" She was anxious to have it; walking was getting very difficult and falling was a real problem now.

She was just getting out of bed when I arrived with the walker, so she tried it right away. She made her way painfully out to the living room, with me and her friend Angela watching. The walker seemed essential. How had she managed with just the cane? She had just settled into the chair when she realized she needed to use the bathroom, so Angela helped her out of the chair, and she used the walker to get to the bathroom.

While she was in the bathroom Angela and I talked. "My husband and I have known Henry for years, and then he married Lauren, and we used to all four get together, have dinner." Then suddenly their invitations were spurned. "For a long time we didn't know what was wrong." Finally Henry told them Lauren was ill, but even then he declined their help, until Angela insisted. She comes one or two days a week for a few hours, and although Lauren will not let her do the laundry, she picks up a little and keeps Lauren company.

Lauren was gone for quite a while, so Angela went to check on her. Moving the walker sideways to get out of the bathroom, Lauren started to return to the living room, but when I suggested trying another pain meditation, she quickly changed direction and headed for the bedroom.

I read Stephen Levine's meditation on exploring pain. She seemed to fall asleep, but as soon as I rose to tiptoe out, she opened her eyes and we talked. After a few minutes I asked her if I should let Angela go home and she said no, to let her wait a few more minutes. She liked the meditation we did last week better, even though it didn't help the pain. I asked her if it was hard to focus on the pain, and she said yes. I told her this was natural and to keep trying, that resistance was often a big part of pain.

Angela came in to say she had to go. Lauren didn't want her to leave, but when I told her I would stay a while, she relented.

We talked of her parents who were due to arrive this evening. She seemed a little apprehensive. "Have you been open with them about all that's happening?" I asked her.

"Pretty much, but I'm not sure whether they realize how sick I am."

"Now is the time to be perfectly frank. The more they know, the more helpful they can be," I urged her. "It's also time to ask any friends who might be able to, to help out by coming to stay with you for a few hours a week."

"I don't like being alone," she admitted, "but everyone is . . . so busy." I mentioned the possibility of attendant care, but she closed her eyes before I could say anymore.

She seemed to drift off and I asked if she wanted me to wait in the living room. With an anxious note in her voice, she asked me, "Could you stay right in here?" When I sat back down, she sighed with relief and closed her eyes. The shades were drawn. The dim light and the rhythmic sound of Lauren's breathing lulled me. I meditated and Lauren slept. It gave me a grounded feeling to know that just my presence here, meditating in the chair beside the bed, was important to Lauren. It didn't really matter that it was me in particular, but in the loneliness of Lauren's life, in the absence of her old friends, I was the one who could be here, and I was glad.

After a little while she opened her eyes. "Oh, are you still here after all this time?" I told her it had been only half an hour, and she remarked that it often feels like it's longer when she sleeps.

Suddenly the doorbell rang. By the time I reached the door, a key turned in the lock and an attractive gray-haired couple came in. It was Lauren's parents, bearing jars of jam and shopping bags full of food and gifts. They looked as if they had just stepped out of an ad for active retirement: healthy, tanned, pleasant-looking people; only the anxiety in their eyes belied the reason for their visit.

They went in to see Lauren, but she told them she wanted to sleep a little longer. Her mother was a bit miffed: "After a month without seeing me, she wants to sleep!"

Both parents were eager to talk to me and find out what resources were available. They will be here a week and are determined to make arrangements for someone to stay with Lauren. They asked about pain control and told me how Lauren has always resisted taking anything that might be addictive. I told them that they should contact the nurse at the agency or Lauren's doctor. They are both very take-charge, and decisive. I sense they have held off interfering, but now are stepping in because they realize decisions need to be made. Henry tends to be reluctant to accept help, so he probably needs their push to take action.

Lauren's mother mentioned that Lauren's Aunt Beth had been very helpful, but it was getting too much for her. Until recently

Lauren has been going there several days a week, but today she didn't feel up to going and said something about her aunt being so busy, there was no point in going.

I left them my telephone number and the agency number. This is a good week for them to be here; Lauren's condition is progressing rapidly. I feel good about today's visit and how I arranged for a massage volunteer and was able to get the walker. My timing on being there when her parents arrived was lucky and I think I made good use of the opportunity. Barbara would be proud of me! I'm proud of me!

Phone calls week of June 7
Her mother answered when I called Monday and immediately passed the phone to Lauren. Lauren said the massage was "wonderful." This was the most enthusiastic response to anything I'd tried to date. I asked her if she wanted me to come on Friday and she readily agreed.

Message from Lauren on my answering machine Wednesday. I called her and she was confused about when I was coming.

June 11
Henry answered the door and led me into the bedroom where Lauren was resting but not asleep. Yesterday various people were to spend time with Lauren, and Henry was to give her the Roxanall at noon when he came home for lunch, but at 9:00 while she was alone for a short time, Lauren got confused and feeling pain took a dose of Roxanall, which on top of the early morning dose really spaced her out. Henry was frightened by this. He called the nurse and she had come out to see how Lauren was doing. Lauren was resting quietly now. "I always left the medications to Lauren before this, but now I can't."

He has arranged for a woman to stay with Lauren starting Monday. Both he and Lauren are thinking of her as more of a companion than a care giver, but it's clear Lauren needs far more than companionship.

Henry took the day off because of the mishap yesterday, and he was grateful for my offer to stay while he went to the bank. There were disability checks to deposit and also a form to be filled out to begin direct deposit. Lauren was nearly asleep, but with a great effort she sat up and pulled her legs into a cross-legged position in the middle of the bed. While Henry investigated the bank forms, she nearly slipped backwards. Still not sure which form she should sign, he decided to have her sign both. She took the pen and began to write in the vicinity of the line, but not on it, so Henry suggested she practice. Over and over Lauren tried to write her name. The "Lauren" sometimes came out pretty well, although sometimes acquiring an extra *n* but the last name never came out as anything more than a *V* lost in curlicues curling over upon themselves. She has been writing *Lauren* all her life so maybe that was easier than a last name she's had only a few years. Henry and I sat on each side of her, encouraging her and willing her to be able to write her name. I told Henry that the checks could be deposited without a signature if they went into a joint account. He was skeptical and Lauren was determined to do it right. Even after Henry took the pad back, she asked to try one more time. I told her it was hard to focus because of the medication, but I feared it might be the tumor pressing on a vital nerve, or a metastasis to the brain. She cannot dial the telephone properly either and gets many wrong numbers.

She continued to sit cross-legged and looked toward Henry standing by the edge of the bed. Slowly and with great effort she stretched her hand toward him and smoothed the hem of his shirt that was turned up at the edge. It was the idle, unconscious gesture of a loving wife, but done now in slow motion, with deliberation. As he left, she called to him, "Did someone important die last night?" He thought she might be thinking of a news story he had told her about, but I heard a deeper query in her question.

While Henry was gone, she slept deeply, breathing noisily and rhythmically. She turned over and I readjusted the down comforter. "Oh, it feels wonderful to turn over!" she told me before she lapsed back into a deep sleep. I sat in the chair and read. Suddenly I realized she had missed a breath and I drew in my own breath, and sat forward. In a moment she resumed the noisy breathing. Again, she missed a breath or two and then continued.

When Henry returned, she awoke and sat up to drink some juice. She had had a good rest, but now the medication was wearing off, and she was dismayed to hear that she had nearly two hours before more could be given. Over and over Henry explained the medication schedule and still she quizzed him about when she would have Roxanall and when the woman was coming and what pills she would give her. "I'm confused," she said sadly, lying down again. I made a mental note to call Lauren's nurse to let her know pain control wasn't good yet.

Throughout the afternoon, Henry had been cheerful, patient and even humorous at times, but when he followed me to the door, I saw the calm expression slip from his face to reveal the lonely anguish that lay just beneath the surface. "I can take the physical, but the mental, I can't. . ."

"You're doing fine, Henry" I told him softly, hoping to comfort this man who never asked for anything.

He continued with despair and terror bubbling up between his halting words. "All along there were little clues . . . and I know what will happen . . . eventually. But now . . . it's happening so fast!"

"Yes, she is changing rapidly now," I agreed. "How hard this must be for you."

"Sometimes I don't know what to do."

"Stay alert to changes in her condition and be ready to make changes in her care. Hiring the woman to stay with her is a good step, but be ready to increase her hours if necessary."

"Well, next week she sees her doctor—if I can get her there. I want to get it straight about these medications."

"It's a good idea to make a list of everything you want to ask the doctor, so that you don't forget anything in the rush of the appointment," I suggested. I could imagine how a high-powered oncologist could easily confuse and intimidate Henry. "And you must not let the doctor rush you. You have a right to answers to your questions." Henry nodded his head numbly without replying. "If you need help getting her there, call me. An extra set of hands helping on the stairs might be good."

"I might have to do that," he replied sounding more open to accepting help than before. I promised to stop by early in the week to see how the new arrangement was working.

June 16
Called Lauren and almost didn't recognize her voice: she sounded so healthy, strong and in-charge again.

Sharon answered the door; she's a cheerful young woman, obviously trying hard to do a good job. No toys were on the floor and the room, though bare as ever, had a just cleaned look. She offered me tea and made some for Lauren, too. Lauren had a hard time finding a comfortable position in the reclining chair, but she seemed generally in much less discomfort, and more alert than she's been. She has finally adjusted to the Roxanall.

Lauren talked of the medications, of Sharon, of the hour each day after Sharon leaves and before Henry returns. She's afraid of being alone. Afraid of dying. Conversation was fragmented. She would doze off midsentence, but after a pause of sometimes nearly a minute, she would continue right where she left off.

Finally, too sleepy to stay up, she decided to go to bed, but she wanted me to stay awhile. She asked me to massage her hip. Conversation is difficult now, so something physical felt satisfying.

June 17

I rushed out my front door, grabbing my mail out of the box without looking at it. I had not a minute to spare if I was to be at Lauren's in time to help Henry take her to the oncologist. The car was hot and stuffy from sitting in the noonday sun. I rolled down the windows and headed down the street.

At the first red light, I glanced at the pile of mail on the seat beside me: amidst the usual junk mail, a thin envelope taken from a motel, addressed in my father's handwriting. I pulled out the single folded sheet, but before I could read it, the light turned, and I had to drive on. At the next light, I unfolded the letter and read:

> We are here at (my sister) Susan's house. Their family has had a bad auto accident in which another car hit their car broadside after running a stop sign. Matthew and Brian escaped with only scratches, but Dennis died twelve hours later.

The light turned and I could read no more; I drove onto the freeway with tears in my eyes. Oh, little Dennis: I never even met him, but the vision of his small body crushed by the car kept tears shooting into my eyes. All the cars on the road around me looked brutal and dangerous; I gripped the steering wheel with unnecessary force, ready to avoid a collision at any moment.

As I exited the freeway, with a start I wondered what had happened to my sister. There was an accident at the first intersection: cars at crazy angles and fire engines with flashing lights. Too-vivid visions floated in my mind: Dennis and my sister crushed and mangled.

At last I made my way past the accident and found a place to pull over and I finished reading the brief letter:

> Unfortunately, Susan has a skull fracture and a broken jaw. She's in intensive care and not as yet fully conscious. We're hoping for the best.

Sitting there in the hot car, reading and rereading the letter, I tried to bring my sister's face to mind. When had I last seen her? 1970, I think, at Gramma's birthday celebration. We had not seen each other in years and had had nothing to say to each other. We'd never been close, but I remembered being disappointed that we couldn't even have a conversation. She had been married a few years, and I was newly divorced. Susan had always been the model of "the good child": quiet, never in any trouble, always pleasing the adults, not really excelling at school, but fitting in much better than I did. She was embarrassed by me: the tall, gawky older sister who got *A*'s and was always causing some sort of disturbance. I envied her her ease with life. I struggled to grow up, while Susan just showed up with her large, dark eyes and her small mouth, and life parted for her.

I have little sense of my sister as a distinct person: she's mostly childhood memories, many of them painful, and disembodied news reports of her life through the years from my mother. I was dazed with the news, my mind a jumble of emotions and images too fragmented, too horrifying even to name. I felt a yanking, tearing sensation in my chest. If this horrible thing could happen to my sister, it could happen to me, no . . . it had somehow happened to me. A submerged, entirely unacknowledged, blood tie was pulled taut and I felt the crunch of metal against soft human flesh.

Choking back the tears and swallowing hard, I rushed on to Lauren's house where she and Henry were ready and waiting.

Getting Lauren down the stairs took great effort on Lauren's part and help from both Henry and me. Two people are now essential to get her up or down the stairs. There are only about eight or ten steps, but Lauren's left leg has no strength whatsoever and without the walker she's immobilized.

While Henry parked the car at the medical building, I wheeled Lauren into the lobby and took her in the elevator up to the fourth floor.

It was a long wait in the waiting room full of cancer patients in various stages of treatment and deterioration. I was nearly suffocated with the weight of anxiety and sadness and suffering within me and around me in that room. I looked at Lauren sitting quietly and patiently in her wheelchair and I thought of my sister, three thousand miles away, lying unconscious in intensive care. They are both the same age, both married and with young children. Actually, Lauren is quite a lot like Susan, I thought to myself. We didn't really have much in common beyond her illness, and we would never have been friends in any other circumstance. Both Lauren and Susan were quiet women who didn't ask much of life: husband, children, home, lunches out and brief vacation trips, good schools and convenient supermarkets.

It was unfair! Just plain wrong! Rage and confusion and fear swelled in my chest. I could scarcely breathe. Why should Lauren be dying of cancer? Why should my sister lose her son and have her skull crushed? It was I who had taken the risks, shunned security, traipsed clear across the country with two little children, traveled by myself, moved about, and changed jobs.

The waiting room was filled, every seat taken by cancer patients: yellow-gray skin, sweaty, clammy foreheads, frightened eyes, thin faces full of pain. I couldn't look any of them in the eyes, but each sat purposefully alone, avoiding contact with the others, unwanted and horrifying mirrors of each other's illness and decline. I sat there in the midst of the dying, embarrassed and confused by my blatantly healthy body.

On the way home, Lauren and Henry discussed the visit. It sounded like they didn't discuss much with Dr. Rosen. Lauren is scheduled for her next appointment in six weeks. Will she live that long? The oncologist gave her another at home chemotherapy pill. Why? I don't think the last one helped her much, and it exhausts her. I never met Dr. Rosen, but I'm beginning to be prejudiced against oncologists. I never see their success stories, only those who are already dying. And I see how awful the treatments are for people, both physically and emotionally. Is it worth it? Patients in a hospice program occasionally had chemotherapy treatments to ease the discomfort of growing tumors, but Lauren's chemotherapy didn't sound like this. I wished again that Lauren could be in a hospice program where she could experience really good pain control and not be put through treatments that only make her uncomfortable.

"By the time Dr. Rosen comes in I'm so tired from just getting there, and from being shuttled from room to room by the nurses, weighed and poked and prodded for the blood tests, that I forget everything I intended to ask. He comes rushing in, flipping through my chart, and barely says hello before he starts writing prescriptions and handing me the chemo pill. He really doesn't say much at all." Lauren shrugged her shoulders and looked out the car window.

Lauren was dreading the chemo pill, but it didn't occur to either of them to question Doctor Rosen's decision to continue chemo. Were they afraid to hear what they already knew, that Lauren was dying? Or were they afraid to be difficult? They were still confused about the pain medication instructions, and they forgot to get a new prescription for Roxanall. All this effort to get Lauren to the doctor, I thought, and for what: a chemo pill that would make her sick and slow her dying not in the least? I sat in the back seat beside Michael's car seat, shifting between annoyance with Lauren and Henry for being so inept, and rage at Dr. Rosen and the medical system for treating people so badly. Finally, I slipped into a generalized despair with the world for allowing a young woman to die and mistreating her in the process.

"Is that the restaurant we went to with my parents?" Lauren asked Henry. As they conversed, recalling dinners out and deciding whether there was enough milk in the refrigerator, I glimpsed their normal life, before they were making trips to the oncologist and dealing with wheelchairs and Roxanall. There was a quiet steadiness between them, and I could see the months and years of a very ordinary married life, now so rudely interrupted. I thought of my sister again, of how her quiet life had been interrupted, too.

We stopped to pick up Michael at day care. He got right into the car seat beside me, without any shyness. Lauren showed her obvious delight and pride in him, and Henry made sure Michael was in the seat before he carefully closed and locked the car door. What a sweet family they make together, now bittersweet with Lauren so sick. At the house, Henry took Michael inside first, then came back to the car and the two of us helped Lauren up the stairs. Up was somehow easier than down, and Lauren heaved a huge sigh of relief and sank into one of the recliner chairs.

Immediately she checked her watch. "Five-fifteen," she said. "Only 45 more minutes." Henry said, "Until what?" I think he knew, but I looked at her, and she and I laughed. Lauren said, "Joan knows." I wondered if she should be feeling extra discomfort in the last hour before the Roxanall was due.

I was tired. Three hours all told in coming, going, and waiting. How much more tired Lauren must be.

June 22

A letter from my brother, full of details of the accident, of the hospital, and of his visit to see Susan touched off my tears, just like the original terse note from my parents. This deep, raw pain I feel is intense and unexpected. I have felt very sad when patients I have been with have died, and I have felt the deep connections of intimate relationships, but this is different. Somehow without a relationship with my sister, it's worse: pain à la carte, with no context, no reassurance, no way to participate, no bigger picture, no picture at all, only the wildly out-of-control pain and grief and fear. The depth and intensity of the brutally anonymous and impersonal pain, reaching back and back into childhood, or beyond, put me in a place no amount of caring for sick and dying strangers could have prepared me for.

I called my parents: they say she has memory loss. Long term or short term, I inquired? "Both! She's all confused!" cried my mother.

"No!" interrupted my father. "She recognized us, so it must be short term." In the sharp exchange I feel their anguish. I try to imagine how I'd react were my own daughter hurt like this. My mind refuses to even conjure up the image: it is too frightening, too horrible to even imagine.

And there's nothing I can do. Except wait and watch, let the pain work its way through me, and hope to comprehend the truth here. I wish I could go there and be with my family during this crisis, but there is no "there." My sister lies in a hospital in one state, my parents make brief visits to the hospital and then retreat to their home in another state, and my brother lives in yet a third state.

Thank God, I have Lauren here, who looks forward to my visits, on whom I can lavish my attentions and caring. If I didn't have her, I might rush into the streets and enfold in my arms the first needy stranger I could find, to ease the pain in my gut, and still the cry in my heart.

June 25
Everything has settled down. Lauren is on a regular medication schedule and no longer appears to be in pain. She's still hazy mentally; words and phrases appear in her mind, which frightens her. "Joan, suddenly it's in my mind to say that I went to the symphony last night and snuck out at intermission to wash my car. Isn't that strange? I know I didn't go to the symphony or wash the car. Yet the thought is there that I did."

"That must be a strange feeling to have that thought and to know that it's not true. Don't be alarmed by these thoughts," I tried to reassure her because I could see that it was disconcerting to her.

Sharon comes every day from eight to four. Some days she's a little late and Lauren worries that she might not "stick with it." Her presence makes a big difference. She does a little housework, and is very attentive to Lauren.

A physical therapist comes two times a week and gives Lauren exercises to do. The nurse and her therapist come once a week, and a volunteer occasionally for massage. Her aunt visits sometimes, but not often enough for Lauren. The visitors break up the day. I hoped someone was visiting my sister.

Lauren has acquired involuntary twitching movements. As she sits in the chair, her leg, her arm, even her whole body twitches slightly. I don't think she notices it. She continues to stop midsentence and doze for a moment before continuing.

July 1

Lauren in the chair, house all clean, Sharon smiling and obviously waiting for me to arrive so she could leave.

Lauren looked tired. "I just don't know whether this Roxanall is the right medication for me." Why did she think that? "Well, I don't know whether it's really doing any good. I'm still in discomfort and it takes so long to work and then wears off so quickly." This doesn't sound right to me. It's obviously doing some good, because her face is not showing the excruciating look of pain it was, but she has been on Roxanall long enough that the dosage should carry her through without peaks and valleys. I encouraged her to discuss it very frankly with her nurse or her doctor.

"Dr. Rosen doesn't really listen," she said with resignation in her voice. She was quiet for a few minutes. "Joan, I just don't know," she said sadly and meaningfully. She couldn't quite express what she meant.

"You have a very difficult situation, Lauren. I can see how exhausting and frightening it must be."

She nodded sadly. With everyone acting so glad the medication was working and that Sharon was now there, I had the feeling she felt a bit lost. Maybe, a feeling of "Hey, I'm still sick and dying in here, despite all these great arrangements." And both the medication and Sharon's presence mean she has less and less control over her own life.

Someone told her about talking books. I told her I would find out how to get them and also I'd bring a book next time so I could read to her. She seemed to like this idea, and we talked of books we had read. I felt excited to have a patient who liked to read, but it soon became clear that Lauren had mostly enjoyed current romance novels, to "pass the time." Again I was reminded of my sister, who as a child had to be required to read an occasional book while I devoured nearly every book in the library. I suggested that she try magazines, that they were easier than books. She scans the daily paper and watches more television than she'd like.

"How long ago was it we went out to lunch?" Lauren queried me.

"Oh, a month or so. Does it seem very long ago?" I asked her. She nodded, yes. "It's not much fun being stuck inside, is it?" I couldn't imagine myself being in such unruffled spirits were it me. "When your two strong brothers are here this weekend, they could easily help you down the stairs. I'm sure you'll get to go out with them." Not being able to manage the stairs frightens her and fills her with the enormity of her situation, I think.

"Well, maybe." She didn't seem very enthusiastic about the visit.

"You sound a little apprehensive about seeing your brothers," I commented.

"Oh, I'm glad they're coming, but I'm just afraid I won't be able to . . . do things with them."

"I'm sure they won't be expecting you to do anything at all and they'll be glad to help you and spend time with you." Was Lauren struggling with her own blood ties? Did seeing her strong, healthy brothers remind her of when they were growing up together, young and healthy, their lives stretching ahead of them?

Suddenly, I remembered a day, or maybe it was many days, during the long, hot muggy summers of my childhood in New Jersey: my sister and I were splashing about in a wading pool in the backyard. I was maybe four or five and Susan, two or three. There we were in matching sunsuits—my mother persisted in dressing us alike, even when she knew I hated it—pouring water from cup to pail, through funnels and strainers, stirring imaginary cakes and stews. Susan, at that age, was still a willing participant in the fantasies I dreamed up, and I remembered her giggling gleefully at some wonderful idea I had, and I remembered feeling a companionable intimacy born of our fantasies in the wading pool. As we grew older, we no longer shared fantasies and we fought more than we played together.

Reports from my parents are vague and confused and quite gloomy. Susan's brain was injured in the accident; she has lost her short-term memory, and has severe depression and difficulty expressing emotions. The doctors can not say whether or how much she will recover. No one knows what to say to her about her son who died in the accident.

For the members of Lauren's family, and for all the hospice families I've spent time with, I have a natural compassion. I see them as doing the very best they can, and if I see imperfections in their ways of relating and coping, it doesn't occur to me to blame them; I merely feel all the more compelled to encourage and support them during their time of need. For my own family though I am horrified to realize that I feel more rage than compassion. In the blinding light of my own pain, I see all their faults and weaknesses, and inwardly I rail at them. I want them to rise to the challenges of this crisis, but they are only themselves, and worst of all they are a mirror of parts of myself that I cannot abide. They are tentative, confused, easily intimidated, vague, and given to fear and panic. I want them to be calm and strong and brave, that I might be, too. I want them to heal my sister with their love and caring, that I might be healed as well.

When Henry arrived with Michael, I realized that he was as vague and confused as my parents. He cared for Lauren with devotion, but at every change in her condition, at every offer of new help, he resisted. Yet I was not angry with Henry; his aloof manner was transparent and I had no trouble seeing the pain and fear and grief he carried within. I saw my parents' pain, too, but it was, I guess, too much also my own pain for me to forgive them their inadequacies in coping with it.

July 8

House full of flowers, including some exotic ones someone brought from Hawaii. Lauren distantly enjoys them.

I asked Lauren about her brothers' visit last weekend. Lauren said she was disappointed. "I made it known that I wanted to get out and everyone said that with my brothers here it would be easy. But it never happened." She was disappointed, I would have been upset and angry.

I brought a stack of books and she was eager to hear a story, but none of the short-story collections I'd brought appealed to her. As an after thought I'd brought along Saint Exupéry's *The Little Prince*. "Oh, that's what I want to hear!" Surprisingly, she'd never read the story before.

I read for a few minutes, uncertain whether she was interested or not, or whether the sound of my voice had put her to sleep. I stopped and immediately, she opened her eyes and said she wanted me to keep reading. Sometimes her breathing sounded as if she had dozed off, but I could feel her listening, so I kept reading. I hope the metaphors in the story will give her a way to think about what is happening in her own life. The story always makes me cry, and I hope when we get to the part about the prince dying that it's not too sad for Lauren. Or for me.

July 15

Lauren looked a bit dazed. "Are you tired today?" I asked her.

"No, I fell down," she grimaced. Both Henry and Sharon had been there, but not right next to her. "I don't know exactly how I fell. I just suddenly found myself on the floor." She was sore now. "I just hope it's nothing neurological," she said with a worried look.

She listened while I read out descriptions of various "talking books" available from the library for the blind. I had been so pleased to discover this wonderful free service that could bring her any of hundreds of books on tape, but none of the titles interested her. I eagerly read her the descriptions of books, suggesting ones I had enjoyed. With my urging, she chose a few books. She seemed more depressed than usual, and after Sharon left we talked more seriously than we had for a while.

"There's just too much going on." What did she mean? "Well, there's the discomfort. And my limitations. And my lack of mobility. My forgetfulness and confusion. The 'Roxanall haze.' " She listed the problems, and I acknowledged that it was a lot to deal with and would be frightening to anyone. "I wonder what the point of my existence is." She looked at me, wanting an answer.

What could I say to her? How often I had struggled with that same question! "Sometimes I don't know what the point is either. I think we have to go on and do the best we can."

"But, there's nothing I can do anymore and I'm such a lot of work for Henry!" she replied despairingly.

"Lauren, you have always been the mother and the wife taking care of other people. Now it's your turn to let others care for you. That too is a gift, but it's a hard one for you. It would be hard for me, too. I think it's easier to be the nurse than the patient."

"It sure is," she agreed.

"I don't think we love people for what they do. Even though you can't do the usual mother and wife tasks, you are still loved just as much. A lot of people care very much for you."

"I know," she said very softly and with sadness in her voice.

"You seem depressed lately," I remarked. She seemed relieved to hear it acknowledged out loud. "You should discuss it with your doctor. There are medications that might help."

"I don't know whether I'm really depressed, or just bored," Lauren replied.

"You've been bored for a long time, and boredom can contribute to depression. You have a lot of difficult things on your mind. It's not surprising that you might be feeling depressed."

"Are you going to finish the story today?" she asked, changing the subject.

I read the rest of *The Little Prince* to her. "But if you tame me, then we shall need each other. To me, you will be unique in all the world. To you I shall be unique in all the world . . ." I paused and let the fox's words float in the afternoon air in Lauren's living room. "Why, this is the same thing we were just talking about." Lauren nodded her head, and I continued the story. For most of the story she was alert and even laughed several times, but toward the end she seemed to doze off. She wrinkled her nose in aversion when she realized that the snake was going to help the little prince die.

We could hear Henry arriving as I raced through the final paragraphs so there was no opportunity to talk about the little prince's dying and returning to his home.

July 29

Lauren doesn't care for the talking books, but she agreed to try one more batch of tapes. She says the newspaper seems easier to read lately. I keep thinking that if I were sick, I would prefer to listen to taped books than daytime television, but I have to remind myself over and over, that it is Lauren who is sick, not me, and that she probably watched more television before she got sick than I do. She appreciated the new group of classical tapes and the large art book I brought her.

She has been getting out occasionally, but not as much as she'd like. The new handrail makes the stairs not such an ordeal. I told her I would take her out, maybe to the park, next week.

We talked of trips we had taken. Before she met Henry she went all by herself to Mexico. As she talked an image floated in my mind, of Lauren sitting on a bench in the plaza by the cathedral in Guadalajara, without the slightest thought that she would have only a few short years before she would find herself dying of cancer and having to leave the husband and child for which she may then have yearned. She was thirty-five when Michael was born, thirty-five, that age many women call the biological clock. The pregnancy started another biological clock for Lauren.

She says she feels less groggy but still experiences funny mental things. A low level discomfort persists in her hip. The swollen ankle doesn't bother her and has improved with diuretics. "Boredom is still my worst problem," she tells me with a bored sigh.

August 5

I arrived later than planned and Lauren was obviously awaiting my arrival so we could go out in the car. Given the late start, we opted to leave the wheelchair and just go for a ride. Without too much trouble Sharon and I helped Lauren down the stairs and into the car. I drove at random on city streets through various neighborhoods. Lauren's face showed her delight at getting out of the house.

Lauren and I spotted a cookie shop at the same moment, so I pulled into a bus zone and handed Sharon a five dollar bill with instructions to get us each a cookie. While she was gone, Lauren dropped into an intimate tone, "I remember how I used to like just walking around the streets. Now I can't walk without a walker or wheelchair. What's the next step?"

"I don't know, Lauren," I told her, "but I think it's probably best not to leap forward to the next step, but to enjoy what you can still do as long as you can."

As we continued back up the hill munching our cookies, I heard myself unaccountably and thoughtlessly extolling the joys of walking these hilly streets! How could I?

We arrived back just in time for Sharon to depart on schedule at 4:00. Though she is late arriving almost every morning, she is religiously punctual in her departure. "Joan," Lauren asked me, "can you stay until Henry gets home?" Being alone is still uncomfortable, but most days she manages the hour alone by going to sleep. She told me how much she liked getting out and we decided to go to lunch next week.

She and Henry and Michael are going out for Mexican food tonight. She said she has to push Henry to get out for dinner once in awhile. I suggested they might enjoy an evening out without Michael. "Yes, I'd like that and my aunt could take care of Michael."

She seemed a bit pale today. "I've felt tired all week. I hope it's the chemo pill I took last week," she said, the implication being that if it were not the pill, then maybe the cancer was progressing. She also showed me some new bumps on her hands that she thought were part of the cancer. Basically, her condition has been stable for some time now, ever since she got on the Roxanall.

August 12
I took Lauren out to lunch with the help of Sharon. Lauren, though a bit confused, seemed to enjoy the lunch. Afterwards we wheeled her up the street, and she enjoyed being part of the hustle and bustle of afternoon shoppers for a few minutes.

Back at the house Sharon and I had quite a time getting Lauren back up the stairs. Halfway up, her legs seemed to dissolve beneath her. Try as she might, she could not drag her left leg up to the next step. She panicked. "I can't! I can't! Oh, no!" Her breath came in short gasps and her forehead gleamed with perspiration.

"Rest a moment, Lauren. No need to run up these stairs." I spoke as calmly as I could, knowing that if she panicked, she would lose what strength she had. "Sharon and I can help you. Don't worry, we'll get you back inside."

Lauren looked up toward the door, and the look on her face said that the few steps remaining might have been a Himalayan peak.

She gripped the railing until her knuckles were white. At last with a burst of energy and determination from some hidden reserve, she managed to propel herself forward and up the last few stairs with Sharon and me practically carrying her.

With relief she lunged upon the walker that I'd positioned at the top of the stairs. Now just the doorsill remained. Her eye on the recliner chair inside, she stumbled toward the chair, leaning heavily on the walker.

Lauren was still heaving great sighs of relief, but Sharon with her eye on the clock, announced that she had to leave. Had the clock struck four while Lauren was still struggling up the stairs, would she have abandoned us then and there, I wondered?

"Can you stay with me a while, Joan?" Lauren inquired. The time after Sharon leaves is getting harder for Lauren to bear. And today, after the excitement of our outing and the ordeal of the stairs, she especially needed not to be left alone. I assured her I'd stay until Henry got home, and she promptly dozed off in the chair.

August 26
I hadn't seen Lauren for two weeks, and was surprised to see new signs of decline after a long stable period. Her stomach is so enlarged that she looks pregnant, and the commode is now positioned in the living room right next to her chair. "I had a bit of incontinence," she admitted to me with embarrassment.

"The diuretic makes you urinate frequently, and there's probably more pressure on your bladder now, too, so it's not your fault," I assured her.

Walking is more and more difficult, so she stays in the chair all day, except to use the commode. She seems to be short of breath, and more frequently now, she dozes off and leaves the conversation without notice.

September 3 and 10
Lauren is continuing to decline. Sharon went with Lauren and Henry to the oncologist this week. As usual he had little to say and told Lauren only to "play it by ear." Another chemo pill to take and come back in six weeks. What an outrage! If I were as sick as Lauren I would want a doctor who would at least talk to me about what was going on.

I read a book to Lauren but the sound of my voice put her right to sleep. She said she likes my reading to her better than the talking books.

The phone rang, it was her aunt calling to see if Lauren's parents were there yet. Lauren had thought they were coming tomorrow and told me she didn't feel prepared to see them today. She seemed suddenly wide-awake and anxious, so I asked her what she was feeling.

"I feel an extreme amount of anxiety, . . . but I don't know exactly why." She seemed surprised and puzzled to discover this anxiety.

"What did you mean," I asked her, "about not feeling pre-pared to see your parents? Is seeing them hard?"

"Well, yes and no. I wish I could do more with them. . ." But this did not seem to be the real issue.

I was unable to get her to express more precisely what made her apprehensive about seeing her family.

In a little while the bell rang and in came her parents, bearing bunches of flowers, containers of food, and assorted boxes and bags. They came in with a whirlwind of anxiety. "Where's our Laurie? Oh, look at the flowers, Lauren! They're from the garden in the backyard. You remember, don't you?" Lauren sat dazedly in her chair and did her best to respond. There was confusion about whether they were to go to her aunt's house. Her mother referred to me as Sharon, and Lauren informed her that I was Joan and not Sharon.

I thought of my own parents, across the country driving anxiously from their home to visit my sister. When they talked about seeing her, there was the same anxiety in their voices that I heard in Lauren's parents. Lauren's mother scurried from kitchen to living room, busy with packages, but not wanting to lose sight of her daughter in the chair. If I was startled to see the changes in her from week to week, how much more devastating it must be for them to have to confront the accumulated changes of six or eight weeks all at once.

Henry and Michael came in before the parental whirlwind subsided. I put on my jacket and told Lauren's parents it was nice to see them again. "Again? Well, you must have been seeing me in your dreams, my dear!" retorted her mother with the distinct flavor of rage to her voice. Lauren's father reminded her that they had met me some months before, but she would not acknowledge this, and immediately turned away from me.

No wonder Lauren feels anxiety in relation to her parents. Her mother has so much rage that her daughter is dying, that it spews out uncontrollably in inappropriate directions. How terrible for Lauren! When she needs comfort, she gets only anxiety and rage. But how else can her parents, any parents, possibly respond to the death of their child? It is an unnatural reversal of the normal ordering of life: parents expect their children to survive them, not the other way around.

September 24

Lauren doesn't say much these days, and she's becoming more uncomfortable when left alone.

"You seem awfully aware of what's going on with me, Joan," she remarked.

"Well, I try to be," I told her. "This is such a hard, hard time for you and even if I can't make it better, at least I can be sensitive to what is going on with you." She smiled broadly, obviously appreciating this.

Apparently my talking to Henry last week about replacing Sharon, if she continues not to show up and to arrive late, spurred him on. He said he had a talk with her. He refused to pay her for the extra hours she said she was due for staying late since she was late arriving several days. "She wasn't happy with this," he said. "You know, once she's here, she's good with Lauren, but I never know when she's going to arrive late. I worry about Lauren being alone."

"Of course, you do. I'm glad you didn't pay her the extra hours. Even if she's good, she shouldn't be paid for hours she isn't here and you are left worrying. No employer would permit her to behave like that. Don't worry, she's not the only person who can take care of Lauren." I had checked with the agency and found that they would be able to help Henry make arrangements for a new attendant.

He followed me out onto the front steps, as if he wanted to say something or ask something, but all he said was, "Thanks for coming. I guess eventually I'll have to get someone to stay with Lauren all the time." He looked so sad and tired, but I couldn't think of anything to say.

October 20

Sharon failed to show up for several days in a row, so the agency arranged for Yolanda, a very experienced attendant, to stay with Lauren from when Henry leaves in the morning until he returns in the evening: no more times for Lauren to be alone.

"Oh, Joan, am I glad to see you!" Lauren cried out when I arrived.

I knelt down next to the chair, and held her hand. "What's the matter, Lauren?"

"I feel like I'm going crazy, Joan! All these changes!" Her leg is terribly swollen again, tight as a drum. She has trouble moving in the chair, but terror flickered in her eyes when Yolanda tried to adjust her position. A hospital bed has arrived, but Yolanda said she will try to get Lauren up and into the recliner chair as long as she can.

Yolanda seems to be a warm and conscientious person. I hope Lauren will relax as she gets used to her. Lauren's parents are due to arrive this weekend.

November 2
Bouquets of flowers and potted plants everywhere, and an unopened box of chocolates on the table. It was Lauren's birthday, but she was completely incoherent and oblivious to this and to everything else.

Yolanda seemed glad to have someone to talk to. We talked quietly while Lauren alternated between deep slumber and anxious restlessness. Her middle is now huge and she looks uncomfortable, no matter how the cushions are arranged. "Her legs are useless now and she's very difficult to transfer from chair to commode. Once she slipped right to the floor and I had to call 911 to get her up," Yolanda confided. "There's no way I could move her once she was down like that."

The egg-crate mattress was drying on the line. "Yes, she's incontinent quite a bit now. You know, I think he's thinking of . . ." —she lowered her voice and mouthed the next—". . .a nursing home." Lauren slept on in the chair. "That poor man is getting awfully tired. I've offered to stay and make dinner, but he always says I should go on home."

"Henry is very independent and it's difficult for him to accept help, but just knowing you are here the whole time he's at work, I know is a relief to him. Keep offering to help with dinner," I urged her.

November 3
I telephoned in the evening to see how Henry was doing. His voice

was weary and raw, but he welcomed my call. "Lauren stayed in bed today. I'm thinking of moving the hospital bed to the dining room, so she can see more. But she doesn't see much anyway . . ." His voice was tight and frightened, full of despair. "The nurse put a catheter in."

"The dining room might be a good idea. Even though she seems unaware of what's going on around her, she still hears everything and may be more aware than you think. Try whatever you can that can keep her there at home with you and Michael."

"I hope I can, but I don't know whether I can much longer. I'm not sure what to do anymore. At least with Yolanda here, I know she's well-taken-care-of during the day."

"Are the nights getting hard?" I asked gently.

"Oh, yeah. I don't get much sleep." I urged Henry to get as much help now as he could, not to try to do it all himself. I asked him about increasing Yolanda's hours so she could help with dinner. He replied that he was "working on it," and told me how he had gone to the grocery store when both Lauren and Michael were asleep. "It was okay I guess, but I worried the whole time."

We talked of Lauren's wish to die at home and whether it might be easier on Michael if his mother died at home rather than disappearing to a nursing home.

November 4

Stopped by for a few minutes on my way home from a meeting. Yolanda was glad to see me. "Lauren has been having a bad time today. I just don't know what to do for her. She's been in bed the last two days. It's impossible to move her anymore."

I went into the bedroom where the hospital bed was set up at the near end and the double bed was pushed up against the window. The blinds were drawn, and Lauren was lying in an awkward heap in the hospital bed. Her eyes were huge in her face and there was so much congestion in her chest that she struggled for each breath. She was drenched in perspiration, yet her skin was not hot, and became cold and clammy as I sat with her.

"She's been awake like this all day," Yolanda told me. "I'm exhausted just watching her." She wiped Lauren's face, and adjusted her pillows. Grateful for my offer to sit with Lauren awhile, she withdrew to the living room.

Anxiety and struggle. Lauren's words made no sense, but her internal struggle was obvious. Life and death warred within her swollen, distorted body. I brought a chair next to the bed and took her hand. "Just relax, Lauren. Rest and relax now. Nothing to do . . . Just let go . . . and rest." She was wide-awake and completely aware of what was happening around her, but unable to respond verbally. Her eyes implored me to help her.

Most of her words were garbled whispers lost in the noise of the congestion in her chest. "I don't know how!" she cried out in a panic.

"Lauren, you know everything you need to know. You truly do. Just listen to your heart and let go. There's nothing to do, except rest. Not a thing. Everything is done," I assured her.

Over and over I stroked her arm and told her, "You can rest now, Lauren. Just let go . . . nothing to do . . . everything is okay, everything will be fine. You have done everything so well. Now you can rest and let go of everything."

She sometimes responded, "Okay," but she continued to struggle and gasp and sweat. Once she gave several distinct smiles. Was she seeing something? Or was it only involuntary movements?

I had only intended to stay a few minutes, but once I sat down beside her and held her hand, I couldn't leave. Her struggle to let go was intense and though part of me wanted to bolt away from that awful rattling, gasping sound of her breath, something told me to stay. I thought about how it would be if I were in the bed, struggling to die, and in horror at the thought, I imagined myself driving away in my car, relieved of this too graphic demonstration of dying. But I was glued to the chair and I couldn't leave. I couldn't escape anymore than Lauren could.

Smoothing her damp hair back from her face, I continued my reassurances. "Rest, Lauren. Just rest and relax. You are doing just fine. Let go of everything. No worries now. Just rest." How would I ever leave this chair? My whole attention was focused on Lauren's noisy breathing and I was a required witness to her struggle. I tried to visualize how peaceful she would be after she got through this difficult time. I remembered how almost every patient I had been with had gone through a time of struggle and anxiety and then had suddenly been released from struggle to spend the last days of life in a deep peaceful slumber of dreams.

The sound of the garage door opening brought a look of . . . I'm not sure what . . . to Lauren's face. It was clear she knew it was Henry arriving home, and his arrival was a cue, vital to her inner struggle.

Henry was shocked to see the change in Lauren just since noon. He looked dumbfounded, but took my suggestion that he call Dr. Rosen while he might still be in the office. I thought oxygen might make Lauren more comfortable, but we all knew that there was little anyone could do for Lauren. How I wished Lauren were a hospice patient and I might call the on-call nurse.

Michael wanted "Sesame Street" turned on. Henry nodded his assent, so I slipped out of the bedroom and left Henry and Yolanda with Lauren. Michael was in his normal coming home routine, seemingly unaware of what was occurring in the bedroom. Lauren and Henry had never shielded Michael from the fact of Lauren's illness, and over the months he had become accustomed to relating to his mother in her chair. He was fascinated with each new piece of medical equipment, and rarely showed much distress. He seemed to have made a gradual shift of dependency from Lauren to Henry.

With Michael settled into "Sesame Street," I returned to the bedroom where Henry and Yolanda were struggling to put a clean, dry shirt on Lauren and readjust her position in the bed. She was extremely difficult to move and no matter what they did her body settled into the same awkward heap. Finally with an assortment of pillows propping her up on all sides, she was more or less on her back in the middle of the bed.

When Yolanda left, I told Henry I could stay a little while, to either sit with Lauren or to give Michael his dinner. He nodded numbly without much acknowledgment, and proceeded to go about getting Lauren her medicine and putting soup on the stove to heat. Henry gave her her medication, and surprisingly she swallowed the pills without too much trouble. I crossed my fingers and hoped the Roxanall would stay down. I wondered why Lauren had never been switched to the liquid Roxanall. Just then Michael appeared in the doorway. Henry looked distraught and preoccupied, so I took Michael into the kitchen to check on the soup. Henry stayed with Lauren while I gave Michael his soup and bread. I ate a small bowl of soup with him and chatted small child dinner talk with him.

Henry came into the kitchen and reached for a bowl. "Maybe Lauren would like some soup, he said." He carried a bowl of soup in to feed her.

In just a few minutes, he cried out loudly, "Joan! Joan!" and I rushed into the bedroom where he was holding Lauren while she vomited. I grabbed towels from the bathroom and began wiping up the vomit.

Lauren lay very still with her head to one side. "I think she's dead!" Henry cried out in a whisper filled with pain and fear and panic. We both tried to find her pulse without success, and Henry began to cry. As I comforted him, a huge gasp came from Lauren's mouth and her face and neck moved. Air was sucked noisily into her nose. So maybe she wasn't dead, I thought. But there was no pulse and she was mostly still.

Henry and I continued to question whether she was dead or not. How I wished I knew more about these things! And how I wished for the hospice on-call nurse. I had never been with someone at the moment of death, and now I saw that perhaps it wasn't really a "moment" at all. Lauren had been busy dying all afternoon and was obviously now dying, but whether she had officially crossed the line from life to death, I couldn't tell.

Henry whirled in the devastation of grief and the shock of loss, compounded by the confusion of not knowing whether she was alive or dead, so I said, "Either she has died or she will very, very shortly. At least she has stopped struggling." Even that bit of clarity seemed to help. The phone rang and we practically knocked each other over deciding who should answer it. Finally, I picked it up.

It was Yolanda and I told her, "I think she's gone."

Back to the bedroom where Henry was still trying to figure out if Lauren had died. She was limp and unmoving now, but like Henry, I had a difficult time knowing —or was it believing?— that Lauren had actually and completely died.

From the kitchen, Michael called out, "Joan Taylor! Come here!" I had completely forgotten Michael. He had eaten all of his soup and was sitting in his chair with soup smeared on his face and dripping down his plastic bib. I cleaned him up and gave him a cookie. He wandered into his room to play with his toys.

Back to the bedroom. I told Henry the doctor should be called and asked him whether he wanted me to call Dr. Rosen. Henry wanted to call him himself. After Henry called the doctor, I asked him if he and Lauren had discussed funeral arrangements. No, they had not, and he didn't know what she would have wanted. How could they not have discussed this! He remembered her once commenting in general that cremation was a good idea, so I told him it was really up to him. If Lauren had been in a hospice program, a social worker would have made sure that she and Henry decided upon funeral arrangements. As it was, here was Henry now struggling alone with the question.

I alternated between amusing Michael in his room and comforting Henry in the dining room. Henry was staring into space, red-eyed and in shock. Michael seemed content to play with intermittent attention, but as the phone began to ring more often, he perked up his ears. I thought of how difficult it would be to tell Michael that his mother had died. Since Lauren's Aunt Beth was on her way over, and Henry was quite dazed, I thought the best thing I could do was to keep Michael content and occupied for a few minutes. This was a very private family, and I knew that Beth and Henry would want to tell Michael themselves.

Soon Lauren's aunt and uncle arrived and while they waited for the coroner, they picked out a funeral home. It seemed unnecessary and maybe an intrusion for me to stay, so I told Henry I would go now. He seemed a little surprised, but he stood up and thanked me for having been there. Without thinking, I hugged him and he hugged me back. I hugged Michael, who by then was on the couch reading a book with Aunt Beth.

Henry followed me out onto the front steps. I was surprised to see that it had rained. The street was wet and the air was moist, and very fresh, almost sweet. The lights of the houses on the hill looked peaceful and bright. We stood there quietly for a minute. I told him the next few days might be tough, and to be sure to call me for anything at all. I touched his arm and he reached for my hand. I squeezed his hand and he thanked me again.

I drove away feeling a curious mixture of exhaustion and elation.

15

Sitting Still Again

It's late afternoon as I walk up the hill into the cemetery. The winter sun, just barely above the crest of the hill, casts the same otherworldly light as I remember here last November, the day of Tom's funeral. Today is the anniversary of his death, and I'm still filled with awe and surprise at the way Lauren died, just yesterday. From now on, there will be two anniversaries to remember in November.

The rows of graves stretch endlessly over the hills. Not knowing exactly where Tom's spot is, I head for the cemetery office. The sign on the door says the office closes at 4:30; I look at my watch: it is 4:35. Oh, well, even if I can't find Tom's grave, just being here fills me with the memories of him.

I remember Bill's vague description after the funeral of where Tom's grave site would be: below the road, just off another road, where they were filling in spaces left in an older section. I veer to the right, down a small road, and I notice that the row of grave markers at the edge of the grassy slope has dates in the summer of last year, and the large white stones in the row behind are from the late 1800s. I walk along and notice that the dates move into the fall—September . . . October, and then November.

Just beyond a tree dropping red berries on the stones below, there it is: Thomas Bryant Noren, April 29, 1936—November 5, 1985. I breathe in sharply with the shock of seeing Tom's name etched in granite. Memories of Tom wash over me, bringing tears to my eyes. "Oh, Tom," I breathe in a whisper.

Several of the nearby graves have bouquets of flowers, but I have come empty-handed. I wish I had flowers, or something to put on Tom's grave, to mark this day, to recall Tom, and to mark my presence in his life and here today. I gather a handful of the fallen red berries and a few sprigs of holly leaves that I find on the damp ground. I bend down and place the berries and leaves in a circle around the grave marker. When I stand up, I feel better. I take in a deep breath of the cool moist air, and I feel a smile on my lips. Now I can look around and see where Tom's resting spot is. To the left is the grave of an elderly man, but to the right is the grave of a man even younger than Tom, a man my own age. It seems that Tom is in good company here under the tree on this hillside.

The cemetery is nearly deserted, but whenever I see someone walking up the hill I look to see if it's Bill. I don't know whether I'm hoping he will come or not. It would seem right for Bill to come; surely he must be thinking of Tom today. But I know that his presence, anyone's presence, would disturb the closeness I feel with Tom, and bring me back to the chilly reality of a late winter afternoon in the cemetery.

I walk on up the hill through the rows and rows of white headstones. The slight sound of gravel crunching under my feet startles me because I am buoyed up by the spirits around me and my feet feel too light on the ground to be making any sound at all. Keenly, I feel the presence of Tom, and of Lauren, and of the strangers buried around me on the hillside. I am a guest here, but I don't feel foreign. It's like visiting a former home: I feel the same sense of recognition of place and recognition of myself and my connection through all time to this place. It doesn't seem odd to feel this recognition for the world of the afterlife. I feel a wave of joy and gratitude for my life, and for my good fortune in being a guest here. I silently thank Tom. And Lauren, so newly out of this world. And Edith, and Anna, and Elizabeth, and all the others who have shared with me their passing from the world.

Rows and rows of gravestones. Lives long past. Human beings now anonymous except for the bare details of names and dates. I read some of the stones trying to conjure up a vision of these people, of their lives. Who were they? I don't know, but now they are all part of the stream of humankind. They all had separate unique lives, just as I think I do now, but in the end, we are all plunged into the stream of humankind that roars around me here. I think of my sister, still struggling to recover some semblance of her former life, and I know that all of the lives of those buried here had tragedies and sufferings, joys and satisfactions. All that is now part of the stream, let loose from personal connection.

I remember Lauren's struggle to let go yesterday: her noisy breathing, her sweating swollen body, her bulging eyes. How difficult it was for her to let go. I wonder if she could have felt the force of this stream of humankind, whether she might have had an easier time. But, no, even being here today fully caught up in the stream, I feel something deep inside me grab on to my separateness, and suddenly I'm aware of my feet walking, step-by-step on the earth, crunching on the gravel, depressing the damp grass, avoiding the muddy spots. Much as I'm reassured and awed by the sense of my oneness with all beings in all times, I'm also, me, one person, here today in this spot on the earth, and I'd not be inclined to give up my life easily.

To be a human being, to be alive, is to live in the world of form and to identify with the separate self, which can only live in the world of form. The separate self serves us well and is the source of all the joys and satisfactions and learnings of the world of form, and it's the only vehicle we have to approach the world of spirit. When the time comes to leave the world of form and enter fully the world of spirit, then we must let go of our separate self. It's no wonder then that we should cling a little, or a lot, and resist this letting go. It's a big leap to make, even when we've had glimpses of the world to which departed friends go.

The sun has now slipped behind the hill, immersing the hillside of white gravestones in deep shadow. The chill settling over me reminds me of the chill of death, and shivering I head toward a small patch of sunlight near the gate. My chest feels tight as I hurry through the rows of gravestones, averting my eyes, walking quickly, as if those long buried here could grab me right out of this world of the living and pull me deep into the cold, dark earth. No, no, not yet! I am filled with the knowledge that, just like those who lie buried here, who have now joined that great stream of humankind, I, too, am just a visitor on this earth. All too soon, I will die. Forty-two years I've had already. If I'm lucky, I'll have another forty, but not much more than that. It's going too quickly! There's so much to learn, and I've only just begun.

Back where I started, I say to myself: sitting still in the midst of not knowing. I've learned that I can be of help to those who are dying, and also to those who come to me needing tax returns and financial statements. Accounting no longer feels like a waste of time; it's just something else I know how to do, neither good nor bad, and ever since I became involved with hospice, I've found it surprisingly satisfying to use this skill, too, as a tool for understanding my life, and for helping other people.

But despite all I've learned, I've only glimpsed the mysteries of living and dying, of life and death, of form and spirit, of being and becoming, but in place of the despair I began with, I'm now filled with excitement and happiness, knowing that sitting still in the midst of whatever I'm doing is exactly what I should be doing. I walk on the earth now, alive and well, blessed with the gift of a human lifetime, and knowing that I am both mortal and immortal, form and spirit.